A STONE ON THE MANTELPIECE

a centenary social history
of the
R S S P C C

A young mother, firmly believing in the Biblical wisdom of 'he who loves his son, punishes him', and who considered that her little boy had deserved a good spanking, sent him into the garden to collect a rod. He came back after a long while, crying: 'I could not find a stick, but here is a stone, you can hit me with that.' The mother looked at her boy and started crying herself. Suddenly she saw it all with the eyes of the child, who must have thought: 'My mother wants to hurt me, so she may as well use a stone.' For a long time they hugged each other, then she put the stone on the mantelpiece and vowed: 'No violence!' Perhaps we should all put a stone on our mantelpiece to remind ourselves and our children: 'No violence!' It might be a tiny contribution towards peace in the world!

Told by Astrid Lindgren, children's author, when receiving the Peace Prize of the German Book Trade (Deutchen Buchhandels).

A STONE ON THE MANTELPIECE

*a centenary social history
of the
RSSPCC*

BRIAN ASHLEY

1985

THE SCOTTISH ACADEMIC PRESS

EDINBURGH

First published in Great Britain, 1985
by
SCOTTISH ACADEMIC PRESS LIMITED
33 Montgomery Street
Edinburgh EH7 5JX

ISBN 0 7073 0360 5

Printed in Great Britain by
Clark Constable, Edinburgh, London, Melbourne

CONTENTS

PHOTOGRAPHS

FOREWORD

Magnus Magnusson
Vice-President RSSPCC

They always called it 'The Cruelty'; and everyone knew what was meant. 'The Cruelty' was the Royal Scottish Society for Prevention of Cruelty to Children, but that was much too long a mouthful. 'The Cruelty', especially in Glasgow when I was working as a reporter on the *Scottish Daily Express*, was what you got reported to, if you didn't look after your children properly.

It is a curious paradox of usage that 'The Cruelty' should have been used for an organisation which stands for exactly the opposite — for kindness, and caring, and compassion, not cruelty. Such are the vagaries of language. But these Glasgow mothers, and their weans, did not think of the 'The Cruelty' as a large organisation with a long and impersonal name; they thought of it chiefly in terms of the men and women who represented the Society, the Inspectors and Women Visitors who were, and are, the front-line troops, the people at the sharp end who saw the suffering and strove to do something about it wherever they found it. As Inspector Cumming, who was in the Motherwell and Wishaw branch of the RSSPCC in the 1930s, once put it, the perfect Inspector would need the patience of Job, the wisdom of Solomon and the decision of Napoleon (*see* Ch. 6, p. 120).

This book can be seen as a most fitting tribute for all those, both young and old, full-time and part-time, professional and amateur, who have worked for and with and through the RSSPCC for the past 100 years. And I consider it a high privilege to be invited to contribute a brief Foreword to it. In my capacity as a Vice-President for several years now, I have had the pleasure of contact with the Society in a variety of ways: compering a splendid Rally of Scottish Fiddlers in Perth's City Hall, for instance, or speaking at the Annual Meeting of the Scottish Children's League (the Junior Branch of the RSSPCC) and being comprehensively upstaged by the enthusiasm and sheer lack of inhibition of these youngsters. All my contacts have been happy and inspiring ones — so much so that I am sometimes tempted to think that the RSSPCC acronym should stand for the Royal Scottish Society for Promotion of Celebration of Children!

In such cheerful surroundings, amongst so many dedicated people, it is all too easy to think only of the present and the future, and to forget the years that have gone by. This Social History provides a fascinating opportunity to reach back into the world of our predecessors — that gas-lit world of the Victorian age whose genteel façade veiled the most appalling deprivation and social squalor. These were days when the child was practically the property of the parents, to do with as they pleased. Consider this single case from the 1880s:

> Four children aged eleven, nine, seven and three were found with their parents begging in the streets on a dreadful stormy night in winter. The children were insufficiently clad and in a deplorable state, their hands and legs deformed and all their bodies one running mass of sores. Their heads were swarming with vermin and putrid matter. The Matron of the Shelter found it impossible to bath one of the girls on account of her state. The parents were brought before Baillie Bertram of Glasgow and charged with cruel and unnatural conduct in exposing their family to the weather. The father stated in Court that he was employed as a Lamplighter and received thirteen shillings per week, but had left this work of his own accord to make more money by singing and begging in the streets with his children, as their miserable appearance roused the sympathy of the public. On the previous day he made seven shillings from 10 a.m. up to the time when he was apprehended.

This was the kind of abuse that the RSSPCC was desperately needed for. Yet, as we can read here, the Founder of the RSSPCC, James Grahame, was at first unable to persuade the Glasgow public of the need to set up a Society (it took a further meeting, on July 23, 1884, to achieve it). Such was the concern regarding any possible infringement of the rights of parents or guardians that the interests of the children were secondary, and it was not until 1889 that the law made formal recognition of their right to be protected against neglect or cruelty.

Things have changed for the better, of course, especially since the last war. Local authorities through their Social Work Departments, Health and Educational services, Children's Panels — there is now an impressive battery of legislation related to child protection and child care. Indeed, there may be too much now — the Annual Report of the RSSPCC for 1983 addresses the need to rationalise the present welter of legislation affecting children — an intriguing echo of the very first Annual Report, a century ago, when the Society was seeking to have legislation introduced for the first time.

Some things have not changed, however. Central to the Society, central indeed to society as a whole, is still the *need* — the needs of children. Lest we become complacent about the advances that the past

100 years have seen, consider another single case, this time from the
1980s:

> A telephone call was received by the Inspector from a teacher
> about a nine year old girl who had sought refuge at her home.
> On examination, the girl was found to be severely bruised, and
> to have both cigarette burns and bite-marks all over her body.
> It transpired that these had been caused by relatives who had
> been looking after the child after the death of her mother. It
> was necessary to make arrangements to admit the child into
> care with the co-operation of the local authority, and a report
> was prepared for submission to the Reporter to the Children's
> Panel.

The RSSPCC continues to respond to the needs which are
presented to it on behalf of children in Scotland — at a rate of more than
10,000 in any average year. And in carrying out this task, it is fulfilling
the role of any voluntary organisation — plugging gaps, monitoring
need and service, providing an independent voice and increasingly
experimenting with innovative work in the field of prevention.

In this Social History we can read of the rich story of a dedicated
organisation, the many struggles against adverse circumstances, the
setbacks as well as the successes, the endless crises. It is told through
earlier records and Minute Books, and also through the personal
recollections of men and women who can still speak of their experiences
in the RSSPCC from the 1930s onwards.

It is the story of a task nobly tackled and doughtily carried out. But
the task is by no means over — indeed, it probably never will be. Much
has been done, but much always remains to be done. However
enlightened the legislation, however thoughtful the legislators, however
practised the practitioners, it will always be incumbent upon us — all of
us — to be ever vigilant about the interests and needs of children. The
long-term solution to child cruelty rests with each and every one of us,
and not just the service professionals and the law-makers.

One of the most important things that an organisation like the
Royal Scottish Society for Prevention of Cruelty to Children does is to
provide us all with the opportunity to be involved, in one capacity or
another, in the work of protecting children.

Sentimental the thought may be; hackneyed it may have become;
but I always remember with warmth the words of John Masefield in his
poem *The Everlasting Mercy*:

> And he who gives a child a treat
> Makes joy-bells ring in Heaven's street,
> And he who gives a child a home
> Builds palaces in Kingdom come.

PREFACE

A response to need

This book sets out to try to convey something of the development of a voluntary organisation which has existed for one hundred years in order to prevent cruelty to children in our society. The underlying assumption is that the origin and development of such an organisation is inextricably interwoven with the social fabric of the time and context. Our understanding is, therefore, dependent upon being able to distance ourselves from the particular view point of our time and our social experience and attempt to learn something of these other times and these other social experiences. We might, from our complacency, be even more tempted to say now, as the Rt. Hon. Mitchell Thompson, Lord Provost of Edinburgh, said in taking the chair at the Annual General Meeting of the Society in 1897, by which time the Society had already been in existence for over ten years, '. . . our feelings must necessarily be mixed when we realise there should be any necessity for a Society like this in Scotland.' Unfortunately most of us are aware that neglect and ill treatment of children still occurs in British society today and, therefore, we might go on to conclude now, as he did then 'Unfortunately, such is the case, and I feel — and I am sure that you all feel — that it is our bounden duty to do all that lies in our power to give this Society all the help that we can'.

So what does this mean? Has all the effort over the ensuing period been of no consequence because the same sentiment and the same statement can still be appropriate? This review of the work of the organisation will suggest that it is not so because the need and circumstances to which the first statement was a response were immeasurably different from the need and circumstances which we may recognise today. The fact that the organisation continues to try to find the appropriate response to the need and cicumstances in order to justify the statement is testimony to its resilient adaptability to change. This profile of the development of the organisation over one hundred years must try to convey something of that resilience and adaptability.

The British voluntary organisation is such a well-established phenomenon, making a necesary and accepted contribution to our national and community life in the widest possible variety of spheres of activity, that it tends to be taken for granted.

However, in other societies, which have taken the principle of public responsibility for communal provision for need even further than we have in Britain, the voluntary organisation is an unnecessary phenomenon, and indicates by its existence a failure in that public responsibility to provide. In such a view the voluntary organisation if it were to exist, would do so merely to demonstrate the need for public provision and would be inevitably preparing for its replacement by that public provision. There would be no case for the continued need for a voluntary organisation to meet a well-established and well-identified community need.

In other societies where the principle of responsibility for others is firmly vested within the primary group of family and kin network then there is little understanding of the motivation or need for people to be interested in such care, support or activity directed towards the need of others. In such a society also, to work for others is only undertaken of necessity and has little status in itself. Therefore to assume tasks on behalf of others or to work for others when this is not necessary and when there can be seen to be no material return has no justification. Here again the voluntary organisation on the British model has no place and cannot be understood.

Other societies with similar social development and a similar social philosophy to Britain have also developed similar voluntary or-ganisations. But they are not universal. They are a particular response to a social situation within a given social contest and they can only be understood on that basis.

These organisations emerge in response to a particular situation, usually to meet an express need, which at a certain point in time, due to some often inexplicable 'trigger' or initiative, becomes particularly significant. At such a stage, a deep underlying current of feeling or need is translated into a specific response. Usually the underlying current has been flowing for some considerable time beneath the surface; and therefore, has its origins deep in the history of the situation in which it suddenly comes to the surface.

The organisation which emerges is shaped partly by that history, partly by the need which it arises to meet and partly by the social circumstances of the time. This history which gives rise to the need has also influenced those people who react to the need and who join together to create the organisation. This history and the attitudes of the time contribute to the development of the philosophy which is embodied within the organisation and to which it gives expression. The methods it develops to meet the need are similarly fashioned and con-ditioned.

It is therefore a very large step which is needed to bridge the gap in consciousness between now and then; between our rather complacent view of our apparently advanced ideas, in comparison with the nature of those which gave birth to the organisation.

The nature of the step required may be illustrated by suggesting that a similar gap in consciousness exists within our time, to understand the present position of children in the Third World, from the relative comfort and security of British society, even though we may feel that we are depressed by a large-scale economic recession.

Henry R. Labouisse, Executive Director of UNICEF, in a foreword to the *Report to UNICEF of the International Year of the Child* in 1979 says:

> The central fact about the situation of children in the developing world is that fully one half of them are living lives which crush their rights as children today and their potential as adults tomorrow. If, as I believe, the well-being of children is an indicator of the degree of civilisation we have attained, then I am afraid that we are living in a kind of planetary Dark Ages.
>
> The statistics are staggering. It is estimated, for example, that out of 100 children born each minute in developing countries, some 15 will die within the year. Of the 85 who survive 75 will have no access to modern medical care in childhood. About one quarter will suffer from malnutrition during the crucial weaning age. During this period, their chance of dying will be 30 to 40 times higher than if they had been born in Europe or North America. Of these who live to school age only 6 out of 10 will ever enter a classroom. Not even few of these will complete their elementary schooling.

And behind the statistics are the faces and the individual people like Keveku the West African boy who told UNICEF:

> A lot of people call me small boy but I am nine years old. My work is I sell chewing gum outside cinema. Plenty boys and girls come buy the P.K. before they see the cinema. I don't go to school because I have no money. My mother died before they born me. My father nobody know. Some woman give me milk when I am little baby. Now I am old so I work. I have no sleeping house. I sleep at lorry petrol station. Don't take photo of me. I don't want people to see me dirty.

The Report states:

> An understanding of the problems which face the developing world's children is a precondition of their solution.

It then itemises some of these problems.

MALNUTRITION

At any given moment an estimated 10 million of the world's
young children are in the grip of severe protein-energy
malnutrition and a further 200 million are inadequately fed.
The result is that half of the 15 million under-fives who die
every year in the developing world are killed by malnutrition
or by diseases which malnutrition makes worse. It has been
estimated, for example, that a malnourished child in the Third
World who contracts measles is four hundred times more likely
to die from it than a child with the same illness in the
industrialised world.

POOR WATER SUPPLY

In sum, the World Health Organisation now estimates that the
worldwide burden of infectious diseases could be reduced by 80
per cent if every family on earth were to have dependable
access to safe water supplies and sanitation. At present more
than 1200 million people in the developing world have no safe
water supply and more than 1400 million have no sanitary
waste disposal facilities.

HEALTH

. . . the task of improving the health of the world's children is
far more a task of prevention than cure.

HOUSING

. . . Often the sleeping area is no more than a small shack
where a piece of clothing hung from the ceiling provides the
only privacy. Other families are crowded into the hastily
partitioned rooms of decaying mansions where sagging
ceilings, rotten beams and the ever-present threat of a
knocked-over kerosene lamp makes the home a place of danger
rather than of security for the child.

EDUCATION

. . . In many developing countries . . . illiteracy has been a
brake binding against almost every aspect of social and
economic development.

And, then, in summary:

For the poor, children often bring the advantages of help in
fields and homes: fetching fuel and water: working and
cleaning: looking after young children and tending animals —
jobs which children can and do perform. In many parts of the
Third World, children become net producers to the family
income, rather than dependants, by the age of eight or nine. By

the time they are adults, they are often the most important
source of their parents' livelihood. And among the poor,
children also bring joy and movement and hope into lives that
are often stagnant with poverty.

As this brief description has unfolded, the conditions in which
children grow up elsewhere in our own time the reader cannot fail to be
appalled by the severity of the conditions. Yet all of us can continue to
live with that realisation because it does not strike continually and
immediately upon our consciousness. We can shield ourselves from the
awareness and distance ourselves from the problem and from the need to
do anything about it. Our consciousness is protected by the remoteness
and by the fact that we live within a different social context. This process
of distancing ourselves is aided by the fact that modern knowledge
permits us to 'understand' the reasons for the problem in terms of
economic processes and movements which we know about but feel we
cannot control. Our conscience is also helped by the fact that modern
knowledge also permits us to believe that we can recognise the remedies
which would remove the problem if these remedies were to be instituted.
Whatever these remedies might be, population control, improved
methods of production, better distribution of resources and so on
through an almost endless list, they remain the responsibility of remote
decision-makers beyond our control and, therefore, outside our
responsibility.

This picture of the conditions and needs of children, apart from
its immense scale, is not much different from the picture which could
have been developed of the conditions of the children of the poor and
disadvantaged in Britain at the end of the nineteenth century. The
difference for the members of the British society at the time, compared
with the position of the contemporary British reader in relation to the
children of the Third World, is that the Victorians were themselves part
of the picture, closer to the conditions and the awareness of the effects,
but also shaped and influenced by the same social context which gave
rise to these conditions.

To the members of Victorian society the condition and problems of
children were part of their own context and their own history. They,
themselves, were products of the same social and historical processes
and, therefore, they saw and understood those conditions, not with the
advantage of our detachment in looking back through the history of one
hundred years: but with eyes and feelings and attitudes which were
influenced and conditioned by the context within which the conditions
manifested themselves.

To understand that consciousness and their response to need as
they saw it we need to understand their social context and the social and
historical process which had helped to produce it.

The underlying current of need to which the organisation in which we are interested was a response emerged from the life styles and patterns of the time. The attitudes to welfare and the basis for the response to welfare needs had their roots deep in social history.

To take this massive step back in social consciousness in order to understand properly our subject it is necessary to explore briefly these social and historical roots.

ACKNOWLEDGEMENTS

The Royal Scottish Society for Prevention of Cruelty to Children wish to acknowledge the help of the following persons in the preparation and production of this History:

Mr Douglas Grant and the Scottish Academic Press for their always helpful advice and assistance.

Mr John McWilliam who designed the cover, Mr Magnus Magnusson for contributing the foreword, Mr and Mrs G. D. H. Dewar of Glasgow who most generously provided sponsorship towards the cost of production,

and

Mr Brian Ashley who, because of his personal interest in the RSSPCC, freely gave of his time and expertise over many months of researching the Society's records and preparing the text.

I
THE SOCIAL CONTEXT

We cannot make the leap in consciousness in order to understand attitudes to welfare in Britain at the end of the nineteenth century without an awareness of the important philosophical movements which helped to shape the social thinking of those days.

Probably first among these influences was the work of Thomas Robert Malthus, a Church of England clergyman and Professor of Political Economy at the East India College, who had published *An Essay on the Principles of Population* in 1798. In this he pointed out that in nature plants and animals were impelled to increase their species and that the repression of the superabundant effects was achieved by 'want of room and nourishment'. Malthus then suggested that man was similarly impelled but could use reason to question whether he should bring beings into the world for which he could not provide support. But, Malthus went on, if man did not listen to this voice of reason then man would constantly endeavour to increase beyond the level of subsistence. Then, said Malthus, the need which man has for nourishment is the absolute check on the growth of the population.

'But' said Malthus, 'this ultimate check is never the immediate check except in cases of actual famine.'

'The immediate check may be stated to consist in all those customs and all those diseases which seem to be generated by a society of the means of subsistence, and all these causes, independent of the society, whether of a moral or physical nature, which tend prematurely to weaken and destroy the human frame. . . .'

Malthus went on to talk of two kinds of check. The preventive, peculiar to man, was that his reasoning allowed him to calculate later consequences of his acts. He could see distress and could estimate the share of resources likely to be available to him and his children and consider whether he could support children he brought into the world. These considerations should be deterrents against too early marriage and the conception of too many children. Except, said Malthus, when it led to vice and promiscuity, which was morally degrading.

The positive checks, according to Malthus, were those causes which shortened human life such as war, plague, famine, and disease.

Mathus, therefore, posited a society with resources just to maintain itself and trends towards increased population were therefore either to be resisted or to result in lower standards of living because the resources would be shared among a greater number.

Therefore, within a society influenced strongly by the views of Malthus there was obviously a difficulty in taking a human and supportive view of poverty and its consequences, particularly in relation to children and their welfare. The poor could improve their condition by keeping down the birth-rate.

Earlier, Adam Smith, a Scottish economist, had published his book *An Inquiry into the Nature and Causes of the Wealth of Nations*. He taught that individual prosperity was inextricably linked to national prosperity and that individual businessmen in pursuing their own advantage inevitably advanced general prosperity. According to Smith individual activity acted through an 'Invisible hand' to improve society. Each man had to work not in the position to which God and birth had called him but in the place into which his own exertions had brought him. Supervising his efforts and ensuring that the sum total of all such activity in the community would result in the greatest possible good was an 'invisible hand'. So in the place of God and birth the economist substituted the invisible hand and competition. All were agreed that the poor should work for the rich and that lavish relief was a mistake. Smith's teaching, therefore, supported the competitive endeavour and the drive to individual profits of the middle class industrialists who developed and extended factory industry. The betterment of society was therefore more likely to come from extension of commercial and industrial activity than from preoccupation with welfare and social conditions which might hinder that extension and development.

The nineteenth century was also strongly influenced by Utilitarianism which was based on the teaching of Jeremy Bentham. He advocated that all human conduct should be directed towards the principle of the 'Greatest Good for the Greatest Number'. He stated that men desire happiness and pleasure and wish to avoid pain. The attainment of pleasure and the avoidance of pain became determinants of behaviour but were also moral acts of right and wrong. He called this the 'Principle of Utility' and said every activity should be judged by it. He realised man would not always do what was right, therefore, he pointed out that there must be alternative choices of action and that the principle would help individuals and governments to choose between these causes of action. He, therefore, associated his ideas with Smith's 'Invisible hand' and believed that individuals working towards their own happiness would increase the general happiness of all. Also the movement based on his teachings claimed that government legislation could steer individuals' wishes for happiness into activities which benefited the greatest number.

The Utilitarians therefore emphasised the importance of the State through law reform but they insisted that the State should interfere with private interests as little as possible. They, therefore, supported Poor Law legislation but were only partially supportive of any legislation to control factory development.

The nineteenth century was not a simple stream of consistent and homogeneous philosophical and political thought. On the contrary, it was a maelstrom of different ideological currents which were continually ebbing and flowing in their influence upon different parts of the society and different movements within it. Though the views which have just been briefly summarised tended to have the ascendancy because they supported each other and provided a useful basis for the predominant and desired trends in the social and economic life of the middle and upper class, nevertheless opposing or questioning views also had their strong adherents. So the nineteenth century also saw the emergence of socialist thinking and particularly the development of the cooperative movement. This was stimulated by the views of people like Robert Owen, a leading Scottish industrialist, who attempted to put his views into practice in his New Lanark Settlement. His views, drawing attention to the importance of history and prevailing conditions upon man's behaviour as well as his individual will, provided a degree of counter-balance to the moralistic and punitive attitudes prompted by the views of Malthus and others. This extract from his *New View of Society* (1813–1814) 3rd essay pages 14–17 expresses the point.

Hitherto, indeed in all ages and in all countries, man seems to have blindly conspired against the happiness of man, and to have remained as ignorant of himself as he was of the solar system prior to the days of Copernicus and Galileo.

Many of the learned and wise among our ancestors were conscious of this ignorance, and deeply lamented its effects; and some of them recommended the partial adoption of those principles which can alone relieve the world from the miserable effects of ignorance.

The time, however, for the emancipation of the human mind had not then arrived: the world was not prepared to receive it. The history of humanity shows it to be an undeviating law of nature, that man shall not prematurely break the shell of ignorance; that he must patiently wait until the principle of knowledge has pervaded the whole mass of the interior, to give it life and strength sufficient to bear the light of day.

Those who have duly reflected on the nature and extent of the mental movements of the world for the last half-century, must be conscious that great changes are in progress; that man is about to advance another important step towards that degree of intelligence which his natural powers seem capable of attaining. Observe the transactions of the passing hours; see the whole mass of mind in full motion; behold it momentarily increasing in vigour, and preparing ere long to burst its confinement. But what is to be the nature of this change? A due attention to the facts around us, and to those transmitted by the invention of printing from former ages, will afford a satisfactory reply.

From the earliest ages it has been the practice of the world to act on the supposition that each individual man forms his own character, and that therefore he is accountable for all his sentiments and habits, and consequently merits reward for some and punishment for others. Every system which has been established among men has been funded on these erroneous principles. When, however, they shall be brought to the test of fair examination, they will be found not only unsupported, but in direct opposition to all experience, and to the evidence of our senses.

This is not a slight mistake, which involves only trivial consequences; it is a fundamental error of the highest possible magnitude; it enters into all our proceedings regarding man from his infancy; and it will be found to be the true and sole origin of evil. It generates and perpetuates ignorance, hatred, and revenge, where, without such error only intelligence, confidence, and kindness would exist. It has hitherto been the Evil Genius of the world. It severs man throughout the various regions of the earth; and makes enemies of those who, but for this gross error, would have enjoyed each other's kind offices and sincere friendship. It is, in short, an error which carries misery in all its consequences.

This error cannot much longer exist; for every day will make it more and more evident *that the character of man is, without a single exception, always formed for him; that it may be, and is, chiefly, created by his predecessors; that they give him, or may give him, his ideas and habits, which are the powers that govern and direct his conduct. Man, therefore, never did, nor is it possible he ever can form his own character.*

The knowledge of this important fact has not been derived from any of the wild and heated speculations of an ardent and ungoverned imagination; on the contrary it proceeds from a long and patient study of the theory and practice of human nature, under many varied circumstances; it will be found to be a deduction drawn from such a multiplicity of facts, as to afford the most complete demonstration.

Many other writers, preachers and thinkers also voiced contrary views to the prevailing philosophy and there was no lack of questioning. That questioning often remained within the intellectual élite, however, and did not always have practical consequences although much charitable and philantropic endeavour received its motivation and support from these dissenters. Sometimes the writing was not simply philosophical but had a hard factual base as shown in this excerpt from the writing of John Dunlop (1789–1868) who was president of the General Temperance Union of Scotland.

The system of rule and regulation, as to times and occasions of drinking, pervades all branches of society in Great Britain — at meals, markets, fairs, baptisms, and funerals; and almost every trade and profession has its own code of strict and well-observed laws on this subject. There are numerous occasions when general custom makes the offer and reception of liquor as imperative as the law of the land. Most other countries have, on the whole, only *one general motive* to use liquor — viz., natural thirst, or desire for it; but in Great Britain there exists a large plurality of motives, derived from etiquette and rule . . .

Scarcely has the stripling commenced his apprenticeship, in some towns, to *the business of the joiner or cabinet-maker*, than he is informed that the custom of the shop is to pay a sum as *an entry*, or gooting, to be disposed of in drink by the workmen. He receives charge of the fire in the premises; and at every failure of kindling, mending, or extinguishing at night, he is fined in a small sum, to be expended in whisky: failure in putting out candles at proper time, or in watching the work at meal-hours, and a number of other petty offences, are met by small amercements for the same purpose. At the ceremony of brothering, ten or twelve shillings are sacrificed in this way; the first wages of a journeyman also are consecrated to the same unhallowed purpose, being in many cases the commencement of a course of inebriation that ends only with poverty and death. If one leaves the shop, his station at a particular bench is *rouped*, i.e. auctioned by the men who remain, and the price spent in drink: sometimes six shillings are thus obtained. When furniture is carried to a customer's house, at moving, packing &c, the employer generally bestows a glass or two. When winter commences, and candles begin to be used, masters give their operatives a *treat* of spirits; and whenever the smallest sum is raised by a fine, the men greedily add to it, and thus a nucleus is easily formed, and drinking perpetuated. The penalties for nonconformity to the usages are various, ingenious, and severe, that it is nearly impossible, as we shall find in the sequel, for an operative to stand out against them and be able to continue in his business. On refusal to comply, men are sent to Coventry; refused assistance and cooperation, which is sometimes essential to carry on work; ridiculed, affronted, maltreated in a variety of ways. A journeyman carpenter, in a town north of the Forth, having declined to pay the customary drink-money, found one morning his tools removed. He received no satisfaction, but in about three months they were found in the side of a dunghill, which was being taken away for agricultural purposes.

In the course of apprenticeship to other occupations, a sum, varying from one to five shillings, is at intervals levied: among *plumbers*, for instance, when the apprentice casts his first sheet of lead. In manufacturing districts when a *blockcutter* cuts his first printing-block, he is bound to pay twenty shillings for the purpose of treating his fellow-workmen with drink. Among *cloth-lappers*, and some other trades, the apprentice not only gives his entry drink; but at successive stages of learning the business, he has to pay drinking usage-money; to all which payments the other workmen contribute a smaller sum, and often a debauch follows. *Entries*, either at admission of apprentices, or new workmen coming to a shop, are general among *founders, coopers, tin-smiths*, and others; and drinking never stops with the occasion of its commencement, but always proceeds in an augmented ratio. A respectable man, having a family, going lately to work at a *black-smith's* shop, refused to pay *entry*; he was maltreated, and finally knocked down and wounded: on the aggressors being summoned, they actually pleaded, in bar of judgment, before a magistrate, the *custom* of the shop having been infringed.

Dunlop was providing information to explain the magnitude of the problem to those he wanted to involve in the temperance movement. Often social reform movements required an intervention into the cultural life and norms which were not known or understood by the middle class who formed the supporters of the movements.

Later in the century the question of intervention was at the basis of the debate about the role of the State and its relationship with individuals as demonstrated by the new Liberalism which developed from the writings of John Stuart Mill. Still, however, there were the opposite views as, for instance, those of Herbert Spencer who feared the State as destructive of liberty.

Generally the nineteenth century embodied a spirit of optimism but there were occasional reminders of the poverty and degradation which still existed. John Ruskin in 1867 exhorted the Low Church members to give up some of their riches and to undertake unpleasant tasks as a demonstration of their beliefs. The High Church were asked to put their attention to the improvement of every day facilities rather than to the decoration and adornment of their church buildings.

This climate of ideas contributed to the nineteenth century attitude to the Poor Laws which had dominated the social response to the poor and needy in Britain since Tudor times. The system assumed that working men were simply motivated by basic wants and also that poverty and destitution were the results of lack of effort and motivation. Therefore society was caught in the dilemma of relieving the obvious destitution without seeming to remove the will of the poor to work and relieve their own situation. This view had been expressed by Bernhard Mandeville in *Fable of the Bees* in 1714 'the poor have nothing to stir them to labour but their wants, which it is wisdom to relieve but folly to cure' (quoted by J. F. C. Harrison in *Society and Politics in England 1780–1960*, published Harper and Row, 1965).

Responsibility for relief was laid upon the parish and wages were fixed by the local magistrates. The destitute were sent to houses of correction where they were given work in return for the relief of their destitution. The system was not capable of meeting the strains imposed upon it by industrialisation and the houses of correction became the mixed work-house where the destitute regardless of cause or sex or physical or mental condition were housed together. Pauline Gregg in her book *Social and Economic History of England 1760–1965*, published George Harrap 1965, quotes from Crabbe's *The Village* in attempting to convey the conditions of these houses of correction at the beginning of the century.

> There, in yon house, that holds the parish poor,
> Whose walls of mud scarce bear the broken door;
> There, where the putrid vapurs, flagging, play,
> And the dull wheel hums doleful through the day —
> There children dwell, who know no parents' care;
> Parents, who know no children's love, dwell there!
> Heartbroken matrons on their joyless bed,
> Forsaken wives, and mothers never wed;
> Dejected widows with unheeded tears;
> And crippled age with more than childhood fears;
> The lame, the blind, and, far the happiest they!
> The moping idiot, and the madman gay.
> Here too the sick their final doom receive,
> Here brought, amid the scenes of grief, to grieve,
> Where the loud groans from some sad chamber flow,
> Mix'd with the clamour of the crowd below,
> Here, sorrowing, they each kindred sorrow scan,
> And the cold charities of man to man.

The deficiencies of the Poor Law system were obvious by the beginning of the nineteenth century and there was set up a Commission to enquire into its activities and the problems. It reported in England in 1834 and recommended new legislation based on two principles 'The Work House Test' and 'Less Eligibility'. By the first no able-bodied man was to be given relief unless he and his whole family moved into the workhouse. The second principle was that the condition of the workhouse inmate was to be 'less eligible' that is of a lower standard than the lowest paid labourer.

This report was based upon the prevailing views earlier summarised. The poor were intended to labour and there must always be an overhanging punishment to ensure that they did so. Beatrice Webb in *English Poor Law History — the Last Hundred Years* quoted a Benthamite, the Rev. J. Townsend, as saying:

> Hunger will tame the fiercest animals. It will teach decency and civility, obedience and subjection to the most brutish, the most obstinate and the most perverse.

Translate those views, held sincerely by a Christian gentleman, into the context of family life and child welfare and it is not difficult to understand, particularly when associated with the principle of non-intervention in the affairs of the private individual, how much harsh behaviour towards children and much degrading poverty could be accepted within society at the time.

There is no evidence that prevailing ideas differed significantly on either side of the Border. The Scottish Poor Law had two distinctive features which influenced its capacity to cope with increasing industrialisation and urbanisation. Firstly, though assessment was legal by an Act of 1574, the poor had always been supported by voluntary contributions in the parish churches and by subsidiary church income. The second characteristic of the Scottish Poor Law was that no relief should be given to the able-bodied. The limited funds of the voluntary system placed a restriction on the effectiveness of the poor relief which was also limited by the harsh interpretation of those entitled to it. Since 1693 there had been in Scotland a distinction between the regular poor, the aged, sick, lame, orphans and destitute children and the occasional poor who only had temporary misfortune. The first group had periodic allowances of right whilst the second group only received relief from the charity of the parish. This was incapable of relieving the destitution in an industrial society. The Scottish Act in 1845 which followed the review by the Commission repeated the principle, however, of withholding right to relief from the able-bodied poor. Subsequently the potato famine forced the Board of Supervision to give relief to the able-bodied but they still had no such right. In England a greater proportion of the population were receiving poor relief and at a greater cost per head of the population. The effectiveness of the Scottish Poor Law was judged by the success of its economy rather than its adequacy as a system of welfare. There was a continuing argument in Scotland throughout the century between those who urged a system based on assessment which would permit a more universal system of relief and those who advocated the voluntary system on the grounds of lower costs and on the basis of the moral responsibility of Christianity. Gradually English ideas had to infiltrate due to the demand of an industrial society. This recognised that social conditions and social problems were broadly comparable although they had particular intensity in certain localities.

There was no doubt, either, about the degrading conditions which prevailed. The population of Scotland increased from 2·66 million in 1831 to over 4 million in 1901. The birth rate reached its peak in 1876 and has since declined. The death rate reached its peak in 1864 and has since declined. In 1861 25% of the Scottish population were under 10 years of age and only 9% were over 60.

W. H. Marwick, *Scotland in Modern Times*, published 1964 by Frank Cass and Co, contains the following summary of social and economic conditions of the nineteenth century:

> The chief feature was the growth of the factory, which increasingly involved an urban environment, the divorce of labour and leisure, of work and home. 'Domestic' work, notably that of the hand-loom weavers, declined; the making of food and clothing tended to leave the home for the factory. Purely industrial towns such as Coatbridge, Addiewell and Clydebank grew up rapidly. Buildings, originally used for other purposes, were frequently adapted for factories; hence some of the deficiencies in lighting, heating and ventilation. There were some 600 underground workshops in Glasgow in 1901. New buildings, like those at Deanston, designed for the purpose, were erected by progressive industrialists; the Border textile industry followed, and the jute mills of Dundee are credited with inspiring a 'school of mill design', whose work 'remained the standard form of construction till the end of the century'.
>
> The labour of women and children was investigated by Commissions of 1842 and 1862; the latter showed that 77,000 under 15 were at work. The limitations imposed by the series of Factory Acts and the Mines Act of 1842 were common to Great Britain. Considerable juvenile employment survived in industries not covered by these Acts, such as bleaching tobacco. Some restriction was put on child labour by the Education Act of 1872, which made schooling compulsory to the age of 13 (raised to 14 in 1883); exemptions from attendance were however freely given in some rural areas, and sometimes for part-time factory work.
>
> About one-fourth of the women employed in Dundee mills were married; to this was attributed the peculiarly high

infant-mortality rate. Some protection for women was secured
by the efforts of the Scottish Council for Women's Trade
founded in 1895 under the Chairmanship of Rev. (afterwards
Principal) Geo. Adam Smith; Miss Margaret Irwin was
secretary throughout its existence.

The duration of the working day was probably no longer
than had been common in 'domestic' work, but the intensity of
labour and discipline were undoubtedly more severe. The
average working week was about 70 hours in the 'forties; it was
reduced to 55–60 by the 'nineties. The Saturday half-day
became more common in the later decades; (Pages 124–125)....

Water supply, especially in larger towns, was frequently
inadequate. Provision of public wells continued till the middle
of the century; thereafter internal piping and sanitation
became general in new construction. Factory effluvia
sometimes occasioned pollution.

Some contagious diseases were virtually endemic, and the
urban death-rate rose in the early decades. Mortality from
smallpox was still over 10,000 per annum. Epidemics of
cholera and typhus ocurred from the 'thirties to the 'sixties.
The average death-rate in Edinburgh and Glasgow in the
'forties was twice that of England, and a third higher than
London. The infant-mortality rate was still well over 100 at the
end of the century.

The traditionally low standard of housing was intensified
by the rapid growth of the towns. One-fifth of the families were
housed in one room in 1861; 25 per cent in Glasgow in 1880.
Rents were relatively high, averaging one-fourth of wages.

Intemperance was rife, due largely to the increase of
whisky drinking. Glasgow was described about 1850 as
'Presbyterian Rome and modern Gomorrah', when the
'Drunken Statistics' showed that 1 in 22 were annually
prosecuted, as compared with 1 in 100 in London.
Gangsterism and sectarian strife were familiar in the area.
Illegitimate births reached a maximum rate of over 10 per cent
in the 'sixties, and were most frequent in rural districts, though
there said to be largely pre-marital. The two best-known
Labour leaders, Keir Hardie and Ramsay Macdonald, were
both illegitimate, as were the novelists S. R. Crocket and Geo.
Douglas Brown. In the light of such facts, the nostalgic
evocation of high Victorian standards of morality and culture
seems to be based on a myth. (Pages 126–127)

Dr George Pryde in the Historical Association pamphlet entitled
Social Life in Scotland Since 1707 and published by G. Bell and Sons in 1934,
gives a similar supporting picture. (Pages 16–18)

If the material progress of the eighteenth century had been
accompanied by a notable social advance, the same cannot be
affirmed of the early nineteenth century. Already by 1851
there had taken place a redistribution, as well as a 75 per cent
increase, of population. The rate of growth was rapid in the
towns, slow in the counties, some of which, like Argyll, Kinross
and Perth, had passed their peak and begun to decline. During
the half-century Glasgow had grown four-fold, Edinburgh,
Dundee and Aberdeen had doubled in size, and after them, in
order, came Paisley, Govan, Greenock, Leith, Coatbridge,
Perth, Airdrie and Kilmarnock. There had thus been a shifting
of the population-centre to the neighbourhood of the Clyde
and a tremendous influx into the towns. Evicted cottars, farm-
labourers displaced by machinery, ambitious and venturesome
peasants, all flocked to the factories in search of high wages. To
them were added, from the 'twenties onwards, many poverty-
stricken Irishmen. The 'hungry 'forties' saw them arriving in
droves, and by mid-century, when the invasion had reached its
maximum, this alien element was considerable — one in six in
Glasgow and Dundee, one in eight in Paisley and Kilmarnock,
one in fourteen over all Scotland. We have no reliable housing
statistics for the greatly augmented population, since a 'house'
might mean anything between a one-room tenement and a
great block of flats; yet the total accommodation seems to have
dropped in relation to the inhabitants between 1801 (546
persons to each hundred houses) and 1851 (780 persons).
Moreover, from 1808 until 1851, a vicious window-tax on
houses of over £5 rental cramped the development of better
dwellings.

Country life showed the fewest departures from
traditional ways. The typical farmhouse was the 'but-and-
ben', or kitchen and best room, with sometimes a small third
room or furnished attic. The garden was usually a kailyard,
though fruit-growing was coming in. House furniture
ordinarily comprised box-beds, straight-backed wooden chairs,
chests, table, press and spinning-wheel. At a short distance
from the farmhouse were the cottages of the married labourers,
whose yearly wages were around £25; these cottages were
often low-roofed, single-roomed, chimneyless and thatched.
Single men, with lower wages, lived in bothies, which, though
varying from farm to farm, were too frequently filthy and
sordid adjuncts of the stables, with men and women
promiscuously crowded together; little wonder that one birth
out of six was illegitimate in some counties. Sanitary ideas very
seldom ran beyond the old-fashioned privy-midden. The
regular diet was as formerly — porridge, with milk or 'small

bear', oatcakes, kail, potatoes and herring, with occasional
bread and flour-scones, mutton or beef. The fare varied in
quantity rather than in kind on the traditional festival —
Hallowe'en, with its characteristic kitchen-games, Hogmanay
marked by 'guisers', rustic tableaux ('Here com I, bold
Slasher') and first-footing, Handsel Monday, the occasion for
family reunions and gifts, Fastern's E'en, with cock-fighting in
schools, the half-yearly Communion, Harvest-home, feeing-
fairs for farm-servants (who were given to frequent changes),
funerals with the subsequent 'draigie', and weddings with
fiddlers and dancing. Whisky was not the least of the
ingredients called for by these functions; the country-dweller
went to horse-races and cattle-shows, ploughing-matches and
local fairs, while shinty and curling were popular in the
Highlands, but, on the whole, large potations of whisky seem
to have been the normal method of relaxation and amusement.

As for the towns, everything points to the conclusion that,
while the nation's energies were directed to the rapid amassing
of wealth, little heed was paid to the human factor, to the need
for decent working conditions, for health and comfort in the
home, for the relief of poverty and overcrowding. Work was
often plentiful but subject to great fluctuations in demand and
supply. Cotton spinners' wages might rise to 21s. and fall to 3s.
Child-labour was unchecked until the 'forties and even then
did not cease entirely. Unemployment was intermittent but
wholesale and terrible in its effects: 10,000 men out of work
constituted no phenomenon in Glasgow or Paisley. Trade
Unions, barely legalized by the Act of 1825, had to work in
underground ways, and, though strikes did occur during
recurring booms and depressions, the masters retained control
through drawing on cheap Irish labour or the half-starved
Scottish peasantry.

While Glasgow manufacturers had imposing mansions in
the West End (now closing up the gap towards Partick) and
Edinburgh lawyers favoured the fashionable New Town,
while, indeed, some of the new wealth was already being
diverted to the acquisition of country seats, for the vast bulk of
people it was a time of discomfort, disease and death. Many
city-dwellings had earthen floors below street-level, more than
one family might occupy a one-roomed 'house', water-closets
and baths, public or private, were rarities, refuse and offal were
disposed of according to personal whim, miners' rows in the
smaller towns, with common garbage-dumps and privy-
middens, were dens of degradation; and darkness, damp and
dirt were universal. Too busily engaged in the mere struggle
for survival, the masses reaped few benefits from the sanitary

improvements of the time. Private water companies were set up in the cities and towns, but public wells, serving as trysting-places for gossiping housewives, were the rule; private wells were scarce and unreliable in either frost or drought. Speculative citizens made profit from their fellows' needs by selling water at a halfpenny per measure. Street-lighting and house-lighting depended on oil lamps until, from about 1820, local gas companies, likewise private concerns, supplied the new illuminant at rates which imposed the severest economy on both public and private users.

Unlit, unpaved streets and closes, dark and dirty entries, the fetid air of overcrowded rooms, unhealthy work in polluted atmosphere — all were an invitation to epidemics. Typhus, the great filth-plague, hung around Glasgow's closes and wynds from 1818 onwards, and cholera swept away thousands in its three chief visitations, in 1832, 1849 and 1854. Smallpox afflicted the Irish workers in particular, and underlying the more spectacular epidemic outbreaks was a chronic festering sore of ill-health and disease. Counter-measures were rudimentary and unsuccessful. Hospitals were few, poor and ill-equipped, nurses little better than drunken slatterns. Anatomical and medical research was hampered by the repercussions of the Burke and Hare scandal; wild rumours (not entirely groundless) of 'resurrectionists' or body-lifters persisted for long afterwards, and popular prejudice delayed progress. It cannot be said that in health, housing and cleanliness the nation was better off in 1850 than in 1800; rather, as a result of the inrush of Scottish peasants and low Irish to towns unprepared to receive them, social evils had been intensified.

This vivid description of social conditions in the first part of the century has been quoted because it provides an understanding of the base from which the welfare later in the century had to proceed. Generations which were contending with these conditions and growing up in this environment brought in to the latter part of the century the experience and the attitudes created at this time. Pryde continues later in his pamphlet:

Real progress was made during the second half of the nineteenth and the opening of the twentieth centuries. The population continued to expand, but at a slower pace, emigration, especially in the 1880's and 1900's, easily exceeding immigration and checking the natural increase. On the eve of the War the chief towns were Glasgow which had absorbed its suburbs to top the million-mark, Edinburgh, with one-third of that number, Dundee and Aberdeen, each one-half, and Paisley, Leith and Greenock, each one-quarter, of the size of the capital. In the larger towns loss by emigration checked the natural increase of the population, and yet it was officially computed that Scotland was three-fourths urban, one-fourth rural. The central fact of the period is the belated awakening of the social conscience, followed by governmental assumption of responsibility for the life and health of all citizens. Reliable statistics fanned public indignation, and town councils in particular were obliged to enter the field of health and hygiene and to administer social services. Opposition was met, for lethargy and complacency died hard. The editor of the *Census Report* of 1871, in commenting on the fact that 6,269 people, mostly Highlanders and Islanders, lived in single-roomed, windowless, chimneyless huts, was able to write: 'One advantage enjoyed by the inhabitants of such districts is the purity of the air and water'. Some manufacturers later objected to fortnightly holidays as being conducive to idleness among the workers. The age, of course, had no monopoly of clumsily disguised selfishness and greed; before the restriction of child labour a Scottish minister opined 'There can be no training of the volatile minds of youth equal to that which is maintained at the factories,' just as in 1933 several Glasgow citizens defended the employment of schoolboys to deliver morning papers and milk as being beneficial to *their* health and character.

From mid-century there were steady improvements, which may best be studied at the point where they were most urgently required — in Glasgow. The great typhus epidemic of 1853–54 was the prelude to the municipalisation of the water-supply and the harnessing of Loch Katrine. Gas followed in 1869 (Glasgow being well behind some others in this respect), electricity in 1891, tramways in 1894. A medical officer was appointed in 1863 and the first fever hospital opened in 1865. The last major outbreak of typhus in 1868 to 1869 led to the appointment of a sanitary inspector, to the adoption of real protective measures and to the ultimate conquest of the twin horrors of typhus and cholera. Improvements Acts of 1866 and later years authorised the destruction or renovation of old buildings and the provision of replacements, and within twenty-five years numerous blocks were demolished and new houses found for some 50,000 displaced inhabitants. After 1890 the authorities carried out slum clearances which swept away well over four thousand houses. Some model lodging-houses were set up on the spot, but there was a marked drift outwards, away from the congested tenements around the High Street, Gallowgate, Trongate and Saltmarket. Much remained to be done, but the fall in the city's death-rate, from 28–34 per thousand in the 'fifties and 'sixties to just over seventeen in the pre-War years, speaks for itself. Infant-mortality also showed a distinct though lesser improvement, from about one death to six births at the opening of the period to about one in eight at its close.

All over Scotland, central and local government undertook new social duties, poor relief, registration, education, public health, sanitation, old age pensions and, on the eve of the War, compulsory national insurance. Above all others lay the need for housing reform. In 1861 there were still nearly 8,000 single-roomed houses devoid of windows, and a half-century passed before they disappeared. In the following year the collapse of a rotten Edinburgh tenement killed twenty-two persons. Glasgow's typical house has been described as a 'gloomy, giant tenement, the colour of mud, built to last for ever, cut up into boxes, with a tap on the staircase' (Mr. Thomas Jones, in *The Times*, March 4, 1932). Buildings had been occupied from generation to generation with the minimum of change — except towards further congestion. The housing returns for 1861 reveal a lamentable state of affairs. Twenty-seven per cent of the people lived in one-roomed houses, nearly thirty-eight per cent in two-roomed houses; hence just over one-third of the population had homes of three or more rooms. Moreover, the smaller dwellings were occupied, on an average, by more than four persons to each house; some single rooms, indeed, were used by large numbers, up to and including fifteen persons. Each succeeding census showed a slight improvement. The number of one-roomed houses was reduced, by 1911, almost by one-half, and the persons using them by more than half. With a growing population, this meant a reduction in the proportion living in them from over thirty-seven to under nine per cent. More two-roomed houses came into use, so that on the eve of the War nearly half the population still lived in houses of one or two rooms, and rather more than half in larger homes. The greatest increase was among those dwelling in three-roomed houses (from thirteen to twenty-two per cent), but all the larger types were doubled in number. The improvement was thus not in the number of dwellings, which merely rose with the population, but in their size: whereas 100 rooms housed 179 persons in 1861, they were occupied by 145 persons in 1911.

Not all districts benefited to an equal degree; there remained great differences between county and county, and still more between town and town. Conditions were most satisfactory in small semi-rural towns and least so in the industrial belt. At Armadale, the worst-housed town in Scotland, over eighty per cent of the inhabitants lived in one- or two-roomed houses, and the proportion was over seventy per cent in ten other typical factory-towns, mostly in the south-west — Galston, Barrhead, Clydebank, Govan, Coatbridge, Airdrie, Motherwell, Wishaw, Kilsyth and Lochgelly. A comparison with England reveals the appalling Scottish inferiority. Of the total English population residing in private dwellings, only 7·5 per cent lived in either one- or two-roomed houses, and practically eighty per cent occupied four-roomed or larger houses. Scotland's largest groups were those in two- and three-roomed houses, England's in four-, five-, and six-roomed houses. Clearly only the major Scottish evils had been dealt with, by way of first aid rather than radical reform; slum clearance was yet in its infancy.

The food of the people showed little change, except that tea and wheaten bread, cheap enough for most purses, came into excessive favour, and, in conjunction with porridge, potatoes and oat-cakes, supplied a starchy and unhealthy national diet. Prices advanced spasmodically but wages more than kept pace with them. By the 'seventies skilled iron-workers, engineers and shipwrights were sure of from £1 to 30s. per week, while male factory-workers, whose pay was subject to the wildest fluctuations as well as utter insecurity, might get an average of 15s. per week. The coal-miner's daily earnings averaged from 3s. 6d. to 4s. throughout the century and sometimes rose as high as 10s. The unequal fight against machines eventually eliminated the hand-loom weavers, whose weekly wages, by comparison, show their pathetic plight: between 1800 and 1870 they fell, with only local and temporary checks, from 30s. to a miserable 4s. 6d. Trade Unions, legalised during the years 1867–76, fought for the workers, not only against low wages and long hours, but also against the iniquitous 'truck' system, whereby masters, by running monopolist stores, defrauded the men out of much of their wages. Insecurity of employment persisted; though everyone benefited from the boom times, there was woeful suffering during the slumps. Bad years threw well over 10,000 men out of work in several towns, and there were said to be 38,000 persons in receipt of poor relief in Glasgow at the time of the panic of 1878. Industrial dislocation, despite the reformed Poor Law of 1845, entailed real destitution until, under Asquith's Administration, the State offered old age pensions and health and unemployment insurance.

This second description by Pryde gives an opportunity to compare the conditions at the end of the century with those in the earlier half. It shows a steady improvement although still the conditions for many of the population were far from ideal. A similar indication of general improvement is given by Thomas Ferguson in *The Dawn of Scottish Welfare* published Nelson 1948.

In his concluding paragraph of the book after detailing the mortality statistics for Scotland until 1863 he says:

> This tale of increasing sickness and death among young
> children does not make encouraging reading, but already in
> 1863 forces were mustering that were ultimately to effect a
> great improvement. Enlightened opinion, like that of Sheriff
> Allison of Glasgow, vigorously denounced the 'vicious state of
> society' that was killing off the infants; the Factory Acts,
> despite their slow and halting progress, were beginning to
> reduce the worse abuses of child employment, while the new
> sanitarians, chief among them Gairdner in Glasgow and
> Littlejohn in Edinburgh, were beginning to make their plea for
> more space for the children, and more of the facilities that
> would help to make possible a reasonably happy childhood.

It is therefore probably not surprising that as part of what Marwick, in the book already referred to, describes as 'the prolific movements for amelioration of these conditions' one of the organisations which emerged towards the end of the century was the Scottish Society for Prevention of Cruelty to Children. This chapter has attempted to describe the origins of the social attitudes and the social conditions which influenced the formation of such an organisation and also the influenced way in which it set about its task. Throughout the profile of the Society which follows in this book it will be possible to trace the consequences of this earlier context. As that profile develops it may be appreciated that attitudes change more slowly than conditions. Indeed it may become apparent that some of the attitudes which we may have been surprised to find underlying policy in the nineteenth century still remain to be questioned and challenged at the present time.

For instance this challenge to what he saw as the complacent atmosphere of the time was published by John Ruskin in 1862 under the title *Unto This Last* and might be regarded by some to be still appropriate today.

> I said . . . that nothing in history had ever been so disgraceful
> to human intellect as the acceptance among us of the common
> doctrines of political economy as a science. I have many
> grounds for saying this, but one of the chief may be given in
> few words. I know no previous instance in history of a nations's
> establishing a systematic disobedience to the first principles of

its professed religion. The writings which we (verbally) esteem
as divine, not only denounce the love of money as the source of
all evil and as an idolatry abhorred of the Deity, but declare
mammon service to be the accurate and irreconcileable
opposite of God's service; and, wherever they speak of riches
absolute, and poverty absolute, declare woe to the rich, and
blessing to the poor. Whereupon we forthwith investigate a
science of becoming rich, as the shortest road to national
prosperity.

And similarly the statement by B. Seebohm Rowntree in his book
Poverty: a Study in Town Life, 1901 when he presented the results of his
survey of York, carried out in 1899 as follows:

In this way 20,302 persons, or 27·84 per cent of the total
population, were returned as living in poverty. Subtracting
those whose poverty is 'primary', we arrive at the number
living in 'secondary' poverty; viz. 13,072, or 17·93 per cent of
the total population. . . .

As the investigation into the conditions of life in this
typical provincial town has proceeded, the writer has been
increasingly impressed with the gravity of the facts which have
unfolded themselves.

That in this land of abounding wealth, during a time of
perhaps unexampled prosperity, probably more than one-
fourth of the population are living in poverty, is a fact which
may well cause great searchings of heart. There is surely need
for a greater concentration of thought by the nation upon the
well-being of its own people; for no civilisation can be sound or
stable which has at its base this mass of stunted human life.
The suffering may be all but voiceless, and we may long
remain ignorant of its extent and severity, but when once we
realise it we see that social questions of profound importance
await solution. What, for instance, are the primary causes of
this poverty? How far is it the result of false social and
economic conditions? If it be due in part to faults in the
national character, what influences can be exerted to impart to
that character greater strength and thoughtfulness?

These views might still be regarded as part of modern debate. Yet
despite the challenge of philosphers and social researchers attitudes died
hard, as shown in this paragraph by Pauline Gregg (in the book already
referred to, p. 7) when she is describing the evidence given to the Poor
Law Commissioners in the review of 1909.

To re-enforce the principle of less eligibility J. S. Davy, the
principal officer of the Poor Law Division, wanted the
applicant for poor relief to suffer

'firstly . . . the loss of personal reputation (what is understood by the stigma of pauperism); secondly the loss of personal freedom which is secured by detention in a workhouse; and thirdly, the loss of political freedom by suffering disenfranchisement.'

When questioned by one of the Commissioners as to the disenfranchisement of men out of work through no fault of their own, the Chief Inspector replied: 'the unemployed man must stand by his accidents; he must suffer for the general good of the body politic.' Davy favoured the able-bodied-test work-house, where work 'both irksome and unskilled' should be the test of relief. Not only the able-bodied but the sick and the children should also be subject to the principle of less eligibility. Conditions had become so agreeable for the old in the work-house that saving for old age was discouraged; . . .

As a summary conclusion to this chapter and as a picture of the challenge to which the Society responded in 1884 there is this extract from *Towards Democracy* by Edward Carpenter published the year before in 1883.

IN A MANUFACTURING TOWN

As I walked restless and despondent through the gloomy city,
And saw the eager unresting to and fro — as of ghosts in some
    sulphurous Hades —
And saw the crowds of tall chimneys going up, and the pall of
    smoke covering the sun, covering the earth, lying heavy
    against the very ground —
And saw the huge refuse-heaps writhing with children picking
    them over,
And the ghastly half-roofless smoke-blackened houses, and the
    black river flowing below, —
As I saw these, and as I saw again far away the Capitalist quarter,
With its villa residences and its high-walled gardens and its well-
    appointed carriages, and its face turned away from the
    wriggling poverty which made it rich, —
As I saw and remembered its drawing-room airs and affectations
    and its wheezy pursy Church-going and its gas-reeking
    heavy-furnished rooms and its scent-bottles and its other
    abominations —
I shuddered:
For I felt stifled, like one who lies half-conscious — knowing not
    clearly the shape of the evil — in the grasp of some heavy
    nightmare.
Then out of the crowd descending towards me came a little
    ragged boy;
Came — from the background of dirt disengaging itself — an

innocent wistful child-face, begrimed like the rest but
strangely pale, and pensive before its time.
And in an instant (it was as if a trumpet had been blown in that
place) I saw it all clearly, the lie I saw and the truth, the false
dream and the awakening.
For the smoke-blackened walls and the tall chimneys, and the
dreary habitations of the poor, and the drearier habitations
of the rich, crumbled and conveyed themselves away as if by
magic;
And instead, in the backward vista of that face, I saw the joy of
free open life under the sun:
The green sun-delighting earth and rolling sea I saw —
The free sufficing life-sweet comradeship, few needs and common
pleasures — the needless endless burdens all cast aside,
Not as a sentimental vision, but as a fact and a necessity existing, I
saw
In the backward vista of that face.

Stronger than all combinations of Capital, wiser than all the
Committees representative of Labour, the simple need and
hunger of the human heart.
Nothing more is needed.
All the books of political economy ever written, all the proved
impossibilities, are of no account.
The smoke-blackened walls and tall chimneys duly crumble and
convey themselves away;
The falsehood of a gorged and satiated society curls and shrivels
together like a withered leaf,
Before the forces which lie dormant in the pale and wistful face of
a little child.

2

THE FORMATIVE YEARS
early successes and conflicts

The analysis of voluntarism in Appendix A indicates the way in which voluntary initiative is often the response to a deep and continuing need which has been vaguely or even explicitly recognised for some time. It also points to the importance often of a 'trigger' of an event or an individual which translates the awareness into effect. It is also true from much evidence that similar conditions existing in different parts of different societies often give rise to similar awareness so that different 'triggers' in these different situations often give rise to similar responses. Sometimes these responses seem to arise in isolation from each other, sometimes they are obviously related to each other and sometimes the relationships although not always obvious on the surface are, nevertheless, influencing the apparently independent activities.

By taking extracts from records of the early days it is possible to see all these processes at work. First from an Occasional Paper of the National Society for the Prevention of Cruelty to Children which is undated but attributed by the Society to the year 1959 and written by Rev. Arthur Morton, O.B.E., M.A., Director of the English Society, entitled *Early Days*. The first paragraphs under the heading 'The Awakening' are as follows:

> In life it is people who count and not things. That is why
> historic movements are always found to arise from individuals.
> As Bergson saw, advances take place when mankind permits
> itself to be shaken and the shaking is always administered by a
> person. The story of the rise of the National Society for the
> Prevention of Cruelty to Children illustrates this truth.

The conviction that such a Society was needed had long been growing on both sides of the Atlantic, but it was to the Americans that the honour fell of being the first to implement this sentiment. There, in the city of New York, occurred one of those incidents which serve to bring into the open forces which have long been gathering momentum. This vital incident cannot be better described than in words used by Colonel E. K. Coulter (General Manager of the New York Society for

the Prevention of Cruelty to Children) at the Society's council meeting
in London in 1934:

A dramatic happening often is necessary to arouse the public
out of slothful, selfish sleep. The story of the founding in New
York of the first Society for the Prevention of Cruelty to
Children in the world is dramatic indeed. A classic with us, for
it marked the promulgation of the first Bill of Children's
Rights. It is fitting it should be related here.

A volunteer missionary found a woman in the last stages
of consumption in the sixth storey of a dilapidated tenement
house in the Hell's Kitchen district of New York. She asked the
woman if she could do anything for her. The whispered reply
was: 'My time is short, but I can only die a peaceful death if
you save the little child next door'. At that moment the visitor
heard blows and the screams of a child. The dying woman said
the child (known as Mary Ellen) was beaten day after day and
night after night by her 'mother'. The missionary knocked on
the door of the adjoining room. A hulking brute of a man
answered and with vile epithets threatened to throw the visitor
down the stairs. She went to the policeman on post. He bluntly
told her he could not break the door without a warrant. She
next went to a police magistrate. 'You have no eye-witnesses,'
he impatiently told the good woman when she finally reached
him. Mrs Wheeler turned to the charitable institutions and
orphanages. 'We cannot take a child without a commitment
from the Court', was the answer. She appealed to lawyers and
those rich men whose names headed lists of philanthropies.
'Madam,' they told her, 'this is a very dangerous thing for you
to undertake. You are not the guardian. The parents have a
right to correct a child. You may be arrested if you interfere in
such a case.' Her spiritual adviser told her the same thing. She
related to me a short time before her death, a few years ago,
'the cries of that child rang in my ears at night. I could not
sleep'.

Finally, she learned there was a Society for the Prevention
of Cruelty to Animals in New York. She laid the case before
Henry Bergh, its founder. Elbridge T. Gerry, that great
pioneer in humanitarian work, who devoted thirty-five years of
his life and thousands of his fortune to the cause of legal
protection of children, was the Counsel of the Animal Society.
'Come to me at once', was the message Mr. Bergh sent to Mr.
Gerry, 'I need your advice and counsel'. Gerry searched the
statute books in vain for some law which would justify the
rescue of the child. There was none. Animals were protected,
but not children. Finally, he decided he might reach the child

as a 'little animal' of the human race — a little animal which
happened to have a soul. Officers of the Animal Society
removed the child, seized the scissors with which her head and
body had been beaten and gashed, arrested the woman; and
brought little Mary Ellen into the only available covering, a
horse blanket, before Justice Lawrence of the Supreme Court.

A reporter at that time for a newspaper told me years
afterwards 'strong men who looked at that bruised, battered
little body, wept like children and wondered how they had
been blind to it all for so many years'. The woman and her
husband, foster-parents, by the way, who had *legally* adopted
the child out of an institution, were convicted and sent to
prison.

The public was now thoroughly aroused. Mr. Gerry, Mr.
Bergh, and Mr. John D. Wright, a Quaker gentleman of
prominence, then signed this famous declaration — our
'inspiration' as we call it:

> We, the undersigned, desirous of rescuing the unprotected
> children of this city from the cruelty and demoralisation
> which neglect and abandonment engender, hereby
> engage to aid with sympathy and support, a children's
> protective society, having in view the realisation of so
> important a purpose.

Men of the greatest prominence have associated
themselves with the movement, and the Society, as now
constituted, came into being.

As the new American Society grew in strength things were moving in
England. More and more people were coming to feel that children were
suffering needlessly and that the community could no longer remain
blind to this fact. Amongst the voices which were being raised one of the
most prophetic was that of the Rev. George Staite, Vicar of Ashton-
haves, Cheshire, who was the author of two letters published in the
Liverpool Mercury in the Spring of 1881, which are important enough to
be quoted at length:

SOCIETY FOR THE PREVENTION OF CRUELTY TO CHILDREN

Gentlemen, — Amongst benevolent institutions there does not
appear to be one for getting at unrevealed cases of cruelty to
children. Most neighbourhoods furnish such instances, which
are freely talked about by neighbours, but receive no further
attention. There seems to be wanted an organisation for
looking into all doubtful cases of real or supposed cruelty and
neglect, and not waiting for them to come to light of
themselves, which many never do.

A case in point was reported last week. A child was

alleged to have been killed by its father dashing it against the wall, and placing it on a stool whence it fell on the fender and subsequently died. The only witness was a child too young to be sworn; and so the case had to be dismissed and would probably never have been heard of but for the accidental killing of the child. Existing agencies are inadequate for reaching such cases. For instance, the district visitor looks upon her avocation as being more spiritual than temporal, and more to the adult than to the children. She leaves her tract with a kindly inquiry for the general spiritual welfare of the family, and is, in most instances, young and inexperienced in the matter of children. The school attendance officer gives an occasional perfunctory call, but his sole business is to get the children to school. If the family want parish relief, the relieving officer calls, and if satisfied of their indigence (the squalid condition of the family being rather a recommendation than otherwise) he relieves them to the extent of two or three shillings a week, and thence his duty ends. Nor can much reliance be placed on neighbours as regards taking the initiative. They will talk freely and in words sympathise, readily giving, when judiciously asked, useful information, but they do not personally wish 'to have any bother' with those perhaps in the same street as themselves, or even next door.

The letter continues with extensive descriptions of cases of severe neglect known to the writer and then concludes:

Let there be formed, say in Liverpool, a society consisting of a committee and organising secretary having for its object something like the following:

1. To appoint voluntary correspondents in different districts (a few to begin with) who would look up any rumoured cases of cruelty and report upon them. Also to get discrete persons to visit such reported cases, and to use their personal influence with the unkind parents and guardians, and by their presence act as a check to them.
2. To show parents and guardians of children their responsibility (of which they are sadly ignorant) as such, by preaching, lecturing, and distributing good, wholesome, salutary literature.
3. To aim generally at doing work for children in their homes, and to influence public opinion upon the subject.

     Some such plan as I have sketched, would not require expensive machinery. It would be a practical, honest, loving work, in which all could join irrespective of religious creed. If any of your readers would be willing to forward such work, the writer would be glad to have their views, and would gladly enter into further details.

A Cheshire Vicar

A second letter from 'A Cheshire Vicar' written in response to intervening correspondence cites more case histories of child neglect and abuse, and then continues:

How can they be dealt with? Surely by some such plan as I have advocated in your columns of the 15th instant, viz. to personally visit these homes: search out the likely cases: enlist the interest of house-to-house visitors: enlighten the ignorant: help with Christian sympathy those mothers who may have great hardships to encounter and overcome, with the paramount object of doing work for those of the flock of whom our Lord said 'of such is the Kingdom of Heaven'. There are children's refuges, homes, hospitals, schools: but there is no system of rescuing the little ones in their homes, who now in vain raise their puny voices and stretch out their emaciated arms for help, whose cry, in countless numbers, never reaches the ear of the great Babylon in which it has been their misfortune to be born.

But for such work as this an organisation is necessary. To those who have laboured much in large and poor districts, and know from experience something of the inner life of even the most abandoned, the work will not appear altogether utopian and impracticable. To ladies generally, and to those especially who occupy the proud position of mothers, I think the work would in time commend itself, and their influence and experience could not fail to have a most salutary effect upon the inner life of those who now furnish the most numerous instances of criminal cruelty and neglect.

A Cheshire Vicar

The Reverend Mr Staite turned to the great Lord Shaftesbury for advice and help which were readily given, but even he quailed at the suggestion that children be given rights in their own homes by Parliament. In a letter of the late summer of 1881 he wrote: 'This evils you state are enormous and indisputable, but they are of so private, internal, and domestic a character as to be beyond the reach of legislation, and the subject, indeed, would not, I think, be entertained in either House of Parliament'. Nevertheless, he gave the project his blessing.

At this very moment, on the other side of the Atlantic, a visiting Englishman to the United States was making enquiries which were destined to have great and lasting results. Mr T. F. A. Agnew, a Liverpool businessman, saw in New York a sign 'Society for the

Prevention of Cruelty to Children'. He was ignorant of what was being said and written at home, but was fascinated by his discovery, and receiving the utmost courtesy from the officials of the New York Society determined to promote the formation of a similar body at home on his return to Liverpool.

And now to turn to the words of Mr Agnew himself in another Occasional Paper again undated (but attributed to 1925) edited by Sir Robert J. Parr O.B.E. who was another distinguished Director of the English Society, from the records and writings of Mr Agnew himself.

In 1882 I returned to Liverpool, bringing with me all the Reports of American societies on which I could lay my hands. I gave them to the Central Relief Society. Mr Henry Cox, its Chairman, Mr Christopher Bushell, its Deputy-Chairman, and Mr William Grisewood all spoke approvingly of them and gave them a place in their next report. I showed them also to Mr Samuel Smith, then MP for Liverpool, and he said: 'This is the very lever we want, the lever for which we have been waiting.'

A few weeks later I met him quite casually in the street, and he said: 'I am on my way to the Town Hall to attend a meeting of the Society for the Prevention of Cruelty to Animals. I have to propose the establishment of a Home for Dogs. Could we not turn it into a Home for Children? Come along with me and see.' So we went together to the Town Hall.

He made an excellent speech for the Home for Dogs, and then most adroitly launched out into an appeal for a Home for Children. Under this heading he gave a very effective sketch of what had been attempted in America. I felt very nervous, for, of course, the whole thing was highly irregular, but to my great delight Mrs Forrer, the President of the Society for protecting animals, said openly: 'I am here for the prevention of cruelty, and I can't draw the line at children': and Dr Manifold, the medical adviser of the Society, said: 'Mr Samuel Smith has not in the least exaggerated the sufferings of children: I know the town well, and I know that such a Society is much needed.' The Mayor, Mr William Radcliffe, turned to me and said: 'If you will get up a requisition, I will call a town's meeting'.

That meeting was a great success. There was not even standing room for all of the great number who came. The Society was formed by a unanimous vote, and Mr J. C. Houghton, one of our leading philanthropists, rose and said: 'This is a red-letter day in the history of the Town Hall'.

Our first duty was to draw up rules, and we were fortunate in having the advice, to keep us right, of such men as Mr W. S. Stewart, afterwards Stipendiary Magistrate:

Captain Eaton, R.N., Superintendent of School Board
Visitors: Mr Arnold Cleaver: and Mr H. J. Hagger, Vestry
Clerk.

We then rented a little house in Nile Street as a Shelter.
We were fortunate in securing Mr and Mrs Brackstone as
Superintendents. She was very kind and judicious in the care
of the children, and he was a man of good judgment,
absolutely fearless in facing the violence and brutality which
then prevailed in the lower parts of the town. One man who
applied for the post of Superintendent, a man of excellent
character, highly recommended, six feet two inches in height,
withdrew his application because he honestly said he could not
face the brutality of the slums.

The first of our cases which attracted public attention was
that of Helen Harrecan. Her father struck her in the eye with
his clenched fist. The mother reported him to the police. He
was arrested and brought before Mr Raffles, the then
Stipendiary. In the Court the poor little girl's black eye and
swollen face told their own tale, and the father was sentenced
to three months' imprisonment. This sounds to us quite right,
but it was not so then. The very reporters in Court could not
believe their ears. What, punish a man for hitting his own
child! In his own house! The newspapers published the
sentence with numerous comments. The Baroness Burdett-
Coutts wrote from London to ask for all particulars; Miss
Hesba Stretton called at the Shelter, and afterwards wrote to
'The Times' that a similar Society was much needed in
London.

And a little later in the pamphlet he describes the function of that
Society.

I explained to Miss Hesba Stretton and to Mr Benjamin
Waugh the course we had followed in Liverpool, and they both
said we could not have a better precedent. Then Mr Waugh
placed his office entirely at our disposal, and I agreed to return
next day with my friend, Mr Charles Reynolds, who was then
a man of leisure, to set to work upon the petition to the Lord
Mayor. The weather was hot to a degree, so Mr Waugh, Mr
Reynolds and I threw off our coats and waistcoats, and it was
for some time a joke against us that we received in our shirt-
sleeves all the big people who called.

In the work of getting up this petition I should have been
helpless but for Mr Benjamin Waugh and Miss Hesba
Stretton. They seemed to know everyone in London, and the
signatures of this immense petition were of great value later on,
for they gave us a large selection of names from which to form

our Committees. These good names put the Society on the broad and national lines on which it afterwards developed. But for these names the Society would certainly have fallen into the hands of a few excellent society people, who might have kept its management and its policy within narrow limits.

Mr Benjamin Waugh was always good at arranging a platform, and on this occasion he excelled himself. The Lord Mayor was in the chair, on his right was the Earl of Shaftesbury, on his left the Baroness Burdett-Coutts. All the speakers were well chosen and did their work well. Among them were Cardinal Manning and Sir Henry Fowler. A quotation by Sir Henry Fowler from Elizabeth Browning seemed to ring through the whole meeting: 'The young, young children, O my brothers!'

Among those who were invited was Sir Mark Collet, afterwards Governor of the Bank of England. I know that at the time he was overwhelmed with work, yet he found time to come to the meeting and sit on the platform. And so it was with many others; they came under circumstances of great difficulty to express their sympathy with suffering children.

Lord Shaftesbury wrote to me before this meeting, suggesting that we should form a National Society, but I explained to him that Liverpool, Birmingham, and Bristol had already formed local Societies, so the new movement was called the London Society. If I had been a prophet, I should have acted on Lord Shaftesbury's suggestion and thereby have averted some amount of controversy.

In this account there is good evidence of all the principles explored in Appendix A on voluntarism. Then in his writing a paragraph or two later is the almost accidental link with the Scottish situation.

While I was working for the London Society, an 'old Edinburgh Academy' boy, Mr James Grahame, of Glasgow, claimed acquaintance with me, and said if I would come down to Glasgow first and to Edinburgh afterwards, he would arrange for two meetings and the formation of two Societies. This he did, and the Edinburgh and Glasgow Societies are still in existence.

Looking at that link from a different point of view we can read the account of the formation of the Scottish Society as reported in the Annual Report of 1908 on the occasion of the Silver Jubilee of the Scottish Society.

FIVE AND TWENTY YEARS AGO

A quarter of a century has now passed since the Society was founded, and it is with thankful hearts that we look back upon the work accomplished in rescuing ill-treated and neglected little children from misery and sorrow, and in restoring to them the brightness and joy which is the birthright of every child.

To America belongs the proud distinction of leading the way in the founding of Societies for the Prevention of Cruelty to Children. Ten years before there was any such Society in Great Britain the New York Society began its beneficent work. It is interesting to recall the circumstances which led to the establishment of a Society for the Prevention of Cruelty to Children in our own country. In the year 1878, Mr James Grahame, C.A., Glasgow, then residing at Auldhouse, Pollokshaws, took his family to a circus about Christmas time. Amongst the performers there was an acrobat with some children — not his own. One little boy of four years of age was forced to undergo such contortions that Mr Grahame left the performance in disgust. Next morning, he went to the Chief Constable and lodged information against the man for cruelty to children. The Chief Constable at once proceeded to take action, but he found that the man had left Glasgow and had gone to Manchester. It was afterwards learned that the law of England was different from that of Scotland, and that no prosecution could be undertaken. In 1881 Mr Grahame paid a visit to America, and almost the first day after his arrival he read in the 'New York Herald' that an acrobat had been arrested for cruelty to a child. Mr Grahame at once went to the Children's Shelter maintained by the New York Society for the Prevention of Cruelty to Children, where he found it was the same child that he had seen performing in Glasgow. Further enquiries brought out the fact that the inhuman acrobat had confessed that he had ill-treated the child with a red-hot poker in order to make him do his tricks. From this object-lesson of the value of the work of the Society for the Prevention of Cruelty to children, Mr Grahame returned to Glasgow fired with the ambition of founding a similar society there. He called a meeting, but did not succeed in making those present believe that such and other atrocities could take place in the city of Glasgow. Three years afterwards, he had again occasion to be in New York, and further experience confirmed the desire to start a Society in Glasgow. On his return to Scotland he was more successful, and on 23rd July 1884 was founded the Glasgow Society for the Prevention of Cruelty to Children. The first Office-bearers were as follows: President; The Earl of Glasgow; Chairman of Executive Committee, Mr James Grahame; Honorary Treasurer, Mr Robert Gourlay; Honorary Secretary, Major Lysons; Law

Agent, Mr C. D. Donald; Consulting Physician, Professor T. McCall Anderson; Physician, Dr W. G. Dun. Work was commenced that same year with a Shelter and three Officers. At the end of the first year it was found that 595 cases, involving 1173 children, had been dealt with. In Edinburgh the movement took shape in the course of the same year, and on 15th October, at a public meeting held in the Music Hall under the chairmanship of Lord Provost Sir George Harrison, the Edinburgh Society for the Prevention of Cruelty to Children was formed. The Office Bearers included the Duchess of Buccleuch, Patroness; Lord Polwarth, President; Professor Grainger Stewart, Hon. Surgeon; Mr R. C. Gray, S.C.C., Law Agent; Mr Andrew Scott, C.A., Honorary Secretary (now Auditor of the Society); and Mr Archibald Langwill, C.A. Honorary Treasurer. Amongst those who took part in the meeting were Mr James Grahame, Glasgow, and Mr Frederick Agnew, Chairman of the Liverpool Society, which was founded in 1883.

Nor was the movement confined to our own country. Across the Border the late Rev. Benjamin Waugh founded in 1884 the London Society for the Prevention of Cruelty to Children. Four years later the London Society, which was extending its work to the English Provinces, assumed the name of the National Society, and it has now an organisation extending over a considerable portion of England, Wales, and Ireland.

The subsequent history of the Societies in Scotland is soon told. In 1886 the Edinburgh Society finding that similar work was being done by the Edinburgh and Leith Children's Aid and Refuge Society, which had been founded by the late Miss Emma Stirling in 1877, joined with that Society, and the Society thus re-enforced united in 1889 with the Glasgow Society under the title of the Scottish National Society for the Prevention of Cruelty to Children. In the following year the Society was honoured by H.R.H. the Prince of Wales, now King Edward VII, becoming its President, and H.R.H. the Duchess of Fife becoming a Patron. After the passing of the Prevention of Cruelty to Children Act in 1894, the Society in Scotland was led to affiliate with the Society in England, and became known the following year as the National Society for the Prevention of Cruelty to Children, Scottish Branch. This continued till July 1907 when, questions having been raised, it was found on enquiry that for some reason which has never been satisfactorily explained the Terms of Affiliation had not been given effect to in the Royal Charter of Incorporation which the Society in England had obtained, and in consequence thereof the English Society subsequently intimated that they were unable to carry out the Terms of Affiliation with the Society in Scotland. As the Society in England declined to take any steps to obtain the requisite powers, the Society in Scotland resumed its independent position, and in July 1907, after due public advertisement, reverted to its former title of the Scottish National Society for the Prevention of Cruelty to Children. A new Constitution was prepared, and it is a matter of much satisfaction that it was adopted unanimously at a special general meeting held on 21st May 1908.

Contained within that report are the indications that the formation of organisations is not always easy and smooth and some of the tensions, competition and defensive reaction which can emerge when there is strong commitment to a movement and to which reference is made in Appendix A are apparent. The events referred to are very clearly documented in the annual report of 1906 as follows:

CONSTITUTIONAL QUESTIONS

We greatly regret that the hope has not been realised which was expressed last year, that a way would be found out of the difficulties which have emerged in connection with the Royal Charter. In explanation of the situation it may be well to begin by stating that in the year 1889 the Edinburgh and Leith Children's Aid and Refuge Society and the Glasgow Society for the Prevention of Cruelty to Children amalgamated under the title of the Scottish National Society for the Prevention of Cruelty to Children. In 1895, at the instance of the National Society for the Prevention of Cruelty to Children, London, we were invited to affiliate with that Society, and became the 'N.S.P.C.C. (Scottish Branch)'. The main conditions insisted on by our Society were that we should retain complete control of our work, funds, and property. It was further agreed, 'that all legacies left by Scottish testators domiciled in Scotland to the National Society for the Prevention of Cruelty to Children (unless directly specified to the contrary) should belong to the Scottish Branch'. This affiliation was entered into with the view of obtaining a Royal Charter of Incorporation to cover the whole of the United Kingdom. The Royal Charter was immediately afterwards granted. The negotiations for the Charter were carried through by the officials of the English Society in London, whose duty it was to see that the conditions of affiliation were given effect to. For ten years or more, and until recently, the affiliation has been acted on by both parties. It has now been ascertained that for some unexplained reason the terms of affiliation were not given effect to in the Charter,

and in these circumstances the English Society are unable to
fulfil the obligations they undertook. To our surprise and
regret the English Society have declined to take any steps to
get the Charter amended so that that they might be in a
position to carry out the conditions agreed upon. We then
offered to make any concessions necessary to overcome the
merely technical difficulties while adhering to the general
principles embodied in the affiliation. We regret that
prolonged negotiations have failed to bring about a solution of
the difficulty owing to the attitude of the English Society,
specially regarding the matter of the Scottish legacies already
referred to. These legacies they now insist upon claiming, and
have intimated that after a very limited period they will retain
them as their absolute property. To this we cannot agree. We
hold that when Scottish people domiciled in Scotland leave
money to the 'N.S.P.C.C.' the intention of the testators is, in
the absence of any indication to the contrary, and in view of
the terms of the agreement of affiliation, that it should be
administered by the Society in Scotland for the benefit of the
children of Scotland. On the whole subject being considered
by the General Council at a special meeting held last March, it
was decided that a petition should be presented to the Crown
praying that the Charter might be amended so as to give effect
to the terms of affiliation. Subsequently the English Society
proposed to refer the whole matter to arbitration. We would
very gladly have accepted this proposal had it been necessary
and possible. We had already offered to meet the views of the
English Society on all points except as concerning the legacies
already referred to, and therefore it was unnecessary; and in
view of the opinion of eminent counsel consulted we found that
as Trustees we were not in a position to submit the matter of
these legacies to arbitration. We have now learned that the
Privy Council have established a rule to the effect that no
application for an amendment can be entertained which does
not come from the governing body of the Association to whom
the Charter has been granted. As the English Society, who
have got the Charter in their name alone, decline to take any
action, it is evident that there is no course open to us but to
resume the position of an independent Scottish Society which
we occupied prior to entering upon the unfortunate affiliation
of 1895.

   We therefore recommend that the former title of the
Society be re-adopted, viz.: 'The Scottish National Society for
the Prevention of Cruelty to Children', and that the
constitution be revised and submitted to a Special General
Meeting as speedily as possible.

These same events are recorded from the point of view of the National Society in England, in a confidential report prepared by the then director Robert Parr in 1907 and here reproduced verbatim in certain parts to indicate the complexity of the relationships of the time:

A Short History of the Relations between the National Society for the Prevention of Cruelty to Children and the Scottish Society for the Prevention of Cruelty to Children.

1. The London Society for the Prevention of Cruelty to Children was founded on the 11th July, 1884. In 1889, the Society having spread its organisation to 31 cities and towns, revised its Constitution and adopted the title of the 'National Society for the Prevention of Cruelty to Children' on May 14th of that year. On the 23rd October, 1894, the Constitution was again revised in order to give Branches a fuller representation in the management of the Society, they having by this time become numerous, and the operations of the Society having extended over the greater part of England, Wales and Ireland.

2. In February, 1894, it was decided, in view of the national importance of the work undertaken by the Society, and the difficulty of obtaining adequate support that application should be made to the Treasury for a grant from the Imperial Funds. This application was not successful, the Chancellor of the Exchequer stating that the Society 'did not come within the scope of Institutions to which it was possible to make public grants.' Enquiries were made, and there was reason to believe that such an application would be likely to meet with better success if the Society possessed legal status such as would be secured by Incorporation. It was thereupon decided to present a petition to Her Majesty Queen Victoria asking that a Royal Charter of Incorporation might be granted to the Society. This Petition was accordingly presented in March, 1895.

3. At this time there was in existence in Scotland a Society called the Scottish National Society for the Prevention of Cruelty to Children. This Society was the outcome of what was termed a 'Federal Union', in the year 1889, between a Society founded in Edinburgh in or about the year 1877 under the name of the Edinburgh and Leith Children's Aid and Refuge, and a similar Society founded in Glasgow. Friendly relations had for some time existed between this Scottish Society and the National Society, the two bodies being often able to assist each other in making investigations into cases.

4. The Scottish Society became aware of the proposal of the National Society to apply for a Charter and a Government Grant, and through Mr John Macdonald, then Secretary of

the Edinburgh Committee of the Scottish Society, it expressed a desire to associate with the English Society in such a way that it might secure a share in these benefits if obtained.

5. It has been alleged by the Scottish Society that their co-operation was sought by the National Society in its efforts to obtain a Royal Charter, and it is even asserted that Her Majesty the late Queen refused to grant a Charter to the National Society unless Scotland was included. This is not true. No demur whatever was made by the Crown Authorities to the National Society's Petition for its Charter, nor is it the fact that the National Society sought the co-operation of the Scottish body. In the Petition no mention whatever was made of Scotland, the Scottish Society, or its work. This allegation was first made in June, 1896, by Mr Grahame, the Managing Director of the Scottish Society. It was repudiated at once by the Rev Benjamin Waugh, the Director of the National Society, who wrote on 11th June of that year.

These meetings are recorded by a paragraph in *The Child's Guardian* a National Society publication of that time as follows:

DECISION OF THE SCOTTISH NATIONAL SOCIETY
UNION OF THE NATION

The Annual Meeting of the Scottish National Society for the Prevention of Cruelty to Children was held on Saturday, the 19th January, in the Freemasons' Hall, George Street, Edinburgh. There was a large attendance, and the Marquis of Tweeddale presided. Mr John Macdonald, secretary, read the report by the Board of Management. In the report it was stated that the Board of Management had decided to recommend that the Society should affiliate itself with the National Society for the Prevention of Cruelty to Children, so as to form a Society comprehending the whole United Kingdom. The Chairman said he thought they would approve of that part of the report which referred to the important proposal to unite the Society with the National Society for the Prevention of Cruelty to Children. He commended the proposal from a financial as well as from an administrative point of view. The Rev Mr Waugh then addressed the Meeting in favour of the recommendation. Mr James Grahame than moved that the Meeting confirm the resolution of the Board of Management, that the Society be united with the National Society, and remit to the Board of Management to carry it out. Dr Littlejohn seconded, and the motions were unanimously agreed to. Mr John Usher, Sir Douglas Maclagan, and Mr J. R. Findlay took part in the further proceedings.

and then later in the same publication:

EXTRAORDINARY MEETING OF THE COUNCIL

On the 22nd of January, at three p.m., at the Holborn Restaurant, an Extraordinary Meeting of the Council was held, under the presidency of Lord Ancaster. There were also present the Marquis and Marchioness of Tweeddale, Earl of Gifford, Countess of Ancaster, Lady Farrer, Hon. and Mrs Stephen Coleridge, Colonel Studdy, W. H. Collingridge, Alderman Rayden, J. Macdonald, J, Mackrell, C. G. Husband, J. Allanson Picton, Rev A. Holborn, M.A., Rev A. H. Hayes, Rev T. Stenhouse, Dr Buchanan, Miss Anderson, C. W. Craddock, W. C. Craggs, T. Hornung, Mrs Hedley, F. D. How, Mrs Hamlyn, W. Clarke Hall, Mrs Henry Lee, D. W. Macleod, C. Kegan Paul, W. B. Robotham, Miss Rayne, H. S. Squance, J. Tijou, H. Wright, T. Gill Williams, Rev B. Waugh.

The first business was to receive a deputation from the Scottish National Society for the Prevention of Cruelty to Children. The deputation consisted of the Marquis of Tweeddale and Mr John Macdonald. Its object was to convey the decision of the Scottish Society to unite with the National Society. Mr Macdonald and the Marquis of Tweeddale both spoke, and the Chairman said he rejoiced that now they would have a union of the British Isles in the service of its children, a fact which he believed would be for the good of every part of the land.

The Chairman having explained the advantages of the Society being incorporated, both as regards its own internal management and its relations to Parliament, Mr Wright, Reading, moved that a count be made. On a count being made, it was found that only thirty-six members were present.

During the discussion of the question of the Charter, which was continued by Mr Alderman Rayden, Mr Mackrell, Mr Squance, Mr Blews Robotham, Mr Kegan Paul, Mrs Hedley, Mr Wright and others, efforts were made to obtain four more members of the Council to make the quorum. These efforts failed, and it was finally agreed that the Council be again summoned to meet on Thursday, the 31st of January next, in the same place, at three p.m. Notices to this effect have been issued.

The confidential report then continues and paragraph 10 indicates the deterioration of relationships:

10. On the 28th May, 1895, a Royal Charter of Incorporation was granted to the National Society, but a

change of Ministry occurring on the 2nd July of that year the idea of making a further application to the Treasury for a grant was abandoned. There is little doubt that when this became known to the Scottish Society, its view of the advantages to be derived from union with the National Society was somewhat modified, while on the part of the National Society there was a growing dissatisfaction at the reluctance on the part of the Scottish Society to loyally adopt the methods of the National Society, and to make the so-called affiliation of practical use to the children of Scotland. An application from the Scottish Society for a loan of £500 was refused by the National Society.

The following paragraphs refer to exchanges of correspondence and visits in which misunderstandings are apparent. Paragraph 15 describes articles about the National Society in London newspapers accusing it of waste and corruption. Paragraph 16 refers to the report of an inquiry under Lord Herschel which cleared the Society. Paragraphs 18 and 19 refer to the absconding of the Secretary of the Scottish Society and how warrants for his arrest brought bad publicity upon the National Society. Paragraph 19 then details:

19. The Committee of the National Society thereupon considered that the time had come when the relations between the two Societies must be placed upon a strictly legal footing. The Legal Advisers of the Society were consulted, and, as the result of careful investigation, the Committee was advised that the so-called Affiliation was non-existent, that it had been entered into not by the Society as an Incorporated body as defined in its Royal Charter, but by the old Society which had previously existed, and that in the absence of any ratification of the affiliation by the National Society, as Incorporated, the Scottish Society had no right or title to use the description of the 'National Society for the Prevention of Cruelty to Children — Scottish Branch' which they had been using for 11 years.

Then follow a number of paragraphs referring to legal disputes over the disposal of legacies from supporters resident in Scotland, in particular a Miss Janet Dow and a Miss Isabella Shiell. Paragraph 27 refers to an attempt at solution:

27. In May, 1906, a Conference was held in London between elected representatives of the Scottish Society and the National Society with a view to discussing future relations between the two Societies, and it was eventually agreed by the representatives of the National Society to recommend that their Executive Committee should entertain proposals for an Affiliation of the Scottish Society on terms similar to those of

1895, but with such modifications as the terms of the Charter Bye-Laws and Regulations demanded. The terms of 1895 were gone through seriatim and agreed to so far as the proviso just referred to allowed, with the exception of the clause relating to legacies, the adjustment of which, it was pointed out, was too complicated for the Conference to deal with and must be a matter for negotiation between the Solicitors of the two Societies. The Conference having been so far in agreement and there appearing to be reasonable hope of a friendly solution of the difficulties, the question of Miss Shiell's bequest was alluded to, and it was mutually agreed between the representatives of both Societies that, if the Scottish Branch would abstain from lodging a claim to the bequest in the action of Multiplepoinding then pending, the National Society would, upon receipt of the amount, pay it over to the Scottish Society.

Further paragraphs then refer to continued legal wrangling and disagreement between the two societies. The period was not easy for the Scottish Society as paragraph 32 describes:

32. That this danger is by no means an impossible one, the unfortunate internal dissensions in the Scottish Society give proof, and it is evident that the Scottish Society, having discovered that the contention of the legal advisers of the National Society was correct, and had no right or title to use its name, have found it extremely difficult to define their present existence and powers. They have reverted to their former title of the Scottish National Society for the Prevention of Cruelty to Children, and are now endeavouring to agree upon a fresh Constitution.

The report of the dispute continues and then concludes on 30 October 1907 with these paragraphs:

36. These proceedings were by a third party, being undertaken by Sir Henry Littlejohn, on behalf of what was originally the Edinburgh Committee of the Scottish Society, who claims that the Scottish Society having ceased to exist, the Edinburgh Committee have reverted to the position they originally held as an independent Society previous to the Federal Union referred to in the earlier portion of this History, and that they, and not the Scottish Society, are entitled to Miss Shiell's bequest, since she was a subscriber to the Edinburgh centre. The National Society feel that these proceedings abundantly justify their position in declining to enter into a fresh affiliation with the Scottish Society, or to hand over any money to it until its legal status is beyond question.

37. The National Society is anxious that it should be made quite clear that it has no wish to take from the Scottish Society bequests properly belonging to that Society. It has no doubt that the majority of bequests to the 'National Society for the Prevention of Cruelty to Children' left by Scottish Testators are intended for the Scottish Society, and apart from the legal position morally belong to it. It is only anxious that by a judicial decision it may be relieved of any charge of improperly handing over sums of money, which are Trust funds, to another body and that one which at present admittedly has no legal status, no constitution, and no sufficiently defined membership to enable it to sue an action.

38. The National Society is anxious also to secure that any legacies bequeathed to it by Scottish subscribers to its funds (of which there are a considerable number), shall be secured to it, and that there shall be no risk of their being paid over to the Scottish Society. It is also determined to prevent the improper and unauthorised use of its name.

This report has been analysed in detail, not only as a record of an important phase in the development of both Societies but also because it so clearly indicates many of the issues referred to in Appendix A, the complexity of the emergence of an organisation including the importance of the personalities involved and effect of their relationships in the negotiations. The difficulty of reconciling deep commitment to local branch autonomy with its feelings of independence and specialised support, with the emerging needs for national coordination and the presentation of a united image to the general public. The influence of the media in emphasising any tensions which existed is highlighted and the dangerous effects upon a voluntary organisation of any suggestion of weakness in administration of voluntary funds. All these issues are clearly apparent and there is little doubt that these difficulties arising early in the history of both Societies, although at the time obviously traumatic and threatening, were also the furnace which tempered the strength of the structures which subsequently emerged.

Fortunately there are also records of the gradual resolution of the difficulty and the recognition of the need for two independent but related and co-operating organisations. This was eventually achieved at an arranged negotiation or conference between the leading executive members of the two Societies for which the following extension of the above report was prepared for National Society participants by the Director, Robert Parr in November 1908.

After referring to the failure of Sir Henry Littlejohn's interdict of the Edinburgh committee because they had no permanent base, the report goes on to refer to a new legal argument over the legacy of a Mr James Crombie of Aberdeen. In hearing this dispute the Sheriff-

Substitute had held that the real question was 'What were the testator's intentions'. Consideration was given to an appeal to the House of Lords but instead a decision was made to try again to arrange agreement.

Therefore the report continues:

> 47. The latter course having been decided upon, the National Society communicated with the Rev P. C. Purves, asking him, as a Member of both Committees, to act as an intermediary between the two parties. This duty Mr Purves kindly undertook, with the result that a Conference was held between Counsel and law Agents acting for both Societies in the Crombie litigation. At this Conference Mr Purves was present, and a settlement was arrived at and signed by Counsel on both sides in the following terms:
>
> 1. The National Society to give a letter to the Scottish Society saying that it might retain the Crombie legacy.
> 2. A joint minute to be lodged by both Societies craving that the diet of proof in the action be discharged.
> 3. A Conference to be held forthwith between representatives of both Societies for the purpose of settling all differences and for providing, by Arbitration or otherwise, for the disposal of future *bequests in dispute, but providing that there should be excluded from the considerations of the Conference the merits of the Crombie bequest, and the merits of the bequest by the late Miss Shiell.*
> 4. At the expiry of three months from the date of settlement a minute to be lodged consenting to dismissal of the Crombie action with full costs to Crombie's Trustees and to the Scottish Society to the amount of £21.
>
> 48. The Conference now arranged for is the result of the above settlement. It must be borne in mind that the National Society desired that the Crombie litigation should be postponed pending the result of this Conference. To this the Scottish Society would not agree, and insisted upon the abandonment of the action with costs against the National Society. In view of this attitude the National Society stipulated that it should be at liberty to retain the amount of the Shiell bequest, which it had obtained by legal process, or, as an alternative, to recoup itself for the whole costs to which it has been put by the dispute with the Scottish Society before handing over to that Society the balance, if any.

The solution was found by this conference. Since 1908 the two national societies have pursued their own separate existence whilst helping each other by exchange of information and coordination of policies and initiatives. Probably the best example is the comparatively recent co-operation in research regarding non-accidental injury to children where the National Society's initiative in setting up special units on 'Non-accidential injury' was followed within Scotland in 1978 by a Special Unit in Glasgow at the Overnewton Centre. However, reference will be made again to these later developments. Having traced and explained the common emergence of the two independent national societies it is possible to go back to the beginning of the Scottish Society and record its separate development.

Whilst the struggle for independence might be seen as an example of Scottish insularity and nationalism it would be better to conclude that it was the result of the fierce local independence which characterised commitment to and involvement with an important cause. The Scottish Society itself was not free of such difficulties in its relation with its own strongly independent Branches. It is a characteristic of the organisation that it has managed to keep the tension between autonomy and independence of branches and coordination and unification of the national system in a productive and developing relationship with each other. Probably this early experience which has just been described helped to establish guidelines for that successful resolution of otherwise negative dissension.

3

ESTABLISHING THE SCOTTISH SOCIETY
the first phase

The early meetings of the Scottish Society were preoccupied with the establishment of a suitable organisation. The minutes of the first two meetings in Glasgow give their whole attention to the selection and appointment of a suitable Collector whose character and image were seen to be crucial to the reputation of the Society. This recognition that one of the first requirements of the organisation was to seek funds for its work and that it was necessary to be seen to be reliable and responsible in the task has continued throughout the life of the organisation. It continued in different branches of the Society later by the appointment of lady collectors who each had a specific district of the city or town as her responsibility and who developed a list of named regular contributors to the Society (in Glasgow in 1897 there were 25 Lady Collectors each with an average of 25 contributors in addition to a long list of subscriptions from individuals, firms and institutions. In Edinburgh in 1897 there were 111 Lady Collectors with a similar number of contributors each.) This practice continued until comparatively recently in the cities (and still exists in some rural areas) and all of the early annual reports contain the names of Lady Collectors, their districts, the names of their list of contributors and the amounts contributed by each individual. This rather unique way of providing for the recognition of individual member involvement would obviously have been, in the early days of a new organisation, a significant way of building up commitment and interest and, at the same time, recognising the need for accountability and responsibility. It is, of course, significant too in terms of the earlier analysis of philanthropy that the full-time Collector appointed by the Society was always a man but that these very important voluntary collectors were all women and that most of the names upon their list of contributors were also women.

The role of women in the development of the Society was everywhere significant, sometimes obvious and sometimes unobtrusive. As the Society gradually extended its operation, new branches were established and the nucleus of each new branch committee usually consisted of women.

Nevertheless in the affairs of the Executive Committee which was the official managing body of the organisation, the preponderance of members were always men and in the first few years exclusively so. Illustrious and important men who were public figures usually showed by attendance at these meetings that the movement had their authoritative support and gave it a public importance but it was often influential women, although by no means exclusively, who provided the charismatic leadership in the developments and who demonstrated a concerned and interested involvement in the work.

So we can read in the annual report of 1891, when the work of the Society was developing to such an extent that it was decided that in Edinburgh some form of more permanent residential care for children was needed, beyond the temporary care of the Shelter which was always a prerequisite of the establishment of branches in most urban areas. This led to the opening of the Murrayfield home, by the Marchioness of Tweeddale.

THE CHILDREN'S HOME, MURRAYFIELD

This Home was opened on the 28th of May by our good friend the Most Noble The Marchioness of Tweeddale, who twelve months before laid the foundation stone of the building. His Grace The Lord High Commissioner and Suite favoured the ceremony with their presence, and there was a large attendance of friends. The proceedings passed off in the most happy manner.

The Home has been found to answer most admirably the purposes for which it was built: it does credit to the architect, Mr Jerdan, and the different contractors. So large a number as 81 children are now resident there, and the benefit of the country air is already visible in the great improvement as to health and appearance of the young people. There has been no epidemic, and little or no sickness. One child died, but it was from a disease of the brain, and occurred a few days after admission to the Home.

The Committee have been fortunate in securing the services of a very efficient Lady Superintendent in Miss Sutter, who, with the assistance of Mr and Mrs Walker, has already gained the confidence and concern of the Committee and the affections of the children.

The elder children attend the Board School in the village of Corstorphine and the headmaster there reports very favourably of their behaviour and their progress. The younger ones are taught in the Home. Their religious training is also carefully looked after, and the Committee have to thank Mrs

POUND DAY AT CROOKSTONHALL, 1911

Neil Fraser and the other ladies who conduct a Sunday School
in the Home. During the year seven boys have been sent to
work: four as page-boys, two as apprentices to trades, and one
as a shop message boy. Three of the working boys have been
admitted to the Industrial Brigade. Two girls have been sent to
service. All the boys and girls who are working are doing well,
with one exception. In the summer vacation the bigger boys
worked at a neighbouring dairy and market-garden, and their
earnings amounted to £2.9.6d.

The Committee are thankful to record that the appeal
which they made to the public two years ago has now been
crowned with success. This beautiful Home, which supplies
such an urgently felt want, is now in full working order, and is
entirely free from debt.

Their thanks are due to those who so liberally subscribed
to the Building Fund, and to the public generally, for the
liberal manner in which they patronised the Bazaar in the
Waverley Market. They also owe their acknowledgements to
the ladies and others who worked so hard to make that Bazaar
a success.

The total cost of the Home, including furniture, fittings,
building Boundary wall and laying out of the garden, legal
expenses, and the expense of raising the fund, amounts in all to
£5086.11.2d.

An interesting comment on that report is both the importance of
the fund-raising for this kind of development and of the cost at that time,
compared with now, of such a development, even if we discount the
decreased value of money.

And again in the report for 1894 there is more evidence of the way
in which the Society gradually extended during this period and also the
important contribution to that development by leading public figures.

The Board of Management have to report that during the past
year the Society has throughout Scotland dealt with 1843
cases, involving the total of 3932 children. These figures do not
include a large number of other cases which are kept under
supervision by the officers of the Society or refer to parents who
have been cautioned, and whose conduct of their children is
closely observed, to the great advantage of the children by the
Society's officers. Of these 1383 have been sheltered and
clothed. Of these cases 182 have been of such a serious nature
that it has been found necessary to have the parents or
guardians prosecuted, and 182 convictions were secured under
the Prevention of Cruelty to Children Acts, 1889–94.

And also the following paragraphs:

The Board of Management would take this opportunity of congratulating the Marchioness of Tweeddale, and her daughter, Lady Clementine Hay, on the very great success that has attended the League of Pity, which was inaugurated by her ladyship last year, and the advantage that the magazine (*City Sparrows*), which is issued by the League, is to the Society. They have also to return their very best thanks to all connected with the League for the £430 received, all which has been devoted to the maintenance of the Children's Home at Murrayfield.

The Board of Management have also to acknowledge the great kindness with which the Duchess of Montrose has received, through the mediation of the Poor Children's Fresh-Air Fortnight Committee and its energetic convener, Mr MacKeith, a large number of children from the Shelter in Glasgow into her 'Holiday Home', to their great benefit and enjoyment during the past year.

This reference to the formation of the Children's League of Pity as Junior Branch of the Society is typical of other initiatives undertaken and further reference will be made to this organisation later.

The same report contains the following section on Edinburgh which again is illustrative of the development of the Society:

In Edinburgh, Leith and district 424 new cases have been inquired into and some hundreds of old cases have been kept under supervision. 390 have been sheltered and clothed. In 50 cases parents or guardians have been prosecuted and conviction secured. 50 children have been sent by order of the Court to Industrial and Training Schools and Ships and other Homes, including the Children's Home at Murrayfield.

The handsome new premises of the office of the Society and Shelter at the High Street have been found to be most convenient and suitable for the work. In February the Marchioness of Tweeddale held a most successful matinée of *tableaux vivants* in the Empire Theatre, which resulted in a donation of £450 to the Fund of the Society and her Ladyship has kindly offered, if necessary, to give another exhibition on the same lines next year. The debt on the Society Buildings is now reduced to £1607, the greater part of the interest on which is paid by the rent received from letting the basement flat.

The first ten years of development of the Society and the way it saw its role in the future was then expressed in the Annual Report of 1895–1896:

It will be remembered that in the beginning of 1895 the terms of affiliation of the Scottish National Society with the National Society for the Prevention of Cruelty to Children were completed, and the sphere of the National Society now embraces the whole of the United Kingdom, making it thus truly a national one.

A short time after the affiliation took place, Her Majesty the Queen, who has long been a Patron of the Society, graciously bestowed upon it a Royal Charter of Incorporation, under the terms of which Scotland is represented by gentlemen who have taken a warm interest in the Society.

Under the circumstances of the affiliation, and the necessity for a Central Office, Mr Grahame, the founder of the Society in Glasgow and the West of Scotland, was offered and accepted the office of Managing Director for Scotland in July last for one year, which terminates 15th August 1896, with the combined objects of establishing a uniformity of method and procedure, and information as to the work throughout Scotland, of bringing the Eastern and Western and other districts into closer union, and of extending the work of the Society throughout Scotland. The advantage of having a Central Office and a recognised Manager will be apparent to all who have these objects in view.

Until October, and somewhat later, the attention of the Managing Director was principally and necessarily directed to the codification of the law in Scotland regarding the safety and protection of children, and to the construction of forms of report by branches, on such a footing as would enable the Managing Director (as he is now able to do) to know exactly the amount and character of the work which has been done in all the various parts of the country on a uniform system.

The Managing Director has been largely indebted to the valuable assistance afforded him by Mr John Macdonald the present Hon. Treasurer of the Eastern District Committee, in matters generally: and in regard to the codification of the law for the instruction of Secretaries and Inspectors, to Mr R. C. Gray, S.S.C., of 37 Frederick Street, Edinburgh, and Mr Henry A. Roxburgh, of Messrs Wright, Johnston, Mackenzie, and Roxburgh, Solicitors, of 150 St Vincent Street, Glasgow, the law advisers to the Eastern and Western Committees.

What remains still as an urgent matter is the work of EXTENSION to which not only personal time and thought has to be applied, but which 'absolutely requires that the General Income of the Scottish Branch should be largely increased, if the Managing Director is to efficiently carry out the work by means of personal visitation of towns and of districts, and by the employment of Inspectors in those places where either the Society is not represented, or where it requires assistance financially'.

CHILDREN'S SHELTER: 142 High Street, Edinburgh.

It can only be by some such aid that the object of the Society can be fully attained, and that justice and protection can be brought within the reach of every suffering child throughout the country, and by which every child will have its legal and moral rights guarded and respected.

The funds of the Scottish Branch are barely sufficient to carry out the work as at present, and an urgent appeal is now made to the generosity of the public to subscribe to the funds, to enable the Society to extend its operations. Subscriptions will be gratefully received and acknowledged by John Macdonald, 3A Pitt Street, as Treasurer to the General Fund of the Scottish Branch; or by the Treasurer in Glasgow, Robert Gourlay, Bank of Scotland; or by the Secretaries of Local or Aid Committees, who will advise the same to Mr Macdonald.

Although various localities are now adequately provided with efficient branches, and Inspectors under their charge, still it is necessary to carry the crusade into districts where it is perfectly well known to the Society that its services are required, and as yet where there is no one whose direct duty it is to look after the interests of the suffering children.

We are met, in places where we had hoped for a totally different response, with the exploded idea that there is no such thing as cruelty and neglect to children within their borders. The Society can prove from numerous instances that some of the most terrible and depraved cases have occurred, not in the slums of our great cities, but in rural localities and country villages.

One has only to send an officer to any town to prove that melancholy truth; and it is no use for people to shut their eyes to evils that are going on amongst them, or close their ears to the appeals which are now being made; and as this is the first report by the Scottish Branch to the people of Scotland as a whole, it may be well to add briefly what the great aim and objects of the Society are.

These are to relieve the sufferings, and to save the lives, and to save the characters, of the neglected children of Scotland. In our great cities the regulations of the police enable them in a manner to cope with forms of cruelty or neglect which are 'apparent on the street'.

Under the Education Act the School Board enforces regular attendance at school, and by means of its inspectors can deal with the class of known but 'not attending school-children'.

The Parochial Board can and does afford considerable assistance to cases of 'sheer poverty', but there are two other spheres in which this Society, and this Society alone, is the

adequate agent of public benevolence; for there are classes in
the population who exist actually unseen by the Police or by
the School Board, or by any charitable or ecclesiastical
institution, and it is there that the greatest neglect and cruelty
naturally takes place.

Unless the victims of this cruelty or neglect are discovered
by one or other of the agencies before mentioned, their case is
sure to be overlooked; and it is the duty of this Society to seek
out and to afford an opportunity to all and sundry of informing
them of these cases of neglect and cruelty which are hidden
from all eyes except the casual eye of a neighbour, the
visitation of Inspectors, or the complaint of the unfortunate
victims themselves.

In short, the main object of the Society is to discover and
relieve acts of cruelty and neglect to children done against
them by their parents or guardians, in places which are
miscalled their 'homes', and where the offences are the result of
parental depravity, or intemperance, or of callous indifference
to the lives and happiness of their children.

The latter is not confined to the poorer classes, but has
been found to exist in quarters where a very different conduct
might have been expected.

The Society has no desire to interfere or to relieve parents
of their moral and legal duties of supporting and maintaining
their children; but they endeavour to enforce the discharge of
those duties and to assert the right of children to protection
against assault, neglect, and starvation, to warn offenders
against neglecting their duties, and in default of their
performance to enforce the law in the interest of the child.

Other charities may relieve parents of their children by
removing them to Homes or Institutions, but this Society exists
solely to enforce the duty of parents and guardians to house,
feed, and clothe the child, and only in extreme cases, where it is
obvious that the child cannot be safely left, the Society places
these children, by the authority of the Sheriff, in Industrial
Schools, Training Ships, or Homes.

The Society has also been the means, by supervision, of
relieving and ameliorating many a home, as can be seen by
inspection of the cases in our books. Many cases which were
the result of careless indifference, or bad habits, or bad
surroundings, on the part of the parents or guardians, have
been ameliorated; and the offenders warned have amended
their ways because they knew that the Society's officers were
there not only observing and warning them against any
infringement of the law, but would bring that law instantly
and effectively into action against them if necessary.

The Society has to look at the cases brought before it in a three-fold aspect.

First, and foremost, there is *The Child* to be considered. If it can be left, after warning, with its parents or guardian with due regard to its immediate future, moral and physical, it is left. It is only when it is perfectly clear that it would suffer both morally and physically that the Society appeals to the law for power to remove it from the charge of its parents or guardians.

The second is the *Advantage to the Community* of the Society's operations. Every child that is rescued from an untimely end and made a useful citizen, or who is saved from becoming a criminal, is a distinct gain to the community. Every child that is prevented from joining the criminal class becomes a useful member of Society, instead of being a perennial cost to the Police and to the Prison Board. We seek to save the flow of infant life before it enters into the channels which lead to prison, and we do a more effective work than even those benevolent Societies who meet the criminals discharged from prison and assist them to lead a new life.

Thirdly, the Society is bound to consider the *Parental Position*, and to refrain from interfering with the sanctity of home life by removing children from the guardianship of their parents, unless it is apparent that the latter are totally unfit to be trusted with their children, and that in the interests of the children and of the community they should be removed from their charge. It may be noted that in removing children to Industrial Schools or other places for protection, the Society invariably endeavours to compel the parents to contribute to their support.

The arguments in favour of the Society are too well known to require more particular expression, but they have been advocated by leading statesmen of all parties in politics, in both Houses of Parliament, and on public platforms, to the complete justification of the existence and operations of the Society.

Let us hope that none will cavil at or depreciate the objects and the work of the Society until they can conscientiously say that they have examined the matter thoroughly for themselves.

Every newspaper almost every day contains cases of cruelty and neglect of children which never would have been touched, or punished, or relieved, but for this Society.

Two Acts of Parliament have been passed, with the cordial approbation of all parties in Parliament — one in 1889, and another in 1894 — and fresh legislation for the protection

ANNE BLYTH — A CHILD AT THE CHILDREN'S SHELTER

142 High Street, Edinburgh.

of child life and nursed children is in progress — a measure
which has received terrible emphasis from a recent case in
England.

The Society appeals to the public on three grounds for
their support.

First, they, and all those 'who know the facts', and who
are convinced that children amongst us are suffering from
cruelty and neglect, are bound to call upon their fellow citizens
to aid them in their work.

Second, the Society, appeals to all the people of Scotland
from the motive of 'patriotism' to render their land 'Sweet and
wholesome', not only at present, but for years to come, by
rescuing infant life from premature termination, and many
young children of Scotland from a career of crime and vice.

Third, it is needless to say that it is a 'most economical
and wholesome way of relieving the ratepayers from the
charges which would otherwise be incurred' if these children
were permitted to become members of the great army of
criminals with which we have to deal, and for whom we have
to provide Reformatories, Industrial Schools, and Training
Ships, all of which must be paid for, not to speak of the
ultimate result of the law — long imprisonments and penal
servitudes.

The public are referred to the particular Reports
appended by the Eastern and Western Committees, and by the
District committee of Perthshire, for the work done in their
localities; and also to the Report showing the whole of the work
done by the Scottish Branch for the six months ending 31st
March 1896.

It will be observed that, imperfect as the constitution of
the Society is, yet, as regards all Scotland, the number of
offenders dealt with was at the rate of over 2600 per annum;
that the number of children affected was at the rate of over
4400 per annum; that of the children so dealt with, who were
clearly being neglected or ill treated, 546 were known to have
their lives insured, which was at the rate of about 1100 per
annum. It has been found necessary to prosecute in 89 cases
during the half-year and the rest of the cases were dealt with by
warnings and other means, and by supervision. It was found
necessary, with the sanction of the authorities, to remove,
under the auspices of the Society, to the Poor House, to
Industrial Schools, to Training Ships and Homes, 220 children
during the half-year, who certainly, but for the Society, would
have become morally or physically ruined. If the Society can
save even 440 children in the year from neglect and physical
degradation, or from becoming members of the criminal class,

who can say that the work does not deserve the heartiest
support of the people of Scotland?

HENRY D. LITTLEJOHN, V.P.,
Chairman, Board of Management
JAMES GRAHAME, V.P.,
Managing Director, pro tem

19th June 1896.

P.S. — It should not be forgotten that a useful and
energetic Society, originated on the movement of the Scottish
National Society, now flourishes in Dundee, although up to the
present time they have not seen their way to become a part of
the National Society.

The Dundee Society published its Fifth Annual Report,
and submitted it to their Subscribers on the 20th January
1896. In it they state 'the painful necessity there is for the
Society's existence' in Dundee, and that during the year 1895
they had taken up 267 cases, involving 411 children. It may be
observed that the number of cases bears a singular and almost
regular proportion to the population of cities and towns under
notice of the Society.

Since the 31st of March to the 30th June, namely, for the
quarter just ended, the Scottish Branch has investigated 464
new cases involving 1015 children.

The Act of 1889 referred to in this report was that which later
became known as the Children's Charter. It greatly enlarged the power
of the law over treatment of and responsibility for children. It restricted
employment of children and made begging by children forbidden. It
also gave the police power to arrest those suspected of ill-treating a child.
It was a significant support for the task of intervening in the affairs of the
family.

In this description of the formation of the Society reference has been
made to the development of the League of Pity, founded in Scotland in
1893 by the Marchioness of Tweeddale and headed by her daughter
Lady Clementine Hay. This followed an earlier initiative in England
which was reported in an Annual Meeting of the Society in 1939 as
follows:

> More than fifty years ago (1891), Benjamin Waugh went to
> speak at a meeting in Richmond, Surrey, and for the first time
> in our Society's history the proceedings were graced by the
> presence of Royalty, and there were present Her later Royal
> Highness the Duchess of Teck and her young daughter,
> Princess May. Benjamin Waugh appealed to the women
> present to form a committee which would collect subscriptions.

Among those who said 'Yes' was Princess May, and she took away a collecting card and a few weeks later there arrived at Waugh's desk that collecting card filled up with her own name and that of her three younger brothers who had each put themselves down for five bob. Now, you have already heard that Waugh was a genius. So he was, and in that moment the idea of a League of Pity was born, for Waugh said: 'If Royal children can give, then all children can give; and we owe the inspiration to the lady we delight to honour as Her Gracious Majesty Queen Mary.

In Scotland the paper circulated to members of the League of Pity was called 'City Sparrows' and it is appropriate to give the flavour of this publication at the time by including excerpts from the issue of 1897 which was the year of the Jubilee of Queen Victoria.

CITY SPARROWS. 3

RESCUED CHILDREN on the Steps of the CHILDREN'S SHELTER.
"They look up with their pale and sunken faces."

GOD SAVE THE QUEEN !

WELL may the children of Great Britain raise that prayer, for to them our Queen has been indeed a mother.

Sixty years ago, when she came to the throne, a young and pretty girl of only eighteen years of age, the children of the nation were, in thousands of instances, being done to death, morally and physically, in wretched homes, in which they slowly pined and starved to death; in factories closely confined, and set to watch the droning, turning wheels, until released sick and faint at night, they crept wearily home with no heart to rejoice in their childhood—no thought but to rest. And worse still, down in the dark mines underground, little, helpless, naked children toiled in the coal-pits. Think what that must have been, you children who love the bright sunshine and the green fields !

4   C I T Y   S P A R R O W S.

Helpless little boys were choked to death in chimneys they had been pushed up to sweep, and the bitter cry of the children echoed throughout the land.

> "They look up with their pale and sunken faces,
>   And their looks are sad to see,
> For the man's hoary anguish draws and presses
>   Down the cheeks of infancy."

But since that joyous June day, sixty years ago, when our bright, young Queen came to the throne, 107 Acts of Parliament have been passed relating to child-life and child-suffering, and only two years ago the Queen gave the Society for the Prevention of Cruelty to Children a Royal Charter, authorising it to carry on its work of helping children in their own homes—of seeking out these helpless, suffering subjects of hers, and protecting them, by making cruel and unnatural parents and guardians do their duty towards them. For, by the Children's Charter of 1889-94—to carry out which the Society exists—the children of the nation were recognised as subjects of the Queen, with legal rights of their own, that can be enforced for them.

And now, you happy children throughout the length and breadth of Scotland, we would appeal to you to commemorate the glorious sixty years' reign of our Queen by joining the League of Pity, and so helping to carry on the work for suffering children she has done so much to further. You will see in our List of Members that two of the Queen's grandchildren— the Princess Ena of Battenberg and the Lady Alexandrina Duff—have joined, and are doing something each year to help.

In Scotland alone, during the past year 1896, over 6000 children have been helped by the Society, and many of them protected from great cruelty ; and there is not the slightest doubt, from the experience gained, that fully that number of children have been left to suffer in districts which, through want of funds, we have been unable to reach.

You children, who have as yet done nothing for them, can now help us to reach them if you will, that we may reform the bad homes and give again to the children the gracious gift of childhood, of which they have been robbed.

In this you will be carrying on the work your Queen began—and of all the boons the Queen has given to the nation, is not this the greatest?— the gift of its children restored to it again.

CITY SPARROWS. 5

For the children are the pledge of the nation's immortality—the hope of the future; without them our old earth would be indeed a weary place for many of us. It is the children that make life worth living for us children of a larger growth, for they possess the master-key which opens to us things invisible—they make the future ours. Whether we realise it or not, it is for them we think and work and pray—those who are to follow after us and enter on the fruits of our labours.

And will not all mothers and fathers, for the sake of their own bright-eyed boys and girls, stretch out a helping hand to these other children?

> " . . . Can we bear
> The sweet looks of our own children
> While those others lean and small,
> Scurf and mildew of the city,
> Spot our streets, convict us all,
> Till we take them into pity?"

The opportunity is given to all, young and old alike, to succour these downtrodden children of the nation—to give them of the wine of the joy of life, the power which childhood possesses of making glad the hearts of men.

Let us then unite one and all with our Queen in doing our utmost, that the children may have their childhood, and rejoice and be glad in it.

FRANCES HEPBURN.

ODE TO QUEEN VICTORIA.

ORIGINAL POEM.

AIL to our Queen!
Longest to reign
Over Great Britain—
Hail to our Queen!

Ruled by her gracious hand,
Prospers our native land.
In one united band,
Praise ye the Queen!

Full sixty years has she
Our ruler been;
Let us for many more
Praise her—OUR QUEEN!
—DOT KIDD (Junior Member).

Lady Alexandra Victoria Alberta Edwina Louise Duff
(The first Member of the League of Pity),

Lady Maud Alexandra Victoria Georgina Bertha Duff,

Children of the Duke of Fife and H.R.H. Princess Louise, Duchess of Fife.

CITY SPARROWS.   7

A PEEP INTO THE CHILDREN'S SHELTER.

BY THE REV. T. HARDY, FOULIS.

NOT long ago I chanced to have a spare afternoon in Auld Reekie, and right pleasantly I spent it—in THE SHELTER. I am ashamed to say that I had never yet seen the place of which I had heard so much. Away down the High Street I wandered in search of it. I could not but wonder *where*, amidst all the racket, and rattle, and clatter of the High Street, they could possibly have managed to find a calm and cosy SHELTER for the bairns! But I know there are—or, at least, were—calm and cosy homes in this same High Street.

Above one door, not far from the Shelter, is a CLAM SHELL, neatly carved in stone, once brightly gilded, but now faded and worn. The whole tenement —the whole *land*—was once proudly titled "THE CLAM SHELL." And the Clam Shell awoke old boyish memories in my mind. On its first floor there dwelt, long ago, an old lady—a "decayed gentlewoman," who, in a highly genteel way, sold pounds and quarter-pounds of excellent tea. She did not live quite alone, for a cat (whose name I forget), and a parrot in a cage, whom I well remember, kept her company. Greatly pleased were we children to be sent to purchase "a pound of 'Miss Millar of the Clam Shell's' four-and-fourpence tea." Tea was *tea* then! and the purchase of the tea involved a formal visit of some length—also a cookie. And "Poley," as Miss Millar called him, joined in the conversation freely, and informed us that "Poley's gotten the cold." But the Clam Shell has long since lost good old Miss Millar, and Poley has ceased to have "gotten the cold."

Since those days, the Children's Shelter found for a time its first home in the old Clam Shell. It has found a bigger and better home now!

I passed on; and, after resisting a strong desire to wander down the "COVENANT CLOSE," and explore it, I reached the happy number, viz. 142, the number by which, in the Directory, the SHELTER is known. A blessed number it has been to many a poor neglected waif, now grown up and going on well!

Does the reader recollect Adam Woodcock and Roland Avenel riding down the High Street towards Holyrood (I think I hear some puzzled reader saying in perplexity—"What's this man *haivering* about next, with his Clam Shells, and his pounds of tea, and his parrots? He is always going off the rail!") —I was referring my reader to Sir Walter's charming story of "The Abbot," in which he tells us how gallant young Roland caught sight of Catharine Seyton, and chased her through an arched passage and across a court, to the door of the mansion of Lord Seyton, her father. I don't say positively that the Shelter was once the residence of the noble Seytons, but I do say that the *Shelter* might very well stand for that which Sir Walter describes.

You pass through a covered passage, or "pend," as the Edinburgh folk call it, and enter a square court. And, fronting you, stands what has no doubt at one time been a very handsome family mansionhouse. Its more ancient history I do not know; but in the early years of the century it was the Commercial Bank, and in that covered archway, passage, or "pend," a tragedy occurred which rang through all Scotland. The bank porter, carrying a large sum of money, was stabbed in that archway; and the murderer escaped to Leith, and left the country, and was never caught. In course of time the Bank fancied a more fashionable site, and the building became a Free Church. In coursé of time the Free Church also followed the fashion; and the old mansionhouse passed into the hands of an incorporated society, the Good Templars, and became its "Hall."

Now, I think the old building has come to its *best*. It reminds one of our old Pantomime days. The clever and benevolent fairy has come in at the end, and by one touch of her magic wand made everything beautiful and everybody happy! The *Shelter* has been well and wisely chosen. Not many yards away from the High Street, and yet the children are as completely screened from its sights and sounds, its rattle and clatter, as though they had the Firth of Forth between Edinburgh and them! And the little creatures occupy a house, whose large, airy, well-lighted and high-roofed rooms many an Edinburgh family would be glad to have.

I am not attempting to give anything like a systematically detailed description of what I saw in the *Shelter*. I am only trying to tell one or two things which struck me. I *know* that if I were put through an examination by a committee of intelligent and experienced females, I should lamentably break down and fail. Such questions as—"How many children did you see? What were their ages? How were they dressed? How many boys? and how many girls? Where did they come from?" Questions like these would puzzle me. I have not female eyes, and I am neither intelligent nor experienced. I can only say I was *amazed* and *delighted*. The children were all so well cared for, so comfortable, and so happy. And *yet* it all seemed to be so very easily done, with no trouble in the world to anybody! *But is that so?* Often have I been told that "to take care of a young bairn, nicht an' day, is *ae wumman's full wark.*" But lo! here were some score and a half of bairns—some at the very troublesome and *steering* ages of three, four, five, six, and seven—wee lassies, and wee laddies; and here were the *more* troublesome "year-olds" and *two*-year-olds, in their restlessness, and their helplessness. And here were utterly helpless *babies—days* old! *weeks* old! *months* old!—hitherto misguided and maltreated, and consequently still wailing, and yammering, and peevish—"no' able to tell what was wrang wi' them," and needing *unceasing* attention!

CITY SPARROWS. 9

And yet, how easily and quietly and simply it seemed all done! How easily a thing is done by one who knows *how to do it!* Oh! Lady Visitors! you have often seen a young mother at her very wits' end, *fechtin'* with a wailing, yammering baby, and I *know* you are gentle and patient with her, for she has not *yet* learned the *art of it.*

My visit began with a pleasant crack in the SECRETARY'S ROOM. There she sat, quietly, busy with no end of accounts and letters and reports and official volumes—an enthusiast on the rescue of children, and her whole heart in it. The lady, sitting so quietly there, and yet guiding the whole business of the institution—to say nothing of editing the *Sparrows* Magazine —made me think of what I often look at when at Perth Railway Station. On the platform there is hurry-skurry, and rushing, and jostling—luggage-barrows flying about, passengers making for all different trains, bells ringing, guards whistling, engines shrieking, trains about to start, north, east, south, and west—*everybody*, in a hurry and a fry. *One man*—and I often look at *him*—is up in a high glass house, yonder, standing coolly and quietly amongst all sorts of unknown machinery-levers, cranks, clocks, and what not. HE is never hurried, never speaks, minds what he is about, attends only to his levers and his signals. Yet that man manages the whole concern—pulls a lever, and off goes the Highland train to Inverness; pulls another, and brings in the Aberdeen. The Secretary, sitting quietly at her busy writing-table, and in close touch always with a wise body of directors, manages all the movements of the Shelter business.

Then I went among the *babies* and the *bairns*. Yes!—comfortable, well-fed, clean and tidy, and happy—but, oh! there are tokens many on the little human frames of early mal-management! A pair of *medical* eyes would see a vast deal more than any of us could. Poor bairns! like "sodgers," they bear *scars*, telling of what they have come through! But it struck me that those Lady Visitors, and other ladies who take an active interest in Shelter work, must see a great deal more clearly than a mere visitor like me could possibly do, the *wonder* and the *beauty* of inside the Shelter. For they have often had occasion to see these poor creatures in the dens of misery from which they have been rescued; and the contrast between what *was* and what *is now* must strike them *very* forcibly. The delight must be very, very great with which these ladies look on the rescued and sheltered bairns, having seen and known the dens from which they were rescued; and greater *still* must their pleasure be in knowing that they themselves bear a helping hand, both in the rescue and in the shelter. Yes! one needs, in order rightly to appreciate the Shelter, to know something of the antecedent condition of the little waifs. We used all to read an advertisement as to "Handwriting taught in Six Lessons," and we remember the difference between "This was my writing before," &c., and "This—after six lessons from Mr Readypen." But, indeed, the capital *photos* which brighten the pages of the *Sparrows*

10   CITY SPARROWS.

Magazine give us vivid peeps into the antecedent conditions, and these do much to aid the work which the Magazine seeks to accomplish.

A sight which I think I shall never forget was that of an infant a few weeks old, rescued a day or two before from one of those illicit "*farms.*" It had been all but starved to death—rescued just in time. Nothing but the care of the Shelter could have pulled it through. How I wished I could have had beside me some of the tender-hearted, couthie, motherly women whom I know here in my own country-side. I can think I hear their

THE BABIES' NURSERY, CHILDREN'S SHELTER.

greetin', and their ejaculations, and their "blessings on the Shelter," and their affectionate embraces of the good Matron, if they had seen, as I did, "the wee darlin' bairn," lying in the neatest, nattiest little crib, and *sookin'* away at its bottle, as if for dear life.

The Matron—as warm-hearted and motherly woman as ever lived—won my heart at once by pointing to a photo-likeness of my late sister ROBINA, and by telling me much about the "wee Davie" and his death, of whom my sister wrote a little book. What a delight that woman seemed to take in the rescued baby! She seemed to me like the woman who found her lost bit of silver.

CITY SPARROWS. 11

Those of the children who had reached the years of discretion as to their *legs*—that is, who could *toddle* along—marched into the schoolroom, guided (and assisted, some of them—for there were some very short legs, and some by no means " soople on the feet ") by their young teacher, who was very gentle with them. There they sang some nice nursery hymns. One hymn took my fancy very much, being sung to some very common *Hielant* song-tune. I am not going to tell *what* it was. It puzzled me, at the time, to " put a name on it," and it was not till next day, on my way home to the Hielants, that I hit upon it. They sang with great goodwill, and they looked quite as intelligent, on the whole, as the children of any school I know. What the Educational *Code* calls " O. and D."—*i.e. order and discipline*—were of course excellent.

Then the playroom ! I have a great weakness for children's toys—always had ;—and the playroom enchanted me. I suppose benevolent fairies and wealthy godfathers flit about the institution unseen, and always add something to the playroom furnishings. A large, handsome, old-fashioned doll-house, with gables, and towers, and verandahs and windows, stood in one corner. It was like a Chinese pagoda, and might have held two or three of the *live* dolls inside. A hobby-horse stood quietly in a window recess, saddled and bridled, and bearing marks of usage—not on its *knees*, but on stirrups and saddle and *tail*. Who knows but the first owner of it may now be some one of Edinburgh's greatest citizens,—a Lord of Session, or a victorious General, or a great medical professor ! A much more humble horse, lower in stature, and bearing *more* marks of usage on main and tail, stood on its wooden wheels—not in galloping attitude, but stock-still. HE brought to memory vividly my own old wooden " BALDY," of long, long ago—long since gone to *sticks !* To conclude the hobby-horse show, I was much taken with a *baby rocking-horse,* or rather a *pair* of horses. Two rocking-horses, each cut out of inch thick deal board, were planted on a rocker about 12 or 14 inches apart, and between them was a perfectly safe *baby-chair.* The tiniest baby could be left sitting there rocking quietly for a good long while, and warranted not to cry or to tumble out.

The walls of nursery, playroom, and dormitory are all decked with charmingly bright, *taking* pictures. And the dormitory is a pleasant place to look into, with its neat little cots, snow-white sheets, and scarlet coverlets, Ah ! poor bairnies ! the beds that you might have still been sleeping in !

Now if anyone imagines from anything I have said that these children are *petted*, and *coddled*, and made too much of with their playroom and dormitory, &c., I wish to say to such a reader, Please go and see for yourself. The whole house is carried on in the very *plainest* fashion. They have the commonest of food and clothing ; they are well disciplined and drilled ; and if kind friends send them old toys for their playroom, where is the harm ? I guess they don't get hobby-horse *every day.* If boys and girls are kept well and properly *in hand*, as these children are, a little play with a doll or a ride on a rocking-horse won't hurt them. Besides, let it be remembered, those in the Shelter are the mere *bairnies*—the *wee things*, the "little ones." In due time they are drafted off to the upper form—the higher school, the harder work—in the institution at Corstorphine. I have a great longing to go to Corstorphine and see what is to be seen; and, if I have a chance of describing Corstorphine for the use of any of my readers who grudge the hobby-horses and the dolls, I shall take rigorous note of anything *there* savouring of luxuries, and I rather think I shall not need to make a "chapter on hobbies" at Corstorphine, finding, perhaps, that rocking-horses there are as scarce as snakes in Ireland. I am thankful to have seen the High Street Shelter. It is a sight *worth* seeing! The two sights I saw in Edinburgh were the Exhibition of the Royal Scottish Academy, *and* the SHELTER. Yes! I think I may say I enjoyed the one quite as much as the other. God speed the CHILDREN'S SHELTER!

"WORK IS HEAVEN'S BEST."

—J. INGELOW.

SPRING, the time of the singing of birds, the time of sprouting hedgerows, primroses, and cowslips, is also the time, as your mothers can tell you, of spring-cleaning. Had any of you called during the past fortnight—and we have had a good many visitors—you would have seen the children "in the rough." Little girls, who simply love a cleaning, clad in working-jackets and petticoats, sweeping, scrubbing, and polishing, all who were old enough to hold a duster doing something; and those who were not, besides being expressly told *not to*, were trying to beat the beds which had been put out on the playground to air. At least this flight of industry happened when they felt an eagle-eye on them, but, free from that fear, they were turning somersaults and performing other tricks.

School was closed last week, being Easter, and then the cleaning got on by leaps and bounds. You should have seen the boys whitewashing, dressed in old clothes—that is, unusually old clothes—and a hat; the latter appears to be always necessary. They seemed to be wildly happy, and worked very hard, that fact being due to the good example shown by Sergeant: one heard them whistling, just like real workmen, from early morn. None of you would have recognised the Band; Pipe-Major, Drummers, all looked like their work, and liked it, which, of course, was quite right.

During April we have received several nice gifts; among others two, notably a Grand Piano, which I enjoy most, and a Noah's Ark,

A more formal view of the Children's Shelter is given by the copy of *Rules and Instructions for the Administration of The Children's Shelter, 142 High Street Edinburgh*, which were printed in 1902 and exist in the records of the Society. This booklet lists the following duties in great detail:

THE MEDICAL OFFICER

RECEPTION AND DISCHARGE OF CHILDREN

HOUSE COMMITTEE

FINANCE COMMITTEE

The working instructions for each official and committee would form admirable job descriptions for similar posts today. There are 20 numbered paragraphs to the job description of the Secretary, including record of letters, granting receipts for money and the organising of entertainments.

There are 30 paragraphs of instruction to the matron including the appointment of staff, the supervision of expenditure and stores, the supervision of cooking and clothing, and the receipt of gifts.

The following paragraphs are repeated verbatim to give a picture of the attitudes to the work at the time:

37. Admission of children — The matron shall see and examine all children brought to the Shelter as soon after admission as possible, and she is responsible that the instructions regarding admissions provided for in Rules 58 to 69 are strictly carried out.

38. Register of admissions, etc. — The matron shall keep a register of admissions and removals, which will be written up daily.

39. Procedure as to infectious disease, etc. — When any child in the Shelter is suspected by the matron and the nurse, or either of them, to be suffering from an infectious or contagious disease, the child shall be removed from the others, and kept in the Observation Room until it has been seen by the medical officer, whose instructions shall be strictly carried out.

40. To accompany medical officer on visits — The matron, when available, shall be always present when the medical officer is visiting, and she shall see that the infants and sick children receive from the nurse the treatment ordered by him.

41. Supervision and cleanliness of infants — When there

are infants in the Nursery, the matron shall satisfy herself, by personal examination, from time to time, that they are kept clean in their persons, and she shall be careful that the Nursery, when occupied, is never without a nurse or properly qualified attendant being present in it.

42. Supervision of all children — When children are in the Play-Room, the matron shall arrange that they are constantly under the supervision of a qualified attendant, and when the weather permits the children shall be ordered to play in the outside courtyard, under the immediate charge of an attendant. The attendants, when so employed, must keep the children bright and cheerful, and take an interest in their amusements.

It is pleasing to note here that the Society was already aware of the importance of play in the development of children and that this should be facilitated by the involvement of interested adults.

43. Supervision in lavatories, etc. — When children are using the lavatories and closets, the matron shall see that they are always under the charge of an attendant, who will constantly have them under supervision. On no occasion shall children of both sexes be allowed to enter the lavatories and closets at the same time. The matron shall see that no child is allowed to wander through any of the lobbies, passages, or apartments of the Shelter unwatched, and in particular that no child shall be allowed to enter the kitchen, scullery, or washing-house, except when allowed by her to help or assist in the work carried on in these places.

44. Cases of sickness — When the matron considers that any child requires immediate attention from the medical officer, she will send information to him at once.

45. Admissions between 10 p.m. and 6 a.m. — The matron shall make arrangements from time to time for the admission of children brought to the Shelter between the hours of 10 p.m. and 6 a.m., and for their proper treatment thereafter.

There are detailed paragraphs for the medical officer in regard to admission, examination and discharge.

There are eleven paragraphs in the Reception and Discharge of Children including:

63. Cases of gross ill-usage, etc. — If, on reception, it appears to the matron that any child has been subjected to gross ill-usage, or is suffering from any physical disability calling for immediate attention, she will report the fact to the medical officer for his instructions, and a copy of the medical

officer's observations, if in writing, shall be given to the secretary, to be put up with the case papers.

There are paragraphs of guidance for the House Committee, which was responsible to the Society for the administration of the Shelter.

These rules of guidance in general are an indication of the extent to which the work of the Society was already being established on a systematic basis.

In this first phase of the development of the Society, the structures of the organisation were therefore steadily being created and confirmed in the shape of the support and involvement of leading public figures especially the clear indication of royal patronage, which in addition to the more informal interests as that shown by Princess May of Teck, was demonstrated by H.R.H. The Prince of Wales assuming the Presidency, and later by the King and Queen agreeing to be patrons in 1912, indicating a support and interest by the Royal Family which has continued in a variety of ways to the present time when Her Royal Highness the Princess Margaret gives active support in her role as President. Also developing at this stage was the formation of national and branch committees, the initiation of subscription and collection networks and the creation of adminstration and staffing.

The establishment of the work had not necessarily been easy and smooth. Both the Society's committees and the Society's Inspectors had to decide upon and to interpret the role of the Society in relation to the behaviour it sought to influence. They had to steer a course between being accused by both the general public and, occasionally, the courts, of intervening too readily in the affairs of the family and, on the other hand, being seen to condone the attitudes of families who were seen to be neglectful of children.

The dilemma was referred to by the Marquis of Tweeddale in his address to the Annual General Meeting receiving the Report for 1897. Recorded in the minutes is the fact that, before the meeting commenced, the Marquis met the officers of the Society, the Inspectors, in a sideroom of the Masonic Hall, George Street, Edinburgh in which the AGM was held. He is recorded as saying to the assembled officers, 'I am very glad to have seen you and to make your acquaintance, so far as I am able to do so to-day. I need hardly tell you that the success of the Society depends — I will not say entirely — but depends in a great measure on the manner in which you discharge your duty: because when the Society first commenced there was an idea that the officials of the Society were disposed to be severe on parents and others. I believe that notion has been entirely dispelled, and, if that is the case, it has been by your exercising a good judgment and tact in dealing with the matters coming before you. I hope you will always continue to act on these lines, because, if so, probably the time will come when you will have little or nothing to do. It will, however, be a long time before such a state of matters is realised, and until then I hope you will exercise yourselves in the same satisfactory manner as in the past. (Applause)'

Later in the meeting itself in moving the Adoption of the Annual Report the Marquis is recorded as saying:

Both Reports agree in one point, and that is that both Societies, the larger and the smaller, have done excellent work during the past year. The number of cases has considerably increased. I find that there were 2,280 cases reported, involving no fewer than 5,500 children. The mere mention of the number of children involved in these cases gives one a faint idea of the amount of good that the Society is doing, because we may feel sure that in each individual case of the 5,500 the children have been suffering either from the neglect or brutality and cruelty of their parents or guardians. There is one feature — a very important one — and it is the decrease in the number of violent cases and assaults. This, I think, shows that, wherever the officials of the Society are operating, a wholesome dread has been established lest the cases of parents or guardians using violence to their children may be brought before the Courts. But, still, there are far too many of such cases. Indeed, it is almost incredible the variety of ways in which parents or guardians are able to and do ill-treat their children. I have a copy here of the Report of the English Society, and they give a list which is astonishing, because in the case of animals we know how very many ways there are of ill-treating them, but there are at least double as many ways of ill-treating children — the important difference being that in the one case the suffering is merely of a purely physical character, whereas in the other the greatest injury, perhaps, is that which is done to the mind and moral condition of the child, making it a still more helpless victim than in the case of the animal. I cannot help thinking that this blot on our boasted civilisation is one which it is indispensable that we should use our best endeavour to remove. (Applause.) I think the public mind is becoming daily more conscious of its responsibility in this matter. There was a time, early in the history of the Society, when the belief prevailed that there was too much interference with what is described as 'the liberty of the parents'. Magistrates showed considerable dislike to convict offenders, and the police were indifferent in affording assistance. There may be, and, perhaps, was at that time — early in the history of the Society — ground for suspicion that the officials of the Society were somewhat too zealous, and were led into doing things which might be considered as undue interference, but I think matters are entirely altered now. There is no ground for any such accusation, and I am happy to say that both the magistrates and the police are giving us a very delicate duty to perform. (Applause.) I have spoken to the officials today, and have pointed out to them how much depends on the manner in which they discharge their duty; and I think a paragraph in the Report affords ample evidence of the way in which they have been discharging their duty, because out of 174 persons prosecuted at the instance of the Society, all but 3 were convicted. That I am sure you will agree, affords the best of all evidence that the officers have been discharging their duty in a thoroughly satisfactory manner (Applause.) I cannot but express the hope that some day or another it will be unnecessary to have recourse to the Magisterial Courts in order to bring offenders to justice. I believe the day will come when it will be sufficient that there should be an official of the Society in the neighbourhood who is prepared to give advice and warning, and when any further proceedings will be rendered unnecessary. It is evident, at all events, that imprisonment in all cases is not of itself resented by those upon whom the punishment is inflicted.

As illustrated in this description of the work the dilemma between punishment and protection was always present in the concern of the early work of the Society. The steady work of prevention however proceeded and in 1899 the annual return of statistics of cases for the year, together with a review of the cases undertaken by the Society in the first fifteen years of its existence showed that by this time the Society was making a significant contribution to the welfare of children in Scotland.

That annual return of cases is reproduced at the end of this chapter, describing the establishment of the Society, but, before doing so, a description of three prosecution cases recorded in the annual report of 1899 illustrates the points which have just been made regarding the nature of intervention and the decisions which had to be made.

NEGLECT AND STARVATION

Case 21/592 — In this case the father, a plasterer, in receipt of 40/- per week, was convicted and sentenced to 30 days, for wilfully neglecting his six children, aged from 14 to 2 years. He was in the habit of drinking the most of his wages, and leaving his wife and children for days unprovided for. The children suffered greatly from want of food and clothing during the winter months. The father was warned several times by the Inspectors of the Society before steps were taken to have him punished. There was a previous conviction in Glasgow for a similar offence in 1897, when he was sentenced to 60 days' imprisonment. The man is now doing much better, and the condition of his family is improved in every way.

RETURN, showing the Number of Cases Investigated in Scotland during the Year 1899.

CLASSIFICATION OF CASES.

COMMITTEE.	Total Number of Complaints.	Number of Offenders Involved.	Total Number of Children Affected.	Number of Children Insured.	Neglect and Starvation.	Ill-treatment and Assault.	Abandonment.	Exposure.	Begging, Singing, and Selling.	Indecent Assault.	Criminal Assault.	Immoral Surroundings.	Other Wrongs.	Dropped after Investigation.
Edinburgh, Leith, and District, - - -	1279	1562	3252	1246	980	48	2	65	67	...	1	8	29	79
Glasgow and District, -	1091	1328	2609	736	697	16	...	25	307	1	...	5	40	...
Ayr and District, - -	147	160	307	...	86	4	1	27	21	..	...	2	6	...
Kilmarnock and District,	148	201	361	79	80	2	...	50	16	...	...	...	...	...
Elgin and Banffshire, -	97	107	239	26	68	4	...	2	2	...	...	...	...	21
Forfarshire, - - -	37	58	114	61	30	...	...	1	6	...	...	...	...	...
Inverness-shire, - -	34	46	128	18	30	3	...	1	...	...	...	...	...	...
Perthshire, - - -	48	69	155	6	39	...	1	1	1	...	...	1	...	5
Kirkcaldy and Fifeshire,	135	190	401	168	121	1	1	3	1	...	...	...	...	8
Monklands District, -	85	108	263	136	44	8	3	20	6	...	...	...	4	...
Totals, - - -	3101	3829	7829	2476	2175	86	8	195	427	1	1	16	79	113

ANALYSIS OF CASES.

COMMITTEE.	Warned.	Sent to Prison.	Fined.	Bound over or adjourned for bet. behavi'r.	Dismissed with Reprimand.	Disch'ged or Acquitted.	Otherwise dealt with.	Number of Persons.	Offences against Children.	Imprisonment. Y.	M.	W.	Fines. £	s.	d.	Supervision Visits by Inspectors.	Children Sheltered.
Edinburgh, Leith, and District, - - -	1007	47	4	9	5	6	122	76	195	4	5	0	9	0	0	2645	687
Glasgow and District, -	902	63	2	3	3	2	116	76	165	17	11	2	26	0	0	2073	563
Ayr and District, - -	112	20	...	...	...	..	15	22	41	1	0	1	9	2	0	207	112
Kilmarnock and District, -	129	11	5	2	...	1	...	19	37	1	7	0	13	5	0	200	70
Elgin and Banffshire, -	67	5	4	...	...	...	...	11	20	0	11	3	13	0	0	550	...
Forfarshire, - - -	36	...	...	...	1	..	...	1	2	Admonished.						46	No Shelter.
Inverness-shire, - -	30	1	2	...	...	1	...	4	4	0	2	1	6	0	0	209	No Shelter.
Perthshire, - - -	36	4	1	2	...	..	...	9	30	0	4	3	1	0	0	887	No Shelter.
Kirkcaldy and Fifeshire, -	106	12	1	5	1	..	2	25	61	1	7	2	1	0	0	431	No Shelter.
Monklands District, -	56	25	..	...	2	...	2	31	71	1	11	3	2	5	0	258	52
Totals, -	2481	188	19	21	12	10	257	274	626	30	1	3	80	12	0	7506	1484

NATIONAL SOCIETY FOR THE PREVENTION OF CRUELTY TO CHILDREN (SCOTTISH BRANCH).

RETURN showing the Work done in Scotland since the formation to 31st December, 1899.

DISTRICT	Year of Formation	Total Number of Complaints	Number of Offenders involved	Total Number of Children Affected	Number of Children insured	CLASSIFICATION OF CASES Neglect and Starvation	Ill-treatment & Assault	Culpable Homicide	Abandonment	Exposure	Begging, Singing, and Selling	Indecent Assault	Criminal Assault	Immoral Surroundings	Other Wrongs	Dropped after investigation	ACTION-TAKEN CASES Warned	Prosecuted. Sent to Prison	Fined	B. over or adj. for better behaviour	Reprimanded	Discharged	Otherwise Dealt with	Convicted. Number of Persons	Offences against Children	PENALTIES. Imprisonment Y. M. W.	Fines £ s. d.	Supervision visits by Inspectors	Children admitted to Shelter	HOW DISPOSED OF. Returned to Parents or Relations	To Industrial Schools	To Poorhouse	To other Homes	Otherwise disposed of
Edinburgh, Leith, and District,	1888	7563	8428	20126	2936	5618	251		64	322	443	2	5	72	541	245	5841	408	24	19	73	10	943	547	1162	27 0 1	160 6 0	11565	4986	2364	650	356	431	585
Glasgow and District,	1885	15859	15990	28273	8689	4837	181		1	525	9302		1	887	123		12895	530	182	3	340	4	1905	1069	2074	77 9 1	306 15 0	13575	12856	8986	2009	1312	337	262
Ayr and District,	1894	759	797	1509	225	342	17		3	161	141			15	80		631	85		7	10		26	107	152	8 11 2	28 14 6	781	525	138	46	98	25	218
Kilmarnock and District,	1894	784	1072	1689	152	294	16			260	191			2	11	1	668	33	44	5	30	1	2	116	223	4 7 2	43 5 6	534	555	427	19	83	14	12
Elgin and Banff-shire,	1897	290	341	870	130	226	6			3	4					51	216	14	6			1	2	25	67	1 8 0	37 0 0	1253						
Forfarshire,	1893	127	180	390	62	111			4	1	8				2		108	7			12			17	58	0 7 2		346						
Inverness-shire,	1899	34	46	128	18	30	3			1					1	5	30	1	2			1		4	4	0 2 1	6 0 0	209						
Perthshire,	1894	251	369	666	22	184	6		10	3	36			5	2	5	210	20	3	9		3		31	82	2 0 0	3 10 0	1237						
Fife,	1898	234	337	743	339	214	1		1	5	2				2	8	195	20	1	5	2		3	37	90	2 5 0	1 0 0	876						
Monklands District,	1890	872	1107	2108	376	442	42		6	165	194			12	11		755	60	9	2	22	1	23	121	196	5 1 0	10 12 6	753	313	188	22	95	9	49
Totals,	..	26773	28667	56502	7949	12298	523		89	1455	10821	4	6	995	772	310	21549	1178	271	50	490	21	2904	2077	4108	180 4 3	597 3 6	31129	18635	12003	2746	1944	816	1126

(No Shelter — applies to Elgin and Banff-shire, Forfarshire, Inverness-shire, Perthshire, and Fife.)

GROSS NEGLECT

Case 22/104 — Husband and wife were each sentenced to 40 days, for wilfully neglecting their three children, aged 7, 5, and 3 years. The father, a scone baker, could easily have earned 6/- per day had he kept sober and attended to his work. He drank heavily, came home at midnight generally in a drunken state, while his wife, who was a very immoral and drunken character, left the helpless children on several occasions alone in an attic room for 8 and 9 hours without food or fire, and in a state of filth and dirt. They were heard crying by the neighbours, who, after warning the parents, and finding no improvement, reported the case at the Shelter. The children were rescued by the Society. Two of them were admitted to Murrayfield Home — the father paying a weekly board for them. This is the second family rescued from these parents. The first family, two boys and a girl, are now grown up and doing very well for themselves. The girl is in service in the country.

ILL-TREATMENT AND NEGLECT

Case 21/275 — The step-father, in this case a house painter, was very much addicted to drink and very cruel to his own child a few months old, and also to his two step-children, boys, aged respectively 9 and 6 years. His wife was almost broken-hearted, her life was so miserable, both she and the two boys dreaded the step-father's home-coming, which meant for them blows and bad language. The boys would plead, 'O, mother, mother, dinna let him in, he will strike us.' The mother was most faithful to her children, and denied herself to give to them. Through the action of the Society the husband was convicted and sentenced to 40 days' imprisonment. The two boys were afterwards sent to Leith Industrial School, where the father will have to pay something towards their maintenance.

4

EXTENDING THE WORK OF PREVENTION

In the previous chapter the early stages of the development of the organisation have been described, during which it passed through the important early phases, of attracting commitment, gaining the support of eminent public figures and royal patronage, establishing a basic policy and method for its work and creating the structures upon which it would depend in the future.

Like all voluntary movements, depending so much upon individual commitment and involvement, the extension of the work during these early phases was not planned but tended to be reactive to need and piecemeal due to the availability of interest and support.

The movement to develop a relationship as a national Scottish body, with the equivalent English national body, though it was fraught with difficulty in negotiation, helped to develop an awareness of the patchiness of the development over Scotland and to put pressure upon the national committee to prepare a conscious policy of extension work.

In 1901 the National Committee took such a decision to extend the work but, of course, still the development had to rely upon resources and also upon the stimulation of local interest and support. The latter could often be achieved by the efforts of eminent supporters, who, as indicated in the last chapter, could appeal to local meetings and attract local commitment. Often these eminent supporters could utilise their own personal network of acquaintances to develop a local nucleus around which the necessary commitment could form and become a local committee and branch.

This, of course, pre-supposed that the Society had a system of identifying where their need required responses to further development.

In this process of identification of need there were two main components. Firstly the recording and analysis of the cases in which the Society was already involved provided some possible indications of trends in behaviour which could be projected to indicate likely need elsewhere. Secondly the experience of Inspectors in the existing cases of intervention also could identify emerging issues upon which the Society could begin to direct its attention, either by developing its own work or by making representations for the recognition of the issue as a matter for national concern and even for legislation.

The importance of accurate recording was recognised and referred to in the Annual Report of 1906 as follows:

RECORDS AND STATISTICS

All the investigations of the Inspectors in dealing with the complaints received are carefully recorded and the results are tabulated. The forms on which this is done have been carefully considered by a committee of the Executive, and as a result of their labours new and improved forms have been prepared, and were brought into use at the beginning of 1907. Instructions for filling up the forms have been issued with the object of securing that the statistics will be compiled on a definite and uniform system, and reflect as nearly as may be the actual work performed by the Society. The Committee were fortunate in having as one of their number Mr W. Donaldson, C.B., formerly Secretary of the Prison Commission, whose expert knowledge of statistics has been of the utmost value in preparing the new forms.

(It is interesting to record here that the author, when asked in the late 1960s by the Society to conduct research into its cases with a view to helping a review of policy found that the case records, though carefully, conscientiously and extensively maintained were not consistent or standardised in the items recorded. The record of statistics retained the same categories as developed in these early stages of the Society's history and subsequent changes in social need and professional practice meant that an analysis based on this experience was no longer helpful. The research (referred to in *Neglected Families*, known to the RSSPCC, B. J. Ashley & H. Cohen, Moray House Publications, 1972) suggested new categories and systems of recording and the Society revised its practice based on these recommendations with the result that significant information is now quickly and easily retrievable.)

Development work, of course, also included the need to review and change existing practice, particularly when limited resources might be needed for new purposes. So the Report of 1906 also includes the following paragraph upon the closure of the Murrayfield Home, of which the proud opening ceremony was referred to in the last chapter.

MURRAYFIELD HOME

The position of the Murrayfield Home in relation to the work of the Society has been the subject of careful enquiry and consideration. The movement for the establishment of this Home dates back from 1889, when there was great difficulty experienced in finding a home for children whom it was deemed necessary to remove from the custody of their parents. It is evident that circumstances have changed very much since then. There are now many institutions open to receive such cases, and experience has shown that they are sufficient for the needs of the Society. The Home at Murrayfield with its limited accommodation could only accommodate a small percentage of our cases. In these circumstances it was decided that as the Home was no longer necessary for the work of the Society it should be closed, and this was accordingly done last September. Some of the children were boarded out, and are under the supervision of the Inspectors in various parts of the country. The League of Pity has kindly undertaken to provide funds for their maintenance. Others were admitted to Industrial Schools; to Highland Orphanage, Inverness; and no fewer than 36 were received into Quarrier's Homes, Bridge of Weir. To the managers of these Institutions our heartiest thanks are due. It should be stated that the Murrayfield Home was admirably conducted under the management of the Edinburgh Committee of the Society. Apart from contributions from the League of Pity for the board of some of the children, the expenses of the Home were a charge upon the general funds of the Society. By closing the Home an important economy has been effected without impairing in any way the efficiency of the work of the Society.

The same report contains an example of how the Society, becoming aware of a particular problem tried to find an adequate response:

Increasing public concern is being attracted to the high death rate among infants, to which we referred in our Report last year. We have had the subject under careful consideration, and believing that a considerable proportion of deaths is due to the ignorance and carelessness of mothers, we have prepared and issued to all our Inspectors a supply of cards containing simple instructions to mothers on the rearing of their infants. The card, which has been revised and approved by several eminent authorities interested in the work of the Society, is entitled 'Mother, save your Baby's Life!' We wish to circulate these cards as widely as possible, and the General Secretary will be glad to send a specimen to anyone on application.

This is the first reference in the records to recognition of the need for educational activity with the parents of the children.

The following year the Annual Report showed how consciousness of the need to impress the public with accountability for funds often preoccupied the Society, whilst also indicating that the pattern of reliance by the Society on legacy income, a dependence which has exercised its financial advisers often over the years since, was already becoming established.

The receipts from legacies during the past year have been exceptionally large, and amounted in all to £3784. 10s., as will be seen from the Abstract of Accounts on page 10. After paying all expenses, the balance on hand at the end of the financial year, including the sum received in 1904 from the League of Pity, amounted to £4998.0s.9d., and this has been carried forward, to be used for purposes as stated.

Dividing the total expenditure of the Society by the number of children dealt with, we arrive at the cost per child. Applying this rule to the last five years, the result is as follows:

	s.	p.
1903 — Cost per child	10	0
1904 — Cost per child	8	8
1905 — Cost per child	8	10
1906 — Cost per child	7	11
1907 — Cost per child	6	11

This table shows a satisfactory reduction in the cost per child, and indicates that as the years go on the affairs of the Society are being conducted with increased economy.

The new financial system inaugurated in the beginning of 1907 has worked well, and has given general satisfaction.

This Report also describes how the Society carried out its responsibility to help to influence new welfare legislation:

CHILDREN'S BILL

Much interest was aroused in the autumn when the announcement was made by the Government of their intention to introduce into Parliament a Children's Bill. In response to an invitation by Mr Herbert Samuel, M.P., Under-Secretary of State for the Home Office, we prepared a Memorandum after consulting Branch Committees, making suggestions regarding various Acts dealing with the welfare of children, for the more efficient achievement of the objects of the Society. These suggestions have been in large measure given effect to in the Bill. The General Secretary gave evidence on behalf of the Society, to the Select Committee of the House of Commons on the Infant Life Protection Act, and the Committee has unanimously reported in favour of the adoption of the views advocated. Amongst other improvements in existing legislation are the provisions for dealing with the too frequent cases of burning and scalding accidents to children, through parents leaving them unattended and exposed to unprotected fires. The overlying in bed of an infant is made an offence. It is said that to these two causes about 3000 deaths are due every year. These provisions, therefore, may save some hundreds of lives annually. Important powers are conferred for committing the children of vagrants to Industrial Schools. Various ambiguities in existing Acts are cleared up, and altogether the Bill marks a distinct advance on the legislation securing the welfare of children. The Bill has been very favourably received by all sections of the House of Commons, and we earnestly trust that it will pass into law.

Behind this simple statement lies a great deal of work by the society to examine the proposed legislation and to consider its effects. The minutes of the Executive Committee for the 22nd July 1908 refer to the detailed recommendations which were submitted to the Home Office. They also refer to the assistance received from Mr J. W. Galland M.P., who had also pressed the view of the Society upon the Home Secretary. This is a good example of the way in which the Society used its influence in the interest of children.

Evidence of the other aspect of extension work is provided by the following report in October 1908 by the General Secretary, Ninian Hill, to the Executive Committee and adopted subsequently by the Council of the Society as policy:

REPORT ON EXTENSION

In accordance with the instructions of the Executive Committee I have considered the subject of the Extension of the Society's work and beg to report as follows:

The scheme for the extension of the Society's work seems to have taken shape in the Report for the year 1902 in which a paragraph entitled 'Looking Ahead' appeared appealing for 19 additional officers. A Table appended to the Report shows that the number of Officers at that time was 26. The number of Officers is now 38 from which it appears that of the 19 then required 12 have already been appointed. The matter stands thus:

	No. of Officers in 1901	No. of Officers in 1908
Aberdeenshire	1	2
Ayrshire	2	2
Banff, Elgin & Nairn	1	1
Caithness, Orkney & Shetland	—	1
Dunbartonshire	1	1
Dumfries, Kirkcudbright & Wigtown	1	2
Edinburgh & Linlithgow	5	5
Fife & Kinross	1	2
Forfarshire & Kincardine	2	1
Inverness	1	1
Lanarkshire	7	14
Perth	1	1
Renfrew	2	2
Ross-shire	—	1
Stirling & Clackmannan	1	1
Total . . .	26	38

It will thus be seen that a considerable amount of extension work has been accomplished since the movement was inaugurated.

There are two districts which I think now call for immediate consideration.

I. The Hebrides and Western Islands. The Hebrides have been visited by Inspector Macdonald, Dingwall, as follows:

1904. Stornoway 24th to 31st October.

1906. Lewis, Harris & North Uist 14th August to 7th September.

1908. Lewis to Barra 5th March to 17th April.
During these visits 42 cases have been dealt with involving the welfare of 164 children.

In 1906 Inspector Macdonald reported:

'I found that the large majority of the Island children living in the houses of the Crofters, Cottars and Fishermen were poorly clothed, many being in rags, shockingly dirty, and evidently rarely washed and very verminous. My attention was drawn to a custom which prevails in the Uist Parish of boarding out pauper children in homes which are in a filthy condition. I found two cases which I reported to the Inspector of Poor. The most of the houses in the Lewis are really shocking, they are rarely cleaned and smell of manure, fish entrails and all kinds of rubbish.

In Stornoway there is a large number of filthy houses. In the Harris District the houses are a little better than those of the Lewis but the condition of the children is somewhat similar.

In the Uist District the houses are much better. As a rule the children are fairly well clad but most of them are in a deplorable state with vermin.

Before I left each District I visited the worst Cases twice and found a great improvement.'

In March 1908 Inspector Macdonald again reported:

'The town of Stornoway can favourably be compared with either towns, but I have seen cases in it as bad as several I have seen in the slums of Glasgow. I found a great deal of improvement in some of the worst cases that I had occasion to warn last year. I booked 10 fresh cases in the Lewis.

Harris. I found the same complaint all over and that is that the children are kept in a dirty and verminous condition. I booked two cases in Harris.

North Uist and Benbecula. I warned several cases in this District last year and I am pleased to say that I found a great improvement in every one of them except one case. Since my visit last year in this District some of the Teachers have what they call "Inspection Day". That is they have certain days in the week for examining the children to see if they are kept clean and one of the worst schools that I visited last year is one of the best this year owing to this inspection day. I booked two cases in the District.

South Uist. In one of the houses I visited I found the cattle in the living room. The children were poorly clothed and dirty and they had to lie upon the bare flooring of the bed as what straw they used to have under them had to be given to the cattle and this was all due to the father being a lazy drunken character. I booked four cases in this District.

Barra. All the teachers were very pleased for my visit as it would assist them in getting the children to attend the school clean. I booked four cases in this District.'

Inspector Macdonald further reports:

'All the cases that I warned in each District I visited a second time and I am pleased to say that I found that they took notice of my warning as matters were much better in each case.'

Captain Finlayson, Chief Constable of Ross-shire, and Honorary Secretary of the Society at Dingwall in forwarding Inspector Macdonald's Report wrote:

'It would be well if an Inspector were permanently appointed in some convenient centre.'

Skye — Portree. In August 1908 Inspector Macdonald visited Portree to investigate a complaint. He reports the general conditions of the children are fairly good but there are some that are not kept clean, mostly owing to their mothers being intemperate and of careless habits during the time their husbands are away at the fishing.

Inspector Maclennan, Inverness, visits Fort-William and Oban from time to time where the Society has some cases under supervision.

Islay. Inspector Brown, Greenock, visited this Island November 27th to December 5th 1906 and reported that generally the children appeared well nourished, fairly clean, but poorly clad. Many of the houses are in a filthy condition. Poverty is very general. The Police were very helpful.

These Reports I submit indicate that there is important work for the Society to undertake in the Hebrides. I should however point out that this must be a somewhat expensive Branch for the Society to work, as little local support can be expected and the travelling expenses must necessarily be heavy.

II. The Border Counties. The Counties of Berwick, Roxburgh, Peebles and Selkirk contain a population of over

100,000. Inspectors from Edinburgh attend to any complaints received from this District. In 1907 the cases at Hawick numbered 19 and at Galashiels 12. The Police authorities give every assistance to our officers. The population of Galashiels is 19,000 and of Hawick 17,000. Other populous places in this District include Innerleithen, Peebles, Selkirk, Melrose, Kelso, Jedburgh, Duns and Eyemouth. During 1907 the Edinburgh Committee received in subscriptions from this District 40:2/- not including contributions from the League of Pity.

I think it may reasonably be anticipated that in the course of a comparatively short time this Branch would become self-supporting.

RECOMMENDATIONS

I beg to recommend:

  I. That an Officer be appointed for the Hebrides and Western Islands generally with residence at Lochmaddy.
  II. That an Officer be appointed for the Border Counties of Berwick, Roxburgh, Peebles and Selkirk with residence at Galashiels.

(Signed) NINIAN HILL
General Secretary
October 1908.

The decision to implement this report was taken in the next year which was the Semi-Jubilee of the Society during which the organisation presented the following address to its founder James Grahame, who had retired to Fort Augustus:

To
JAMES GRAHAME, ESQUIRE
Fort-Augustus

Sir,

We are directed by the Executive Committee of the Scottish National Society for the Prevention of Cruelty to Children to offer you their heartiest greetings and congratulations on the occasion of the Semi-Jubilee of the Society.

We recall with much satisfaction that it is now twenty-five years ago since, in the good providence of God, you were moved to take steps for the establishment in our own Country of a Society for the Prevention of Cruelty to Children. Founded by you in 1884 at Glasgow, the Society has since extended its beneficent work throughout Scotland, from the Pentland to the Solway, and has become a truly Scottish National Institution. With its staff of forty Inspectors, stationed at twenty-six different centres, it protected last year more than

Twenty Thousand Helpless Children in distress. During the past quarter of a century Tens of Thousands of Little Children have had reason to bless your honoured name, for you have been the means of drying their tears, and bringing joy and brightness into their lives.

We rejoice in the privilege of being associated with you in the great work of the Society which, with the generous support of the people of Scotland, we shall ever strive to maintain in the highest state of efficiency; and in offering to you our congratulations on this occasion we earnestly pray that every blessing may be yours.

In name of the Executive Committee,

(sgd) JAMES KIRKWOOD . Chairman

WILLIAM DONALDSON Vice-Chairman

May 29th, 1909. NINIAN HILL General Secretary

No doubt, many people who have been responsible for similar significant voluntary initiatives would have found such an appreciation a very valuable part of their memorabilia!

The implementation of the report by the General Secretary of the precious year to extend the work of the Society meant that the Society could confidently review its development over twenty-five years in the following way:

THE PROGRESS OF THE SOCIETY

Ten years after the Society was founded, there were Branches at work in Edinburgh and Glasgow, each equipped with Shelters and each having a staff of 5 Inspectors, and at Ayr, Kilmarnock, Coatbridge, and Perth there were also Branches with 1 Inspector each, making a total of 6 branches and 14 Inspectors. In 1893 the Scottish Children's League of Pity, which has been of such great value to the Society, was founded by the Marchioness of Tweeddale and Lady Clementine Waring. In the Annual Report for 1901 a table appeared showing that there were at that time 15 Branches and 26 Inspectors, and an appeal was made for 19 more Inspectors, so as to bring up the number of Inspectors to an everage of 1 per 100,000 of the population of Scotland. The extension movement culminated in a great bazaar, organised by the League of Pity, held in the Waverley Market, Edinburgh, in October 1903. As a result of this effort it is now found that of the 19 additional Inspectors then required no fewer than 14 have been appointed, and consideration is again being given to the demand for more Inspectors in needy districts. In 1901, when the extension movement began, 4034 complaints involving 11,365 children were dealt with in that year. Below we give the figures for the last five years:

Year	Cases	Children
1904	6237	18,747
1905	6121	18,382
1906	6215	18,772
1907	6994	20,990
1908	7326	21,993

The increase of cases is largely due to the vigilance of the Society and its officers, and to the extension of its work in various districts.

A later paragraph in the Report of the same year shows how the Society continued to maintain its interest and influence in the development of national legislation:

THE CHILDREN ACT, 1908

In the course of His Majesty's speech from the Throne at the prorogation of Parliament, the King stated that a 'measure has been passed largely extending in a variety of directions the law for the protection of children from cruelty, danger, and neglect, and reforming the methods for dealing with juvenile offenders'. The Children Act is well described thus. It comprises 134 clauses, and will greatly strengthen the hands of the Society both in dealing with cruel and neglectful parents, and in rescuing children from their power and evil influence. We welcome especially the sections providing for the appointment by Parish Councils of Infant Protection Visitors;- the registration of farmed-out infants and children up to seven years of age;- the voidance of insurance by baby-farmers on the lives of infants committed to their charge;- the declaration that a father cannot get rid of the custody of his children by deserting them, and that a father is responsible for the maintenance of his children even when kind friends out of pity for the children step in and provide for them while the father is idling or drinking;- the making it an offence to leave children in a room with an open and unguarded fire whereby they may have got burnt or scalded;- the declaration that it is to be deemed neglect if a woman going to bed drunk overlays and causes the death of an infant;- the several valuable sections which will enable the Society to rescue many children and young persons from the contaminating influences of immoral surroundings;- the power to send the children of tramps and vagrants in certain circumstances to Industrial Schools;- the permission given to Parish Councils to contribute to the Society;- the institution of Juvenile Courts;- the exclusion of children from the bar of any licensed premises. It is of the utmost importance that these and other provisions of the Act

should be efficiently administered, and that they should not be
allowed to become a dead letter. We would, therefore,
earnestly appeal to all the members of our various District
Committees in every part of the country to take all possible
steps to secure for the children the full benefit of the Act.

No doubt it was partly the confidence deriving from this
contribution to a new and publicly declared policy of children's welfare
and the desire to build upon the climate created by trying to increase
public commitment to its cause that led the Society to take the positive
promotional policy displayed within its Report of the next year:

THE YEAR'S WORK

The work of seeking out and protecting ill-treated and
neglected children has been steadily pursued throughout the
past year with the greatest benefit to many a poor child. We
have now a staff of 42 Inspectors, who devote their whole time
to this work. They are stationed at 27 centres of population
from the extreme north to the extreme south, and they work in
every county of Scotland. The number of cases dealt with
during the past year has been 7514, involving the welfare of
22,224 children, and this shows a slight increase over the
numbers reported last year. Cases of ill-treatment and assault
numbered but 180 as compared with 6262 cases of neglect and
starvation, and this appears to indicate that cruelty to children
in Scotland arises more from want of thought than from want
of heart. There can be no doubt that the work of the Society
during the past quarter of a century has resulted in a marked
reduction in the number of horrible assaults on children. Such
cases were much more frequent than they have happily now
become. Inhumanely inclined parents have learned that
children have rights which must be respected, and that the law
severely punishes cases of wanton ill-treatment. One feature of
the cases dealt with during the past year which is not shown in
the statistical tables may be mentioned. There has been a
notable decrease in the number of cases of mothers found
drunk in charge of a child. This, we think, may be attributed
to the Children Act, which prohibits persons from taking
children into public-houses. The company of children is, no
doubt, often the means of preventing women going into public
houses.

the Report then goes on:

THE SOCIETY'S PRINCIPLES

It may be well to repeat and emphasise the principles upon
which the work of the Society is carried on. The Society seeks
to enforce the responsibility upon parents of properly treating

and properly providing for their children. When a child is found neglected and destitute, while we give immediate protection, we do not immediately rush off and provide for that child. We enquire who is responsible for the condition of the child, and why the child is neglected and destitute. Needless to say, in the great majority of cases there is no sufficient reason, and the parent is advised in a kindly but firm manner that the child must be properly treated and properly provided for; and the good advice is enforced by a warning that the child has a right to be properly treated, and if it is not properly treated, the law provides for a serious penalty on the neglectful parent. We hold that when parents have the means and are able to provide for their children, it is wrong in principle to relieve them of their responsibilities, to step in and provide the children with clothing and food, or to remove them to Institutions at the public expense. Such a method can only aggravate the disease it is sought to cure, and while relieving an individual child, cannot but encourage parents to neglect their children, and so lead to an increase of such cases. The aim of the Society, therefore, is not to destroy parental responsibility, but to encourage and enforce it; not to break up a family, but to reform it; not to create paupers, but to promote self help; not to create criminals, but to turn idle, drunken parents into industrious, sober citizens. It is not denied, of course, that in carrying out this policy there are numerous disappointments met with. There are those who turn a deaf ear alike to good advice and warning. They have to be reported to the Procurator-Fiscal, and a conviction and term of imprisonment in many cases does no good for the culprits who immediately resume their former life and commit similar offences over again. Such cases point to a lack in our penal system, that calls for reform. In too many cases a term of imprisonment is no remedy; it neither punishes nor reforms. There is a consensus of opinion that habitual criminals require prolonged detention in a labour colony under circumstances which would alike be penal and reformative. In no class of crime would such treatment be of more benefit, or is it more urgently needed than in cases of continued neglect and ill-treatment of children.

This paragraph indicates not only that the Society was already trying to work with parents in a way that would be regarded as similar to the objectives of modern child care but was also still wrestling with the punitive and controlling attitudes of society at that time. In fact the paragraph indicates that the Society embodied within itself that conflict and that dilemma.

The Report of that year then goes on to try to explain this dilemma to the general public, or at least to the members of the Society, and also gives one of the first authoritative summaries by the Society of the role of the Inspector of the Society.

THE SOCIETY'S METHODS

The question is sometimes asked — Why should there be a Society for the Prevention of Cruelty to Children? The answer is to be found in the peculiar nature of the problems with which we have to deal. The offence of Cruelty with which we have to deal. The offence of Cruelty to Children is unlike many other breaches of the law. It takes place in the privacy of the home. People do not often neglect and ill-treat their children in public. If children do appear ragged and ill-clad out of doors, it is usually but a feeble indication of their neglected condition at home. It is difficult to get at the facts. To accomplish this requires tact, skill, and experience, such as can only be attained by concentration of effort. Kindly disposed neighbours are more ready to give information to the Society than to call in the Police. The Society in the course of years has formed a staff of carefully selected and highly trained officers, whose whole time and energies are devoted to their duties. Experience has proved that they are well qualified to undertake this work. They possess no special powers or privileges, but it rarely happens that they meet with any serious obstacles in making their investigations, which are of a very thorough nature. The persons, clothing, and bedding of the children must be carefully examined and reported upon. If an infant is in a cradle, it must be lifted out so that its real condition may be seen. The feeding bottle if there be one, must be examined to see that it is not sour and poisonous. The Inspector does not go as a mere amateur detective seeking to get up a prosecution. He goes to prevent cruelty in the widest sense of the term, and he does so by giving good advice in a friendly manner. He points out what is wrong, he tells what the children need — it may be food, clothing, bedding, cleansing, or medical aid. All this is done with sound discretion and tact. The responsibility which rests on the parents for providing things necessary for their children is impressed upon them, and the advice is enforced by warning of the serious consequences that will result if the neglect or ill-treatment continues. After this, the case is not lost sight of. It is kept under supervision, and this is a most important part of our officers' work. In the great majority of cases the advice and warnings produce good results, and after a few visits it becomes evident that the neglect or ill-treatment has ceased, and that there is no further need for the Society's intervention. If, however, the advice and warnings are unheeded, then the Inspector collects evidence and reports the case to the Procurator-Fiscal, who decides whether or not the case must be prosecuted. There is no public authority in a position to undertake all the work of the Society. The ordinary Police Constable has multifarious duties to perform, and has neither the time, experience, nor training to enable him to undertake this work. On receiving a complaint from the public, a constable's duty is this. If there is a contravention of the Act, he must report it for prosecution forthwith; if there is no contravention, he has no right to take further action. Cases of cruelty, however, are not usually so

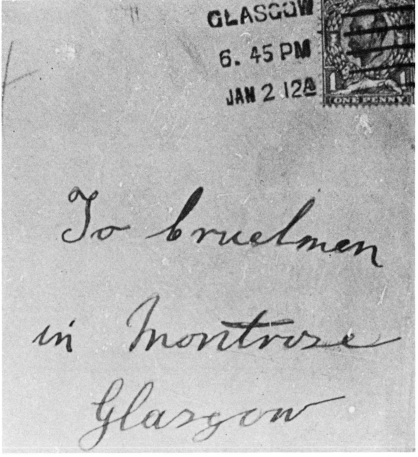

ANONYMOUS COMPLAINT ABOUT CHILD
Addressed to 'Cruelmen' at the Glasgow Office, Montrose Street. To this day more than ten per cent of the Society's referrals are anonymous.

clear and simple that either course can prove satisfactory.
More frequently it is found that there is not sufficient evidence
to convict, but too much evidence to justify dropping the case.
In such circumstances what is needed is constant supervision.
This work is undertaken by the Society's Inspectors. The
Society, while working in co-operation with the Police
Authorities, is under no obligation to report for prosecution.
Its policy is to reform the home and to preserve the unity of the
family. School Boards are not called upon to take cognisance of
children under school age, the very time when, in some cases,
supervision is most needed. Parish Councils are only charged
with the visitation of boarded-out infants and the care of
destitute Children. Churches, Charitable Societies, Cripple
Aid Societies, Training Schools, Orphanages, Industrial
Schools, Asylums, Hospitals, Convalescent Homes, Fresh Air
Fortnight Funds, and other philanthropic agencies are all
providing for the manifold needs of poor children. The
Society's Inspector is the child's friend. He specialises in the
subject, and through the ready and valued co-operation of the
various public authorities and charitable agencies, he is in a
unique position to secure for the child all that the law and
charity provide. In the *Children Act*, Societies for the Prevention
of the Cruelty to Children are more fully recognised than
before, and they have been given increased opportunities of
usefulness. Testimony to the good work that such Societies are
doing is seen in the fact that power is given to Parish Councils,
subject to the approval of the Local Government Board, to
contribute to their funds. Already a number of contributions
have been received from Parish Councils, which shows that the
principles and methods of the Society are thoroughly
appreciated.

Finally this Report also gives another indication of the way the
Society used the experience of its Inspectors to influence the
development of welfare legislation:

STREET TRADING

The subject of street trading by children and young persons
has been under enquiry by a Departmental Committee
appointed by the Secretary for Scotland, and the Society was
afforded an opportunity of giving evidence and expressing its
views. Before doing this, enquiries were made by the staff of
Inspectors, and a report was submitted to the Council. After
full consideration of the facts, it was unanimously agreed that
street trading was most demoralising to children and young
persons, and should be prohibited by law under the age of
eighteen years. It has been clearly established that street

trading is virtually an apprenticeship to casual labour at the
most critical period in life, when it is of the utmost importance
that children and young persons should be acquiring habits of
industry and discipline to fit them to become useful citizens.
This view has been so widely adopted that we hope it may be
given effect soon by Act of Parliament.

By 1910 the Society was not only well established with its views on
welfare being recognised but could report 40 Inspectors; of these 10 were
stationed in Glasgow, 5 in Edinburgh, 2 in Aberdeen and 1 in 23 other
centres from Wick to Stranraer:

> The Society operates in every county in Scotland, and thus
> establishes its claim to be a truly Scottish National Institution.
> It is composed of 26 District Branches, with 1452 members of
> District Councils. There are 65 District Committees, and 758
> Hon. Lady Collectors, During the past year the number of
> cases investigated amounted to 7677, involving the welfare of
> 23,140 children. These figures compare with 7514 cases, and
> 22,224 children in the previous year. On an average, every day
> a fresh group of 66 children claims the protection of the
> Society. The past year has been notable for the large number
> of complaints received from School Board Officials as a result
> of the medical inspection of children, and applications for food
> and clothing made by lazy or drunken parents for their
> children. The complaints are made with increasing confidence,
> for it is now well known that the Society does not prosecute
> until good advice and warnings, generally oft repeated, have
> failed to bring about the desired improvement in the condition
> of the children.

The nature of the work at that time is shown clearly because the
Report goes on:

NEGLECT AND STARVATION

> Out of 7677 cases investigated last year, no fewer than 6708
> were classified under the heading of neglect and starvation.
> Surely a neglected child is one of the most pathetic sights in
> God's fair world. The wrongs of children are for the most part
> suffered in the privacy of the home, all unknown to the great
> outside world. The passer-by little thinks of the long-drawn-
> out tragedy being enacted behind the stone walls of the house
> that looks so commonplace and is so familiar. And yet behind
> such walls there are children crying out their little hearts,
> when there ought to be nothing but joy and laughter. They are
> hungry, for there is no food. They are cold, for there is no fire.
> They are in rags, filth, and vermin. They are lonely and

miserable, for there is no one to comfort or care for them. They may have a drunken mother. Possibly their father is lazy and heedless of them. They are neglected and starved. The passer-by sees none of this. He knows it not. Yet, there it is — in the great cities, the country town, even in villages and rural districts. Or, if a casual visitor enters a house, he may perhaps find it well furnished, comfortable, and cosy, but he does not know that under the stair there is a dark, cold closet in which a poor, hungry boy sits crouching and cramped, locked in for long, dreary hours at a time by a wicked guardian. Again, it

OUTSIDE THE CHILDREN'S SHELTER: 142 High Street, Edinburgh.

may be in a cottage amid romantic scenery in the Highlands. The children are gathered round a cheerful fire in the kitchen. But all alone, in a cold, bare garret upstairs, lying in an old orange box in an indescribable condition, is a frail little cripple girl. The policeman, making his nightly rounds, visits a 'model' lodging regularly as clockwork, yet he never thinks of looking into the coalhole, where an unwelcome infant is being starved to death. Yet such cases have been found, and similar horrors are doubtless still taking place. The Society's officers are indeed doing a work of infinite mercy. They rescue the children when

OUTSIDE THE CHILDREN'S SHELTER: 142 High Street, Edinburgh.

necessary, and in other cases watch over them until their proper treatment is assured.

ILL-TREATMENT AND ASSAULT

Cases of ill-treatment and assault happily show a welcome reduction in number, viz., 164 against 180 in the previous year. Those who have taken part in the work of the Society longest assure us that in former years such cases were of much more frequent occurrence. Parents, when remonstrated with for assaulting their children, used to ask: Is the child not mine? Can I not do with it as I like? It is now widely known that every child has its rights, which must be respected, and that no one, not even a parent, can ill-treat a child with impunity. Still, every now and then we are startled by the discovery of wicked cruelty to some helpless child or even to an infant. What caused those marks on that infant's face? Babies cannot speak. The rough, brutal-looking father says it fell. No one saw it done, but the neighbours declare he was drunk and violent, and they believe he did it. A wild woman loses her temper because her little boy won't go out to fetch her more liquor, and she kicks him on the face. An infuriated father beats his four young children with the flat of a large bread knife and a strop, and their poor little bodies are found painfully bruised, blistered, and swollen. An 'adopted' boy, four years old, disappears from sight, but is heard crying by the neighbours as they pass the house. It is discovered that the foster parents thrash him and keep him in a cold bath. These are some of the more painful cases we have come across recently. Those who thus ill-treat children are, for the most part, craven cowards, and if a case is not so serious as to demand immediate prosecution, an emphatic warning from our Officer is often sufficient to ensure good treatment for the children in future.

ABANDONMENT

Forty-two cases were dealt with by the Society last year in which children were abandoned by their parents or guardians. In such circumstances the child is usually taken to the Poorhouse at once and the offenders sought for. A child found wandering and having no home may be sent to Industrial School. Sometimes a young mother will abandon an unwelcome child. In other cases a widower will leave his children in a lodging house and desert them. Cases in which a father deserts his wife and family and neglects to provide for them are classed under the heading of Neglect and Starvation. Such cases are far more numerous than cases of abandonment.

EXPOSURE

During the past year 273 cases of exposure were dealt with by the Society's Officers. Cases classified thus are of various types. Perhaps the most common is the familiar one of a wretched-looking woman singing on the streets on a wet day, or on a wet night, with an infant in her arms — the child wet and blue with cold and frequently asleep. Thoughtless persons give alms to these unworthy women, and reward them for exposing their infants, and thus cruelty is encouraged. Cases of mothers found drunk in charge of children are classed as exposure. These cases have decreased in number since the public-houses have been closed to children. But women still get drunk and forget

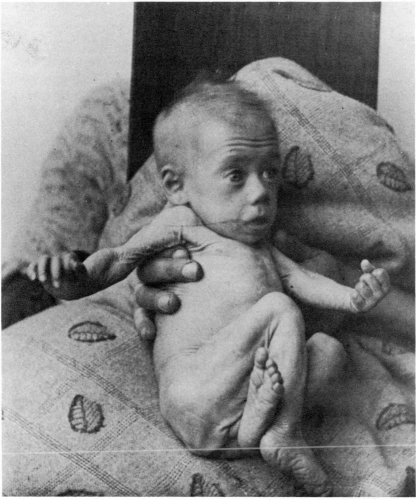

NEGLECT

about their children. Not long ago one of our Officers rescued
an infant only ten days old from its mother, a tramp, who was
drunk. Sometimes vagrants buy a bottle of whisky, get drunk,
and fall asleep on the roadside, heedless of their children, who
cry bitterly from cold and exposure.

BEGGING, SINGING, AND SELLING

Cases of children found begging, and of children street-trading
contrary to law, are classified under this heading, partly for
convenience and partly because it is sometimes difficult to say
whether a child who offers a box of matches or a flower is in
fact selling or begging. These cases numbered 229 against 441
in the previous year. The reduction in number is noteworthy
and encouraging. It indicates that public opinion is being
aroused against the evils of street-trading, and the harm done
by giving to children who beg.

IMMORALITY

Cases of offences against children, whilst by no means
unknown, are not frequently met with. In dealing with cases,
the great difficulty is to obtain sufficient evidence. As matters of
serious crime they are at once reported to the police
authorities. More frequent by far are cases of children living
with vicious parents. The prospect of the reform of the home is
usually so remote, that steps are generally taken at once to
rescue the children by removing them to institutions. Cases of
children living in immoral surroundings numbered 44 during
the past year.

OTHER WRONGS

Two hundred and fourteen cases were entered under the
heading of 'Other Wrongs' during the past year. They were of
a very miscellaneous character, and are of interest as showing
that our Officers take no narrow view of their duties, but are
always willing to be of any assistance where the welfare of a
child is concerned. Cases of vagrants wandering about and
failing to educate their children are entered under this
heading. A child who goes off with some hawkers in a caravan
is sought for. A little boy in the Highlands with a deformed foot
is sent to the Infirmary, and greatly benefited by the treatment
received. Weakly children are sent to Convalescent and
Holiday Homes. A wild lassie is persuaded to go into a training
home. A lad found tramping is sent to a Working Boys Home.
Another lad going astray is sent to a Farm Colony. Such are
some of the other wrongs which the Society helps to right.

It is the duty of this profile to record without too much comment but the modern reader must have some questions about the general social attitudes which were still underlying the caring activities of the Society.

Nevertheless there is no doubt as to the indefatigable way in which the Society pursued its objectives and used the combined experience of its staff and Inspectors to promote the cause of children's welfare. A particular concern throughout its history has been the welfare of the children of the tinker or traveller fraternity. Often it was only the Society which could collect national evidence and present a national case for these children. So in 1912 the Annual Report has a paragraph upon Vagrant Children.

Before reporting the paragraph, however, it is interesting to record the work within the Society which preceded the Report.

So in December 1909 the Executive Committee received the following report from the General Secretary:

S.N.S.P.C.C.
REPORT to the EXECUTIVE COMMITTEE

I beg to report as follows for the consideration of Executive Committee and to draw their attention to one of the Objects of the Society as stated in the Constitution, viz., — 'To take action for the enforcement of the laws for their (all young persons) protection'.

CHILDREN OF VAGRANTS

I have made enquiries regarding the children of vagrants throughout all the Branches of the Society including the Hebrides, Orkney and Shetland, who at the end of November were living out-of-doors. From the returns received it is only possible to frame a thorough estimate, but it would appear that there were probably somewhere about 361 families with 913 children so living. Of these 109 were living in Vans, 197 in Tents, and 55 otherwise, chiefly in out-houses and such like. At the beginning of November the numbers will have been very much higher but the severe weather occurring about the middle of the month caused a great many vagrants to seek shelter in country towns where the lodging houses are now crowded. The children living in vans are mostly fairly comfortable and clean and are attending school. The children living in tents are far otherwise. Few if any are receiving any education whatever and in the inclement winter weather must be exposed to many hardships and much suffering.

Under the *Children Act, Section 12* obligation is laid on parents and guardians to provide adequate lodging for their children.

STREET TRADING

From recent enquiries made it appears that in certain of the
larger towns a more or less considerable amount of street
trading takes place in contravention of Local Bye-Laws and of
the Employment of Children Act 1903 Sect. 3, and the P.C.C.
Act 1904 Sect. 2.

NINIAN HILL
General Secretary
December 1909

and then on the 19th January 1910 the Council of the Society received
the following report:

REPORT TO THE COUNCIL
VAGRANT CHILDREN

In accordance with the instructions of the Executive
Committee we beg to report regarding the children of
Vagrants who are living out of doors during winter.

1. As already reported to the Executive Committee it appears
   from inquiries made by the Society that at the end of
   November there were throughout all Scotland, including
   the Hebrides, Orkney and Shetland, somewhere about 361
   families with 913 children living in tents, 109 in vans and 55
   otherwise, mostly in sheds, out-houses, and such like.

2. For the most part children of Vagrants are healthy, well
   nourished, fairly clean, sufficiently clad and are happy in
   their open air life. They are however reeiving no education,
   nor any industrial training, and in winter are exposed to
   many hardships and privations.

3. From time to time the Society has taken proceedings and
   has secured convictions for neglect in cases of children living
   in tents, and as a result children have been committed to
   Industrial Schools.

4. *The Children Act 1908, Section 12*, provides that a parent or
   guardian shall be deemed to have neglected a child or
   young person 'in a manner likely to cause injury to his
   health if he fails to provide adequate food, clothing, medical
   aid, or *lodging*.'

5. We are not aware of any cases reported by the Society to
   Procurators Fiscal for failing to provide 'adequate lodging'
   alone, but if this provision could be enforced it would clear
   the country of Vagrant Children, and secure for them
   proper maintenance and education.

6. From the information received by the Society it appears
   that the children of Showmen, living in vans, are for the

most part settled in the immediate neighbourhood of towns
and are attending school regularly. The children living in
tents, probably without exception are not attending school
or receiving any education whatever.

7. *The Children Act 1908, Section 118,* makes it an offence
   punishable by a fine of 20/- for a parent or guardian who
   habitually wanders from place to place and thus prevents
   his children from receiving education. A difficulty has arisen
   in getting Vagrant children admitted to Industrial Schools
   owing to it not being obligatory on the part of School
   Boards to maintain such children, and the Society is
   pressing the matter upon the attention of the Scottish
   Office. *The Education (Scotland) Act 1908* makes 'efficient
   education' of all children between the ages of 5 and 14
   compulsory.

8. It is understood that School Boards in country districts
   frequently neglect to enforce the law as the presence of
   Vagrant children is not welcomed in Schools.

RECOMMENDATION

Having considered the remit we are of opinion and beg to
recommend:

1. That before taking other steps to secure adequate lodging
   for the children of Vagrants, a communication on the
   subject be made to the Crown Office, and advice asked as to
   competency of the suggested proceedings.

2. That the Society should formally report all cases of
   children, Vagrant or otherwise, not receiving efficient
   education to the Local School Board, and if proper action is
   not then taken that the matter should be reported to the
   Scotch Education Department.

We have only to add that in our opinion it lies within the
province of the Society to adopt the course recommended in
accordance with the Constitution, Art. 11, (2) which is as
follows: 'To take action for the enforcement of the law for their
(i.e. all young persons) protection'.

R. C. GRAY	Hon: Law Agents.
R. T. PATERSON	
NINIAN HILL	General Secretary.

and then this finally resulted in the following paragraph in the Annual
Report of 1912:

VAGRANT CHILDREN

The condition of vagrant children is a subject that has received
much serious consideration by the Society for many years past.

It is a matter of great satisfaction to us to be able to report that substantial progress has now been made in suppressing vagrancy among children. The full extent of the evil is not always recognised by those whose only acquaintance of vagrants is obtained through a visit to tinker camp in Summer. Far different is the condition in Winter of these poor children lying in a miserable tent or cave exposed to all the rigours of our northern climate. But serious as is the physical suffering, the moral wrong inflicted on these children is even greater. They are not brought up like other children. They are outcasts in the midst of a civilised Christian state. They grow up in ignorance and idleness. Vagrants contribute nothing to the commonwealth of the country. They live the parasite life, subsisting on the industry and thrift of others. No greater cruelty can be inflicted on a Scottish child than to permit it to grow up in such conditions — without ever learning the meaning of the word self-respect, let alone still higher things. It is generally admitted that it is well-nigh hopeless to attempt to reclaim the adult vagrant. The best hope lies in saving the children. The law provides great and far-reaching powers for rescuing children from a life of vagrancy. We have the utmost satisfaction in reporting that the difficulties which have hitherto prevented the law from being put into operation have been satisfactorily overcome. The thanks of the Society are due to the Authorities for the readiness with which they have received the representations we have from time to time put before them, and for the orders they have issued for the due administration of the Children Act for the benefit of vagrant children. The provisions referred to are these: (1) Lodging — Under Section 12 it is enacted that every child or young person is entitled to adequate lodging, and failure to provide adequate lodging is deemed to be neglect, and is a crime punishable on summary conviction by six months' imprisonment with or without hard labour. In order to overcome some uncertainty which existed, Procurators-Fiscal have now been directed to prosecute in cases where parents or guardians have failed to provide adequate lodging in contravention of the Act. Thus it is now acknowledged to be a crime to expose children to the inclemency of the weather in tents and caves, in a manner likely to cause unnecessary suffering or injury to health. (2) Education — Section 118 empowers any constable to arrest without warrant any vagrant habitually wandering from place to place and taking with him any child above five years of age, whereby it is prevented from receiving efficient elementary education, and following on conviction the child may be committed to an Industrial School. The serious difficulty which presented itself as to the maintenance of vagrant children thus committed has now been overcome, the Scottish Education Department having agreed to provide for the expense out of the Education (Scotland) Fund.

The Society's Officers have been actively engaged warning vagrants that they must settle down and send their children to school. The great lever in enforcing this has been, not so much the fear of prosecution and imprisonment as the fear that their children would be taken from them and sent to Industrial Schools. Many tinkers and hawkers, more especially in the Highlands, have thus, with the assistance of the Officers, found houses and work and have sent their children to school. These children have not proved nearly such objectionable schoolmates as might have been anticipated. In many cases their conduct has been highly spoken of by schoolmasters. Testimony has also been given to the reflex influence on the parents themselves through the children attending school like other children and bringing back to the new home new and wider interests. This, then, is the policy we would pursue with the tinker — not to rob him indiscriminately of his children, but to induce him to settle down and work for the maintenance of himself and his family, and to educate his children so that they may grow up respectable and useful citizens.

As regards the ordinary tramp, the outlook is less hopeful. He is distinctly of a lower type than the tinker. He is usually unemployed because he is unemployable — sodden with drink and vice, at once repulsive and pitiable. The female tramp is even sadder as she wanders about in a circuit from the poorhouse, where her children — usually illegitimate — are born, to lodging-house, prison, barn, and roadside, homeless and friendless, till at last she sinks, worn out before her time, into a pauper's grave. In such cases it is a clear duty to save the children. Those of school age are committed to Industrial Schools. Younger children present greater difficulties. Some are admitted to Homes and Institutions. Our Officers warn vagrant mothers to go into the Poorhouse with their children, but no one can compel them to remain there, and thus they easily evade the Society's supervision. For no pauper of the 'in and out' class is compulsory detention more needed than for the female tramp with young children.

Still the noticeable admixture of caring concern and punitive value judgements but also good evidence of a determination to use legislation to extend its application to the benefit of children. The *Children Act* was obviously being heavily utilised when helpful but the Society did not

hesitate to point to shortcomings and disappointments because the
report then continues:

OVERLYING OF INFANTS

Another unsuccessful attempt in the same Act to deal with a
serious matter is made in the section concerning the overlaying
of infants. In order to secure a conviction it is necessary to
prove that the woman on going to bed was under the influence
of drink. The difficulty of obtaining evidence in a matter of this
kind is obvious. The evil goes on in spite of many efforts made
to warn mothers of the danger, and to advise them to get
cradles for their infants. The number of deaths of children
under 5 years of age from suffocation in the eight principal
towns of Scotland during the past five years has been as
follows: 1907, 63; 1908, 59; 1910, 44; 1911, 55.

BURNING AND SCALDING ACCIDENTS

A praiseworthy attempt — unfortunately futile — was made in
the *Children Act* towards mitigating the prevalence of burning
and scalding accidents to little children. An offence, punishable
by a fine not exceeding £10, is committed only if a child under
seven years of age is killed or suffers serious injury through an
open fire-grate not being sufficiently protected. The fine is a
feeble anti-climax to the tragedy, and has proved as useless as
might be expected. Our Officers are continually warning
mothers against going out and leaving their children alone in
the house with an unprotected fire. These distressing accidents
continue unabated, and they are far more frequent and fatal
than the public is generally aware of. The number of deaths of
children under 5 years of age from burns and scalds in the eight
principal towns of Scotland during the past five years has been
as follows: 1907, 98; 1908, 104; 1909, 118; 1910, 97; 1911, 100.
The *Children Act* came into operation on 1st April 1909. These
figures give no cause for satisfaction. The number of accidents
which do not terminate fatally must be very considerable.

This chapter, therefore, has traced the components of the extension
of the work of the Society. Within the first thirty years the characteristics
of the Society and the way it was to proceed were clearly recognisable.

The structure of the Society described in the last chapter had by
this period extended over the whole of the country through the pattern
of district Branches and committees.

The work was firmly based on a widespread staff of Inspectors
whose role was now clearly understood, recognised and respected.

The Society was already using its national structure and its
widespread staff coverage not only to pursue its objectives of prevention
of cruelty to children by its direct work with cases presented to it but also

to collect and use evidence to promote new welfare developments both within its own practice and in the wider provision by public authorities.

It had established its right to be consulted about and had demonstrated its ability to contribute to the development of welfare legislation and had shown its capacity to use that legislation both directly and by acting as an agent for the authorities.

All of this was being sustained by a strong commitment of voluntary support at all levels of society. This pattern of support was already well expressed financially in the form of individual subscriptions, public fund-raising efforts, and an extensive contribution from legacies.

Having recorded the progress of the Society to the point of national stability and recognition in some chronological detail this profile will now begin to take a more kaleidoscopic view of the next stages of development.

5

RESPONSE TO A NATIONAL CRISIS

It is doubtful if it is possible to imagine a greater national crisis in the past hundred years than was embarked upon in August 1914. It is certain that the scale of that crisis and the effect it would have upon life in this country could not have been envisaged at the time. Yet there is something, admirable, about the sense of continuity conveyed by the records of the Society while at the same time containing the evidence of the unusual events which were taking place. Thus, taken from the page of the Staff Committee Minute Book which records the events of this committee chronologically, there is the simple and poignant reference to the routine affairs which concluded the previous meeting followed by the minute of an Emergency Meeting:

> It was resolved to approve of the application by Inspector Shedden, Ayr, dated 16th July 1914, to be supplied with a bicycle.

> ## MINUTE OF EMERGENCY MEETING OF STAFF COMMITTEE ON 11th AUGUST
>
> The General Secretary intimated that Inspectors Mathieson Glasgow, and A. D. Rutherford, Greenock, both Army Reservists, had rejoined the Colours on general mobilisation.
>
> A letter was submitted from Mr R. T. Paterson, Secretary Glasgow Committee, dated 5th August, regarding Inspectors whose services may be temporarily lost to the Society owing to the War. In connection with this letter Mr Paterson intimated that although as yet only one Inspector from the Glasgow Staff had left, others might have to leave later. The Committee decided to continue consideration of this matter until occasion arose for further action being taken.
>
> A letter from Inspector Hugh Murdoch, Peterhead, and a telegram from Inspector McGillivray, Elgin, asking permission to volunteer, the former with the Ayrshire Territorials, and that latter for ambulance work under the Red Cross Society, were submitted. Permission was granted in both cases, and the

General Secretary was instructed to intimate to these men accordingly, and to state that they would be re-instated at the end of the War. It was resolved to deal with any similar requests in like manner.

A letter was submitted from Miss Hepburn, Secretary, Edinburgh District Branch, dated 7th August, asking the Staff Committee's permission to allow the two Women Inspectors, Mrs Roscrop and Miss Kirkpatrick to volunteer for service under the Red Cross Society. It was resolved to deal with these applications in the same way as with those of the men. It was remitted to Miss Trotter and Miss Dingwall Fordyce to appoint one or more women Inspectors in place of Mrs Moscrop and Miss Kirkpatrick.

It was resolved to remit to the General Secretary to deal in his discretion with the question of allowance to be made to the wives and families of Inspectors during their absence on service in connection with the War.

With reference to the carrying on of the Society's work in the Buchan Branch during Inspector Murdoch's absence, the General Secretary was instructed to write to the Chief Constable of the County, asking him to instruct the Police Constables in the Buchan District to report any cases of cruelty or neglect to the Society's Hon. Secretary at Peterhead.

Good evidence here of an enlightened policy with regard to the reinstatement of men released on war service and also of equal treatment of men and women staff.

The work of the Society proceeded, however, and the next item to be recorded shows how the Society continued to try to influence the application of the *Children Act 1908*. The Executive Committee, responding to information from Inspectors and Branches, decided to offer advice to the courts of Scotland in an attempt to maintain the authority of the Inspector in cases where prosecution was sought. There is interesting evidence in this memorandum of the way in which the Society used its extensive network to build up its case and also of the ambivalence felt by an organisation which, whilst concerned to maintain a caring concern and objective still also had to try to ensure that the sanctions to which it had recourse as a final response, were effective.

MEMORIAL from Executive Committee, Scottish National Society for the Prevention of Cruelty to Children to the Sheriffs and Sheriffs-Substitute of Scotland regarding the system of deferring sentence in prosecutions under the Children Act (1908).
The Executive of the Scottish National Society for the Prevention of Cruelty to Children desire respectfully to call the

attention of the Sheriffs and Sheriffs-Substitute of Scotland to the following matter.

In cases of prosecution for Cruelty to Children, it frequently happens that the Sheriff or Sheriffs-Substitute before whom the case calls, after the offender has been convicted, *defers sentence* for a period of say two or three months. The offender is told that he must come back again on a certain date, and that if his behaviour to the children is then reported as being satisfactory that will be taken into consideration in pronouncing sentence. If, when he returns, his conduct is reported to have improved, he is, generally speaking, dismissed with an admonition.

At first sight this seems a reasonable course to follow, but, after much careful consideration and investigation, the Executive Committee of the S.N.S.P.C.C. have come to the conclusion that this system of deferred sentence does not work out satisfactorily, and that it does not conduce either to the reformation of the offender, or act as a deterrent to others.

It is to be remembered that in every case dealt with by the S.N.S.P.C.C., before information for a prosecution for neglect is lodged with the Procurator Fiscal, the offender has been frequently remonstrated with by the Inspectors of the Society, and has been warned that if his conduct does not improve he will be prosecuted. From the very nature of the offence, it is one which must have been often repeated or continued over a considerable period, for prosecutions for actual cruelty in the ordinary meaning of the term (assaults, etc.;) are now of very rare occurrence. The conduct complained of is almost invariably *neglect*, caused by failure to work or by drink, the result being that it is impossible to feed, clothe, or properly care for the children. The offence, therefore, is not a single act, but a habit, and has always been long continued before prosecution is brought. If the offender is at last prosecuted, and if, though convicted, he finally escapes punishment, the power and influence of the Society and of their Inspectors as a preventive agency in the early stages of child neglect is weakened, — a result greatly to be deplored, for there are innumerable cases which never come before the Court at all, but in which the offender is induced to amend his ways by the remonstrances of the Society, and by the fear of punishment.

It may be said that, though sentence is deferred, the offender will not escape punishment unless he meantime amend his conduct. But experience shows that amendment in such circumstances is often to be attributed to the knowledge that the offender has soon to appear again before the Sheriff, and is therefore rarely of a permanent nature, and so soon as the period of probation is over, he relapses into his former misconduct.

It is generally admitted that the object of punishment is, not so much to reform the offender, as to warn others from doing the like, but 'dismissal with an admonition' is not, in the experience of the Society, of the slightest benefit *as a warning to others*.

In order to obtain the opinion of all parts of Scotland upon this question, enquiries were recently sent to all the Society's local Secretaries. Of the replies received, 24 were against the system of deferred sentence, 7 were in favour of it, and 3 were neutral. Most of those in favour of it were from country districts, and it is possible that there may be little objection to the system there, where the offender is well-known to his neighbours, and where accordingly a prosecution, irrespective of the sentence, is of itself a disgrace, and is much more likely to act as a deterrent to others than in towns.

The Executive trust that the Sheriffs and Sheriffs-Substitute of Scotland will pardon the liberty they have taken in thus respectfully calling their attention to this system of procedure, which the Executive are humbly of opinion is not calculated to promote the object for which their Society exists.

Ex Provost KIRKWOOD
Chairman, Executive Committee
CHARLES T. GORDON
General Secretary

The next item recorded is again a reminder of the national situation and the emergencies to which a response had to be found. The meeting of the Staff Committee on 23rd September 1914 contains:

The question of making further temporary appointments to the Inspectors Staff was considered and the suggestion made that the remaining vacancies might be filled by appointing men and women over the recruiting age. Miss Hepburn, Secretary, Edinburgh District Committee, stated that in the event of Chief Inspector Shirran's offer of his services being accepted, she would be prepared to take over his duties at the Edinburgh Shelter during his absence on War service. The Committee expressed their cordial appreciation of Miss Hepburn's offer, and it was resolved to authorise her and the General Secretary to make any temporary appointments to the Inspectors' Staff at the Shelter from time to time in their discretion, subject to confirmation by the Staff Committee, and to authorise Mr R. T. Paterson, Secretary, Glasgow Committee, and the General Secretary to act in like manner with regard to the Glasgow Staff — these powers to include the

appointment of an additional woman Inspector if found
necessary.

And yet again a nice reminder that the Society was probably in the
van of the movement to recognise the equality of the sexes. They were
already employing a few women as Inspectors and then the following
minute refers to another woman member of staff.

> A letter was submitted from Miss Hepburn, Secretary,
> Edinburgh District Committee, dated 8th September, 1914,
> enclosing letters from Mrs Ponder, senior woman Inspector,
> Edinburgh Shelter, dated 2nd and 21st September 1914. In
> view of the statement made by Mrs Ponder in her second letter
> that acting on her medical advice, she is obliged to ask to be
> relieved of her duties at the Shelter at present in order that she
> may have a complete rest for some months, it was resolved that
> she should be placed on the same footing as regards the
> payment of wages during her temporary absence as the
> Society's men Inspectors who are temporarily disabled from
> duty on account of illness.

And, from the minutes of this meeting in the early months of the
War, this rather pleasing excerpt which draws attention both to the
character of the work of Inspectors in rather remote areas and the
continuing evenness of tenure in these areas.

> A letter was submitted from Colonel Paton, Hon. Secretary,
> Greenock, dated 4th August, 1914, in which he stated his
> opinion that the subsistence allowance to Inspectors when
> travelling is not suitable for journey by boat. The Committee
> resolved to recommend that in the circumstances referred to,
> actual outlays may be charged by the Inspector in his
> paysheet.

The work of the Society was quietly brought back into the
realisation of the effect of the War because on the 30th September a
Special Meeting of the Executive Committee was called and the minute
states:

> The Chairman stated that the object of calling the Meeting
> was to consider an application by the General Secretary for
> permission to his accepting an appointment in the Territorial
> Force. The General Secretary, after recording letters which
> had been received from Miss Trotter and Mr John M.
> Macleod, who expressed approval of his application, stated
> that he had been asked to join a new Reserve Battalion of the
> 9th Battalion, Royal Scots (Highlanders), which is now being
> formed in Perthshire and that he felt, at a time like the present,
> it was incumbent upon all who could be of any use in this way

to offer their services if practicable. After making certain suggestions as to the carrying on of the Society's work both at the Head Office and in the Country Branches during his temporary absence, if his application were granted, he placed himself unreservedly in the hands of the Committee. The General Secretary then withdrew.

It was unanimously agreed to grant Mr Gordon's request for leave of absence.

There was then considerable discussion as to ways of meeting the needs of the headquarters office in his absence.

It was understood that any temporary appointment run to the date of the next Annual Meeting (or till the end of the War should that come first) and that a re-appointment could be made at the Annual Meeting. . . .

The General Secretary was then recalled and the decision come to intimated to him. He cordially thanked the committee for the exceeding kind and considerate manner in which they dealt with his application and expressed the earnest hope that the temporary break in his work would not be very prolonged.

This was subsequently found, of course, to be a very optimistic view of the position because Major Gordon did not return to the Society but after a considerable period of War service was later appointed to the public legal service as a Sheriff-Substitute.

The work of the Society continued and the meetings of different committees on the 21st October 1914 show the nature of that work and also the new demands it might have to meet during the national emergency.

The Executive Committee Minutes of October 21st 1914 record that a letter had been received from the Falkirk District Committee expressing their concern at having significant evidence of the wastage of allowance money in drinking by wives of men on active service.

This was also supported by evidence from the Edinburgh Committee and the Executive decided to ask for any further evidence from other areas.

The Council meeting of the same day, 21st October, held in the Religious Institution Rooms, Glasgow in reporting on the work of the Society shows an admixture of the routine, the progressive and the special events of the time.

The Chairman submitted the following report upon some of the principal points in connection with the work of the Society since last meeting of the Council:

In July a Branch Directory was issued to all Hon. Secretaries of Branches and Branch Inspectors. This little book, which was compiled with a view of gaining a closer co-operation between the Branch Committees and the Executive, and also of aiding the Society's Inspectors in the discharge of their duties, has been favourably received. At the same time an Inspectors' Manual was issued to all the Society's Inspectors. This Manual is the *Children Act* of 1908 in condensed form, and arranged so that the Inspector on consulting it, can find out exactly what steps to take in dealing with the cases which come under his notice and supervision.

New local Committees have been formed in several of the Branches. In the Ross and Cromarty Branch a Committee has been formed at Stornoway, one at Tobermory, one at Lochmaddy and the other at Lochgilphead. A Committee has also been established at Port Ellen (Islay), which comes within the boundaries of the Greenock Branch. In the East Fife Branch Committees have been formed at St Andrews and Leven, and the St Andrews Committee has met and mapped out the boundaries of its operations. It is felt that through this further extension of our work in these districts additional interest will be taken in our work by the local public.

On the establishment of the Prince of Wales' National Relief Fund at the outbreak of War, the General Secretary after consultation with the Hon. Secretary of the Scottish Advisory Committee appointed to deal with the administration of the Relief Fund in Scotland, sent a letter to the Secretaries of the different local Committees throughout Scotland suggesting that the members of each district should be represented on the National Relief Fund Local Committees, and in practically every instance this suggestion has been adopted, many of these Committees being of the opinion that the experience of the Society's Officials and Inspectors will be of great value in sifting the applications for relief received, and in the proper administration of the Fund. It has also been suggested to the Committee that representation might with advantage be given to the Society's Executive upon the Scottish Advisory Committee, and at the last meeting of the Executive Committee, the General Secretary was instructed to make application to the Advisory Committee for a grant from the Prince of Wales' National Relief Fund in aid of the Society's work. This has been done.

At the beginning of the War two or three of the Inspectors who were Army Reservists were called up for duty, others asked permission to volunteer for active service, and up to date twelve Inspectors have gone away on military duty, and there is a possibility of two more at least of the Glasgow Staff having to go off very shortly. To carry on the work of the Branches, where Inspectors have gone away, the co-operation of the

Committees in neighbouring Branches has been sought in order that the services of the Inspectors under their control might be utilised in those districts where there is now no resident Inspector. Through this arrangement, the only appointments that have been made to fill vacancies have been on the Glasgow Staff where two temporary Inspectors have been appointed, and on the Edinburgh Staff where one temporary appointment has been made. One of the two Women Inspectors who volunteered for service with the Red Cross was accepted and has gone to the front. Several of the Society's Hon. Secretaries have rejoined their regiments, but we have been fortunate in each case to secure the help of other prominent men in the different districts to fill the vacancies.

The General Secretary was at the end of September allowed to accept an appointment with the 9th Battalion (Highlanders) Royal Scots and at a Special Meeting of the Executive Committee held on 30th September, received permission to accept this appointment.

In the minutes of the Executive Committee in November 1914 there is an interesting reference to the way in which the subscription income of the Society was maintained.

The following statement of work done by Miss Macrae was submitted:

Miss Macrae started duty on 5th November and continued till Saturday 14th November. She visited Dowanhill, Partick, Dennistoun, Crosshill (all districts in Glasgow), Old Kilpatrick, Clydebank and Cambuslang. She obtained six collectors. She also made calls in Clydebank and Dalmuir at the request of the Local Superintendent upon the works of Messrs. Beardmore, Brown Ltd., Napier and Miller, and D. & J. Tullis, to endeavour to obtain subscriptions from the Workmen's Funds when same come to be allocated.

But then the serious matter of the concern over the behaviour of wives of men on active service is returned to as the minute shows.

The Executive resumed consideration of the subject brought forward at the last meeting with regard to intemperance amongst women whose husbands are on Military Service. With regard to the information desired by the Executive replies had been received reporting that there had been trouble in this direction from the following Branch Committees: Aberdeen, Greenock, Falkirk, Ayr, Dunoon, Dunfermline, Dumbarton, Hamilton, Arbroath, Kilmarnock, Kirkcaldy and Leith. The following Committees had had no complaints within their district namely Wishaw, Forfar,

Airdrie, Nairn, Buckie, Forres, Peterhead, Dingwall, Coatbridge, Montrose, Cupar, Portree, Lerwick, Campbeltown, Keith, Galashiels, Oban and Brechin. No reply had yet been received from the following: Fraserburgh, Jedburgh, Dumfries, Paisley, Elgin, Inverness, Perth, Motherwell, and North Ayrshire. Letters had also been received in reply from Col. Etheridge, Territorial Force Association, Edinburgh, and from the Secretary of the Soldiers' and Sailors' Families' Association, Glasgow. Col. Etheridge stated that he had not found that the evil of Intemperance amongst women was widespread and he promised if any case were put before him to have it investigated. He further stated that the Army Council were willing, on the request of any soldier who applied to them on account of his wife's intemperance, to make payment of the separation allowance to any Approved Society to be disbursed for behoof of any children who were neglected. The Army Council also had intimated that in any case where a woman was proved to be guilty of gross neglect to her children they may withhold the issue of a separation allowance from her and direct it to be paid at a higher rate to some person in trust for the children. The Secretary of the Soldiers' and Sailors' Families' Association, Glasgow, stated that his Association withdrew any allowance to a woman who was found to have given way to intemperance. Mr Galbraith supplemented these replies by reporting that the Glasgow District Committee were endeavouring to get the Town Council to convene a meeting of all Societies interested with a view to concerting some form of joint action.

The Committee having received these replies and considered the whole position, resolved that, as it had been brought to their knowledge that other Societies more particularly interested in the matter were approaching the Government direct, there was no need for this Society taking action meantime, but expressed their willingness to co-operate with any Association in concerting measures of relief in any case where the welfare of children was involved.

It was further resolved that a letter be sent to the Secretaries of all Branches of the Soldiers' and Sailors' Families' Association inviting intimation to be made to the Local Inspector in any case of a woman giving way to intemperance where children were concerned.

During the Great War the influence of the Society upon significant legislation was maintained as shown in this excerpt from the Executive Committee meeting of December 19th, 1917.

The Executive resumed consideration of the working of the Mental Deficiency Act when the General Secretary submitted the following memorandum prepared on the instructions of the Executive:

The Mental Deficiency Act which came into force on 16th May 1914 was designed to improve and extend the Lunacy Acts. The older law dealt almost entirely with provision of treatment for the insane, while this new Act is designed to deal with those who, while not insane, are of weak intellect or feeble-minded.

Special care is taken in this Act for young persons, and clauses are enacted for the education of those who are capable of receiving education. It is the duty of parents and guardians of all children between the ages 5 and 16 who are mentally defective to make provision for their education if they are able to receive education, or for their due care and supervision if they are not educable. If a parent is not able, by reason of the expense to provide the necessary education, the duty is then thrown upon the School Board of the District to provide the education, and if the child is so defective as not to be capable of education, then his care, in case of the parents not being able to meet the expense, falls upon the Parish Council.

It is the duty of every School Board to ascertain what children within its area are mentally defective and which of them are capable of receiving instruction. These clauses of the Act make it imperative on School Boards to carry out what was merely permissive in the *Act for the Education of Defective Children* of 1906. By that Act School Boards had power conferred upon them, if they thought fit, of making special provision for the education of defective children. Now the Mental Deficiency Act makes it imperative on School Boards to provide for the education of defective children, who are capable of receiving instruction, presumably by making special provision for them. To meet the objection that some School Boards may be too small to carry this out for themselves, power is given to any two or more Boards to unite for the making of the special provision for the defectives under their care. A special duty is thrown upon School Boards with regard to children, who in addition to being defective, are found neglected, abandoned or without visible means of support, or are being cruelty treated.

So far not much has been done for the carrying out of the Act. The War is blamed for preventing special buildings being erected, and there is danger that after the War, the provisions of the Act may be forgotten.

Unless special provision be made for the education of

defective children, there is grave danger that they may grow up without any improvement of their mental faculties. When placed in the ordinary school along with more quick-witted children, they are apt to be left behind. In classes of the usual size there is little time to give to any one particular individual, and it is generally a choice between the keeping back of the class for the sake of the individual, and the neglecting of the individual for the sake of the class; and in such dilemma it is easy to predict on which side the decision will rest.

From reports received from different parts of the country, one gathers that some of the smaller School Boards are not carrying out the duties imposed on them of providing such education for defective children as they are capable of receiving, where the parents are unable to provide this for themselves. To incur expense in giving such instruction as defectives can take in is money well spent. Without it they grow up dull and useless, a trouble to themselves and a burden upon others. With boys growing up like this it is bad; with girls it is deplorable.

The report was supplemented by the following extract from the Annual Report of the Board of Control, submitted by Dr Fraser and read at his request:

'For reasons of economy the operations of the *Mental Deficiency Act* have had to be curtailed, and no expenditure upon new buildings for the care of Mental Defectives has been undertaken since the outbreak of War. Under these circumstances we have not considered it advisable to press local authorities to put the provisions of the Act into force by the certification of Mental Defectives for whom no accommodation exists.'

The Executive received the Memorandum and resolved that word should be sent to the Society's Inspectors to report any case coming under their notice of children who were mentally deficient and of the means taken to meet each case when, if necessary, further action could follow.

So the work of the Society continued throughout the Great War. Over half the permanent staff undertook active service. Two Inspectors were killed on active service and a number were wounded and invalided. The end of the fighting on the continent was not, however, necessarily a time for relaxation at home as the Report for the year 1918 shows.

During the year the work of the Society has proceeded satisfactorily though under difficulty, so many of the regular Staff being still on military duty, but the victorious end of the long struggle in arms promises a more hopeful future. On the signing of the Armistice, as it seemed unlikely there would be any renewal of hostilities, we applied to have our Inspectors released from military service as early as possible. Experience gained on the termination of the South African War showed that the period of demobilisation was a time of much disquiet and unrest, and we therefore desired that the Society's Inspectors should be at their posts forthwith.

After a war on such a large scale, with forces in numbers beyond all previous experience, the Executive foresee a long and difficult time of readjustment. Industrial conditions have completely changed in character during the period of the war. Many industries employing large numbers of men in peace time have perforce been closed; the activities of all classes, both men and women, have been directed into new channels. All these activities, so essential to the proper conduct of the war, are no longer required, and there must be difficulties to be encountered in the restoration of normal conditions.

Where there is any disturbance in the economic or social life of the country, the children generally suffer. It is distressing how little active care for their welfare is exercised by many parents and guardians, even by those who mean well. Ignorance plays a part in this state of matters, and so does carelessness, both of which, if good feeling exists, can be removed, and it is a real pleasure to see the improvement which takes place when bad conditions have been brought about by want of thought, where there is a desire to do better. But if parents are indifferent to what their children require, and what they are entitled to receive, then the matter assumes a more serious aspect and is more difficult to treat.

The work of the Society is closely connected with the life of the people in every aspect, and so improvement in the standard of living, on the one hand, and economic conditions becoming more acute on the other hand, are factors which affect the rise or fall of the work of the Society. Where economic conditions are severe and household incomes on a modest scale the lot of children is hard; they are the first to feel the effects of a small family income, and in the growing stage of life it is they upon whom such conditions tell most adversely.

Taking a retrospect of the state of matters prevailing during the period of the war, one notes a considerable decrease in the number of cases brought under the Society's care. There have been happily two main lines of genuine improvement in the past four years which have had a distinct bearing upon the welfare of the children. While the war lasted work was plentiful, and with wages high there was a very real improvement in the conditions of the homes of the people.

Incomes were good and the effect was that children received better care and better feeding, and this improvement was recognised by no class more than the parents of the children themselves when they discovered how much stronger and healthier these had become. A recognition of improvement often brings with it an intention, even if unconscious, to continue what has been so well begun.

Of even greater value has been the enhanced interest of all classes in the importance of the life of children and a desire to remove all causes of disease and trouble. A genuine feeling of the interdependence of the whole community has been aroused. Former class feeling has been broken down, and poor and rich, high and low, have felt, as never before in the history of the country, how much each one is a part of the whole. There has arisen a new outlook upon life and the social state and a sense of the reality of the brotherhood of man, coupled with a realisation that no one section of the community can suffer through being deprived of the necessities and amenities of life without all classes suffering also. Any apathetic individualism, which does not trouble about what is going on in other parts of the country, has gone, and the effect will be seen in days to come by a wise endeavour to better the conditions of living in those ranks of society which need most help and sympathy.

Even although there has been a steady decline in the number of cases brought under the notice of the Society during the years of war, we have still in 1918 been called upon to deal with a very large number, so large as to make one feel at times greatly concerned about the home life of our people. One argues that if so many as 5775 cases have had to be treated there must be many more, there may be thousands of them, in which the conduct of the parents is just above the border line which lies between proper care for the children and utter neglect. The total number of children concerned in these cases cared for by the Society's Inspectors amounted in 1918 to 17,952, and this great number, coupled with the fact that the Inspectors in their daily rounds paid no fewer than 52,594 visits to the homes of the people in investigating and supervising, gives some idea of the magnitude of the Society's operations and of the value of its service to the State.

6

NEW CHALLENGES
AND A NEW CRISIS

The last chapter which traced the effects of a national crisis upon the Society concluded with paragraphs from the 1918 report which may have been prophetic. They referred to the close connection between the welfare of the community and its economic well-being. When the Society reached its Jubilee in 1934, merely sixteen years later, the country was deep in the effects of recession with high unemployment.

Over the intervening years the most significant event for the Society had been the granting of the Royal Charter in 1922. This was the culmination of the steady progress towards a distinctive national organisation and a formal recognition of the position the Society had reached in the field of child welfare in Scotland. There is no doubt that it was greeted with great enthusiasm by those who had always wished to emphasise the different needs of Scotland and the special contribution which had to be made within the Scottish content.

This may be partly due to the fact that the social and economic history of Scotland gives evidence that many of the resounding social and economic issues are felt with particular severity in Scotland, for example the depopulation of rural areas, the deterioration within the older basic industries and the low standard housing which is a relic of rapid urbanisation during the later Industrial Revolution. Therefore when Britain was plunged into depression in the early 1930s with serious unemployment the effects were strongly felt in Scotland.

As has been indicated earlier in this profile the main sensors of the social effects of such changes, so far as the Society was concerned, were the Inspectors of the Society. The Executive Committee had a practice of requesting regular reports from each of its District Inspectors in turn and giving the report close attention in an effort to keep in touch with developments throughout the country.

So in the minutes of the Executive Committee of January 18th 1932 is evidence first of the feelings of Scottish distinctiveness and then secondly of the comprehensive reporting which formed the basis of much Society policy-making.

One other matter which has constantly caused trouble is the lack of adequate accommodation for mental defectives and the Committee recommend that a fresh message be sent to the Board of Control asking that something should be done to provide sufficient accommodation. In the existing Institutions at Larbert and Baldovan there are long waiting lists of children to be admitted for proper training. Mr Johnston speaking in support of the proposals in this Report said it was greatly to be regretted that Bills applying to the whole of the United Kingdom should be drafted in London without due consideration being given to Scottish views and he explained that the Committee had done what was possible to counteract this. One method he said was to approach the Secretary of State direct, as proposed by the Committee, and he concluded by moving that the Report with all the proposals therein be approved. This motion was adopted.

INVERNESS BRANCH

In accordance with the arrangement, the following report from Inspector Shennan on the work in the Area covered by the Inverness-shire Branch was submitted as follows.

'Inverness-shire alone has an area of 4,200 sq. miles: has the longest and the deepest lochs; and the highest mountains in the British Isles. Great glens intersect the County; and long arms of the sea indent its coast.

The same topographical features are found in Argyll, Ross and Cromarty, Caithness and the North Isles; and as far as the Society's work is concerned, the problems arising in each are very much the same. Agriculture, Fishing, Weaving, and in this County, Aluminium production are the staple industries. The inhabitants are on the whole stolid, unemotional, and not easily swayed one way or another — but human nature is the same in the Highlands as elsewhere; and the Society is as necessary a body as any other preventative institution.

The majority of complaints may be classified under General Neglect, and are chiefly economic at their source, by which is meant an over-sufficient family and an insufficient income administered by inefficient parents. The father, if he neither drinks nor gambles, is of the easy-going type, who leaves the greater burden to be borne by the mother; she loses heart and becomes generally careless; her ill-clad and poorly nourished children become easy victims to childhood's ailments. Sometimes there is a decline from a good economic position to poverty and slumdom, due to mesalliance or folly — leading to the disruption of the home and neglect of children.

The verminous condition of children at school is a
common complaint, and strangely enough is considered by
many parents as not sufficient cause for complaint — on the
plea that such a state was indicative of robust health.

The benefits of personal hygiene are becoming widely
known, and dispelling such ridiculous ideas.

Complaints of children being ill-nourished usually come
from the Outer Isles, which on investigation are found to be
due to bad harvest, poor fishing, and sometimes to exploitation
of cattle buyers who give starvation prices for animals upon
which the crofters' livelihood chiefly depends.

Quite a third of the parents dealt with are of the feckless,
thriftless type, with a slum complex and hereditary handicap,
who breed prolifically.

Where there is an unselfish, enlightened body of men and
women on local councils, whose humanitarian ideas impel
them to provide a better environment for the slum-bound, they
prove beyond doubt the wisdom of their counsels in not only
making a fine municipal investment, but enormously reduce
and sometimes finally overcome the handicap of bad heredity.

On the whole, offenders in the Highlands are perhaps
more sensitive to rebuke than offenders in the South, and very
often one visit to a household is sufficient. In the Outer Isles a
strong rebuke to one is sufficient to produce a mild
repercussion in the whole community, because of the close ties
of kindred.

In the general neglect cases the homes are of one or two
apartments poorly furnished, dirty and untidy. In the crofting
districts a poor house is a woe-begone spectacle; with earthen
floor and leaky roof sagging in places. It is not wise however to
judge by exteriors, as some of the finest men living issued from
croft houses. The old Black Houses are fast disappearing, so too
is the auld clay biggin', and in their stead are arising all over
the landscape (with which by the way they do not harmonise)
— houses of a modern type. New or old, the windows are kept
shut — because, they say 'You can get plenty of fresh air
outside'. The artisan class do not give much trouble and have
clean, comfortable homes.

The problem of the housing of the poor is as acute here as
elsewhere, but good progress is being made.

Such a problem as housing requires not only a change of
mental attitude in the mass, but also the application of the best
brains in the country to investigate the causes out of which
such problems arise — and produce a cure. Meanwhile, good
progress is being made in the Highlands; and the idea here as
elsewhere is; that if his house is condemned that he be removed

to a new house provided for him by the Municipality and his old abode abolished.

Now it is always difficult to get rent out of a slum tenant, because he is ever in a chronic state of poverty, he was either born in such surroundings or gravitated there due to external stress or else folly.

However that may be without any training in how to make the best use of new property he is transported to his new home, slum mind, furniture and all. In his unprepared state he will yet make a bold effort to establish himself and family, if he fails, he will gravitate back to some other slum, where his latter state may well be worse than his first. The majority thus removed elect to fight on. The destructive tendencies of the children have to be held in check; he refuses to put his coals in the bath; gradually the bedding is improved; boots and better clothing acquired; coupled with all this added expenditure a bigger rent has to be paid out of the same slum income. Somehow the family struggles on and after bitter hardships, and the discipline imposed upon them by their state and surroundings — 'with the inevitability of gradualness' — cease to be active sores on the Body Politic.

When the great tunnel was being driven through the Nevis Range the Inspector had to deal with men from all parts of the British Isles. This service is still being rendered at the Dam construction works near Tulloch, and Road Camps along the Caledonian Canal. The conditions as described in Patrick McGill's book *The Children of the Dean End* of the old Kinlochleven days are now gone. Contractors now realise that if a man is treated fairly he will give a fair return in labour. Owing to the dangerous nature of tunnel driving work, it is not always easy to get the right class of men. Many undesirables therefore got into the Camps — usually the type who had deserted their wives and children; or other fugitives from Justice. Arrests effected at the instigation of the old Parish Council were common, but nowadays are infrequent.

On the whole the British navvy is a hard working man and after a week of hard toil, it is not surprising that he has a bit of a fling. He will have a drink or two and a throw of the dice or cards, but before doing so will send off to his wife a proportion of his earnings. With a few drinks and gambling claims he may lose what was so hardly won by pick and shovel. On many occasions the Inspector's services were in request to warn men for failing to provide: men who said that they had no desire to evade their responsibility.

On leaving home to tramp to Fort William they had painted a glowing picture of how they were going to make provision — to find after a week of tramping, sleeping and begging by the way that work was not immediately available. After further delay, a start is made, and from the first wage of say 50/-, 23/- plus another 23/- is deducted for board and fore-handed board. Strong boots and clothing have to be purchased — debt is incurred — which is gradually paid off: but all this time not a word to the wife as to how things stand. The woman complains, and after the Inspector has gone into the matter and duly warned and advised the man, weekly payments are made and continued.

It is sometimes quite impossible for tunnel and road worker to make adequate provision, because in the first instance the wage is divided, and in the second instance bad weather upsets the whole arrangement, because wages are not paid for hours thus lost. Married men on such work who try to do well deserve full consideration and sympathy. Many have to throw up the job and risk getting into trouble through no fault of their own.'

The Report was regarded as very satisfactory and on the motion of the Chairman the General Secretary was instructed to write and thank Inspector Shennan.

The meeting concluded by discussion of two cases which showed how strongly the Society felt about the nature of Court decisions in the areas in which it had an interest.

The General Secretary reported that he had received a letter from the Assistant Manager of a Picture House in Leith reporting that a criminal assault had been committed in the Picture House upon a young girl six years of age. The matter had been brought to the notice of the Police and through an arrangement made by them, the girl had again attended the Picture House and the same man came and would have again committed a criminal assault upon her but was arrested and brought before the Court when he had been sentenced to three months' imprisonment. The Assistant Manager reported this because no doubt he wished to vindicate his own place of public entertainment while the parents of the child were most indignant at the paltry sentence. The General Secretary was instructed to write to the Lord Advocate and draw his attention to the light sentence imposed when even penal servitude might have been inflicted.

Mr Blakely mentioned as of the same character a case in which a couple had while under the influence of drink upset a bottle of some corrosive acid and one of their children, 2 years of age crawling about had come upon this fluid and had been so severely injured that it had died. The matter had been

brought before the Court when the case against the mother
had been dropped. As regards the father Sheriff Berry before
whom the case came said that as the man was intoxicated at
the time there was some excuse for him and had sentenced him
to short imprisonment. Mr Blakeley said in his view the offence
was all the worse because of the parents having contributed to
what happened by their conduct. Agreed to bring cases to the
notice of Lord Advocate.

On the 20th April 1932 the Executive Committee received the
following report from an Inspector which makes direct reference to the
effects of the recession and unemployment.

In accordance with the arrangement for a report of the work
in some part of the country the following report was
submitted from Inspector Cumming of the Motherwell and
Wishaw Branch.
'Dealing first with the nature of the complaints received,
"failing to provide" is an easy first and next to actual brutality
it is the worst form of complaint. When one thinks of a child
being kept hungry through the selfishmess of either of the
parents, it often makes one wish he had the right to give those
parents what they so richly deserve. The area covered by the
Branch is mixed, a very large industrial population and a large
district made up of people who follow agricultural and fruit-
growing pursuits. It is in the industrial area where the most of
the complaints arise and "failing to provide" is the most
numerous. The reason for this, so far as experience goes, is the
gambling fever which is making such havoc among so many
families at present. There has been much ink spilled regarding
the Betting Laws of the country and more especially in
connection with the "Street Bookie"; he is certainly a nuisance
and a danger, especially to women betting, but compared to
the "gambling school" his responsibility for the "failing to
provide" complaint is not as great as might be thought. Every
weekend from Friday till Sunday night great "gambling
schools" gather at different places and play at "pitch and toss"
and it is not an infrequent occurrence for men to stand at the
"school" and gamble away all the money they have received
from the Labour Exchange or in a few cases their wages. The
mother in such cases is usually the complainer, but it is
remarkable how often one finds that she is very unwilling to
take the extreme step of having her husband reported to the
Procurator Fiscal. The Inspector has then to get to work
getting relatives roped in to provide for the children, and
generally this is not difficult if the offender is going to "get a
chance". The whole affair is made so impressive that the

delinquent is heartily glad to take the chance and for a very long time, at least, he is an absentee from the "school". Regarding the character of the parents, they are not much, if any, worse than will be found elsewhere. There is the problem of the unmarried mother which has always been with us, but the present want of work is to a large extent making the problem more acute. There are so many young men and women with nothing to do that they are thrown into each other's company much too often and when the disaster does take place, no money can be found to pay for the maintenance of the child. Sometimes marriage takes place and they live "on the Buroo" but those marriages are rarely successful and lead to a life of quarrelling and misery. The housing conditions for the most part are little short of deplorable and a great number of the houses in Motherwell have become untenantable owing to underground workings, and the need to provide houses for those who occupy them has to some extent hindered the dealing with slum areas. The reluctance of factors and owners to do anything except absolutely necessary repairs and the shortage of money by the tenants all contribute to make the houses anything but comfortable homes.

In spite of those drawbacks it is remarkable how most people respond to the advice and hints the Inspector is able to give them and the eagerness with which some of them seek advice as to how to do certain things. One case was where the woodwork round the sink was rotten and causing a very bad smell. Unfortunately the tenants were behind with their rent and when they asked the factor to do the repair he told them to do it themselves. They were afraid to complain to the Sanitary Inspector, but not to the "Cruelty man". The Inspector examined the place and then told them what do do. The job is finished now, the smell is gone, everybody, even the factor, is pleased, and so the work goes on.

There have been a few cases lately of parents complaining they could not find housing accommodation; their story generally is that they are in a room and are being turned out as the tenant has to undergo the "means test' and as their payment towards the rent of the house will be taken into account they must clear out. This raises a very difficult matter to deal with; nearly everybody who sub-lets a room is in the same position and no factor will take any notice of persons who perhaps have never had a house of their own. The Burgh or County Housing officials cannot do anything to help those people, as they do not come under the class to be dealt with under the *Slum Clearance Act*. The Inspector has been somewhat lucky in being able to get some of those unfortunate people

placed in rooms, and in two or three cases, owing to the
tenants removing the "folk in the room" have become the
tenant of the house.

Much has been said regarding the ill effects, moral and
physical, of families living in one-apartment houses and it is
difficult for some people to imagine anything worse, but bad
though that be, two families in two apartments of the same
house is infinitely worse. The number of sub-lets in the Burgh
of Motherwell and Wishaw is in the neighbourhood of 300, so
it will be readily understood that the provision of houses at
rents which are not outwith the means of the "roomer" are
urgently required. This condition may be pretty general
throughout the whole country, but the industrial areas have
much more to contend with regarding housing than the
country districts.

There is a splendid School for defective and cripple
children in Motherwell under the charge of a lady who has a
very real interest in the children and no one could estimate the
amount of good that is done in and from this centre.

The Sanitary Officers throughout the whole area are
always very willing to co-operate and should any of them come
across dirty or neglected children the Inspector is sure to be
informed. On the other hand should any of the houses visited
be dirty and smelling the Sanitary Officers are notified so that
between the various officials there is sure to be a very
considerable improvement in a short time. The dirty
verminous type of case is becoming less, the medical
supervision in the Schools having done much to reduce the
number, but parents in general are paying more attention to
the cleanliness of the children. This may not be done because
they like to do it, because there are cases where, if they thought
the "Cruelty man" would not come back, the children would
receive scant attention and it is because of the possibility of his
dropping in at any time which keeps the parents, especially the
mother, up to as near perfection as one can reasonably expect
them, or her, to be.

There seems to be no end to the advice asked for by
parents. The Inspector was once asked by a friend what were
the qualifications required to make an Inspector of the Society,
to which the reply was given that if one had the patience of
Job, the wisdom of Solomon, and the decision of Napoleon I,
he would make a perfect Inspector. Unfortunately very few
people possess all those qualifications and yet in the work of the
Society one requires to exercise one or other of them to the
utmost of his capability. Throughout the whole of this area
there is no one in any official position who would refuse to do

all he or she could to help the Inspector in carrying out his duty, or by giving assistance in any case recommended by him. Also a work of praise is due to the Press for the willingness to give our District Committee Meetings such valuable space in their papers for much good is done by those reports in letting the general public know that the work of the Society goes steadily on to save the children.'

The Chairman drew attention to what was mentioned in the Report about gambling and asked Mr Fordyce about this. Mr Fordyce replied that the matter seemed to be gaining a very serious hold in the districts round Motherwell and Wishaw, perhaps due to the greater amount of idleness and to young men having nothing else to do. The evil seemed to be increasing and where men assembled for gambling this had come to be known as a 'Gambling School'. The Chairman said that the Report was very interesting and he moved that a message of thanks be sent to Inspector Cumming, which was adopted.

These reports not only continue to give the flavour of the work but also give strong evidence of both the variety of work undertaken by Inspectors and also their rather distinctive personal approach to that work. The strong personal attitudes of the individual Inspector come through the basic approach which is a firmness based on a conviction of moral standards which, probably even at this time, were old-fashioned and would not necessarily have received consensus of agreement within the community. Nevertheless there is evidence that such strong guidance was not resented within communities which were accustomed to look for this kind of model for behaviour.

Also within the reports are clear indications of both the difficulties associated with problems like slum clearance and the necessary policy antidotes which were required. Yet these same problems and a search for the remedy were still being repeated in reports and study literature even twenty or thirty years later.

There is no doubt that within the collected wisdom of experienced officers like these of the Society there was much of relevance to the policy-makers within the statutory context. Unfortunately so often this wisdom and experience lie locked within the files of organisations and are not applied to the widest potentiality of its usefulness.

As has been shown the Society often collected such experience on specific issues but too often there is not generally the flow of inter-communication between those closely involved with social problems and those who seek the remedies.

The Society often used this basic information to inform the public through the Annual Report, as for instance in the year of 1933 which refers to the fifty years of experience of the Society and after reviewing the history of the Society and its growth from dealing with 595 families in the first year to 8,160 families involving 24,077 children in 1933, including the comment, as one gentleman wrote:

> Think not only of one year, take the vast number of children whom the Society has cared for, and multiply it by fifty for the fifty years of the Society's existence.

Then later continues:

> One can best judge the work of the Society, how it comes into contact with the lives of the people, and what good it actually accomplished, by reading some of the tales told by the Inspectors. Selfishness, laziness, thriftlessness, and careless indifference, amounting at times to utter callousness, are ever with us.
>
> At the present time gambling is one of the serious evils, very often due to the fact that men are unemployed, and so take to gambling as a means of passing the time. Also there have been instances of people who are hard up hoping that by venturing a few shillings they may 'win a prize' as they term it, and so get money to tide them over the hard times. But there have been very bad cases of men out of employment and dependent upon the money which they drew from the Labour Exchange spending the whole sum in gambling, quite heedless of their dependents. In one case a young man, married, with one child, who was unemployed and dependent upon the allowance received from the Labour Exchange began to gamble, and at times most of the money received went to satisfy this craving. The Inspector heard of this and called and warned the man severely, and even went further, and for some weeks accompanied him when he went to the Labour Exchange, and saw that the whole amount was handed over to the wife. Then efforts were made to break up the gambling habits of the people who consorted together, with the result, so far as this individual was concerned, that there was so great improvement that the wife told the Inspector that life was now worth living.
>
> A frequent cause of children suffering hardship is where there is quarrelling between the parents, which when continued is a never-ending source of trouble. In one household the father had become so careless and indifferent to the claims of his wife and children that he spent a large part of his weekly wage upon himself, which caused continual quarrelling between the parents. The inevitable result was that there was not enough money to feed the children properly, and because they were under-nourished some of them required

medical attention, sores having broken out upon them. The Inspector got a hold of the man and dealt with him severely, and in the long run he admitted that he had been altogether in the wrong. He began to do better, with the result that there was what the Inspector described as a complete transformation in the home. It did not look like the same place, and the children's appearance showed how much they had benefited.

Then desire for constant amusement and pleasure-seeking may work disaster. A young wife was so fond of dancing that she went out night after night, and thought nothing at all of the claims of her two very young children, but left them by themselves in the house. The husband was on the night shift and could not be at home, but both parents were to blame, for the husband knew what was going on, and made no attempt to improve matters until the Inspector tackled both, and spoke very sternly to them. Both parents promised to mend their ways, and this they did so effectively that soon anyone calling at the house could see a great improvement, and, as the wife remarked to the Inspector, she had learned that dancing was 'not her mission in life'.

Then if dancing does not appeal to a man he can neglect his duties by other methods, such as in the case of one whose whole desire was to go out night after night and drink with his companions. He had a good wage, but as two boys of the

CHILDREN
Outside the Children's Shelter, 142 High Street, Edinburgh (1930s).

family were at work, the father took it for granted that they would hand over their money to the mother, and so he was quite reckless of the consequences. The Inspector found the house very poorly furnished; the bedding and bed-clothes needed renewal, and the children were in a very poor and neglected state. The mother was losing heart, and although she had done her best she could not do what was needed. Warning seemed to have no effect on the man, and so he was brought before the Court with, as the outcome, a complete change: reformation in the man's conduct and improvement of their whole condition. The man admitted that he had never realised the state of things until he had been brought to book, and he promised to behave in future. The mother, it was quite evident, realised what a benefit the Society was, so happy and contented did she look.

Some parents do not realise that failure to obtain medical aid for a child who is ill is a punishable offence. There was a case in a remote part of the country where, if the family income was not large at least there was something to go on with. The house was poorly furnished, but the mother was doing her best to keep it clean and comfortable. The younger child was in need of medical attention, but neither father nor mother seemed to think anything about this. Fortunately, the Inspector heard about it, and went at once to the house. The infant was in a very emaciated condition, and although the child looked almost as if dying no doctor had been brought in. The Inspector at once arranged for the Medical Officer of Health to send one of his Assistants to see the child and for the District Nurse to call. At once, because of the advice given and the Inspector's warning that the medical man's instructions must be followed, a change for the better set in, and the Inspector was able to report that in subsequent visits the child was making steady progress. Had it not been for the intervention of the Society the child would have died.

With careless parents it is at times hard to know what to do, advice seems so futile. Thus in one case both parents were of a thriftless nature, and each of them seemed quite indifferent as to how the children, of whom there were eight, would get on. They were not only thriftless but also lazy and they were constantly quarrelling. The Inspector tackled both father and mother, and warned them of their responsibilities, and also what might happen if they did not do better. This warning had to be repeated over and over again, but in the end both parents admitted to the Inspector that they had been living a life of misery, and that the children had suffered because of the continual quarrelling going on. They said they now realised

the injustice done to the innocent children, and promised that
in future proper care and attention would be paid to them.
The promise was carried out with the result that the children
were soon properly nourished and properly clothed, and all
had a very different appearance to what they had when the
Inspector first called. The Inspector had the pleasure, more
than once, of being stopped in the street by the father, who said
to him that the home life had completely changed, and
everyone was happy.

It is not only parents with whom the Society has to do,
but also there are times when guardians have to be dealt with
— persons, that is, with whom children have been placed to be
cared for, for whom payment is made. There was one case
where a gentleman called at the Inspector's office and told him
of three children who were boarded out with a guardian near
at hand; the children were sent out every morning to deliver
newspapers, and then in the house the guardian made them do
household work, washing and cleaning, and after school was
over they had again to go out with newspapers. The father of
the children was a widower, and as he had no one at home to
look after them it was he who had placed them with this
guardian. When he was told of the state of matters he took
them away at once, though it seems curious that a father
should take so little interest in how his children were being
brought up as not to know at all of the condition of matters
until the Society's Inspector had drawn his attention to it. The
Inspector found that the mere fact of his intervention in this
case had a good effect upon others who were keeping children,
knowing that they too might get into trouble if they did not
fulfil their duty properly.

Apart altogether from the cases of cruelty and neglect
which it is the constant work of the Society to check, a great
deal of work is thrown upon the Inspectors, which gives
opportunity to them to be of assistance. Thus an Inspector
heard of a family in which the parents were highly respectable
but in very poor circumstances. He called at the house as a
friend and spoke to the mother, who said that her husband was
out of work, that he had no Unemployment Benefit, and that
the family were hard up. The man had done his best to find
work, but though he had failed he would not dream of going to
the Public Assistance department as he had never asked for
charity all his life, and he would not care to be in receipt of
public relief. The only income was that of a daughter who was
employed and brought in 10s a week. To provide food, many
articles of clothing and of furniture had been pawned. The
Inspector reasoned with the man, and then himself went to the

Public Assistance Officer, who at once granted relief, which the
man, however unwillingly, accepted for the sake of the
children. The Inspector further helped the man to get a grant
from the regimental association of the regiment in which he
had served during the War. Also the Inspector was able to help
the father to get work after some little time, and life then for
this family became a different thing altogether. The mother
said that they had gone through a terrible time during the
period of unemployment, and that they had tried to hide their
poverty even when things were at their worst.

What is impressive to the observer is the continued experience of
the extreme conditions which seem almost to be repetitive of the earliest
descriptions of cases, despite the reference to improving general
conditions and a better social environment. This indicates that the
nature of the Society and the image presented by the Inspector resulted
in it continuing to work at the lowest end of the social system amongst
those who continually found themselves in the direst circumstances.

The case quoted in the 1934 Report, however, shows that the
Society was often basically supportive and helpful, and by no means
always emphasising its authority.

The Inspectors have many different duties to perform and have
to give advice on many topics. There was one case where the
father had died at an early age and the mother died also within
a twelvemonth later. There were five children, the eldest a lad
of eighteen, and upon the second, a girl of fifteen, fell all the
care of the household. The house was well furnished and of
good size, but this girl did not know how to manage, and
although she had money given to her every week both by the
eldest boy and the Public Assistance Department she did not
know what to do. So she came to the Inspector crying bitterly,
and told him that she was in great distress because she did not
know what to do or how to keep control of the youngest boys.
The Inspector got in touch with an aunt who promised to take
charge of the house till something else could be arranged; the
Inspector made enquiries amongst relatives, and the three
youngest boys were taken by them and for the girl he found a
situation as a domestic servant. Both this girl and the relatives
later on expressed their gratitude to the Society for what had
been done.

There was another case where the father was out of work
and in receipt of Public Assistance allowance, but through
pure ignorance of how to spend the money the mother never
had enough to do what was required. At the Inspector's
request a grocery book was produced, and on examination it
was found that she had been buying expensive food and not

proper food at all, so the Inspector told the woman that she
was wasting money in the way she spent it, and he wrote out a
list of things which she should purchase which would be
beneficial for the children's health. The woman was wise
enough to be guided by the Inspector, and somewhat to her
surprise she found that her grocery bill was at once reduced by
over 7s a week. She was quite proud of how she had
accomplished this, and the Inspector found she was trying to
cut it down even more. The money saved from the useless
things she was purchasing was then used to buy clothing and
footwear.

A different way to use the information and expertise developed by
the Inspectors was to use it as a basis for articles to educate young
supporters through the League of Pity and its journal *City Sparrows* as
this description of the Tinker Community published a year later
indicates.

THE TINKER COMMUNITY

All over Europe there have been bands of people called by
various names in the countries through which they passed,
people who never cared to settle, but having the wandering
instinct strongly implanted have gone here and there pretty
much as the spirit moved them. These people called 'Gypsies',
when they came to our shores have been, on the whole, quiet
and peaceable, with a form of religion of their own. Yet they
were not liked nor welcomed in most of the countries in which
they were found and many edicts were enacted to cast them
forth.

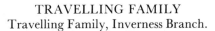

TRAVELLING FAMILY
Travelling Family, Inverness Branch.

Some of these wandering people reached Scotland as early as the sixteenth century, but being law-abiding they were not only not expelled but were even encouraged to remain. The name by which they were known in Scotland, Gypsy, is a variant of the form in use in different parts of Europe, 'Gypsy' being a corruption of 'Egyptian', due to the belief that they had originally come from Egypt, a belief that has much to support it.

The same wandering spirit which had driven them over many parts of Europe still remained with them and prevented any desire to settle down for long in any district. They had in their own community different ranks, and the Chief to whom all looked for such rule as they were prepared to accept was known as Faw or Faa. The Chief usually lived in the south east of Scotland and there too was found the Queen of the Gypsies, one to whom all honour was given, but beyond a certain barren honour the Queen obtained little else.

In places the Gypsies had a certain evil repute, because it was believed they practised black magic, a belief which probably arose from the fact that certain Gypsy women professed to foretell anyone's fortune; and many a country lad and country lass were willing to have their fortune told, and if they were credulous enough to believe what they learned then often they, perhaps unconsciously, helped to fulfil the 'fortune' which had been given. The Gypsy wife, be it noted, required to have her palm crossed with silver before she read the fortune of the consultant and with many of the shrewder ones this was a lucrative trade.

Of the Gypsies wandering about the countryside, the better ones had some trade or occupation. Thus many of them learned a certain amount of the work of a tinsmith; they took with them pots, pans, kettles and similar articles, and in the days when there was little going to and fro many a housewife in out-of-the-way places was glad to have them come when she needed a new kettle, for it supplied a present need and it might have been days before she could travel to the nearest town. So, too, repair work of a kind was entrusted to these travelling tinsmiths. Thus arose the name 'Tinker', the man who dealt in tinware.

Others were more interested in china, and their stock-in-trade consisted of small household ware which could be easily carried, and china cups or mugs forming a principal part of what they carried, these traders were known as 'Muggers'. Many of the more skilful were good at mending broken china ware, by cement usually, but some could even rivet broken china.

The aristocrats among these wandering classes were the men who knew something about horses; they bought and sold horses and were thus most useful to many a farmer or to a small dealer who could get a cart but required a horse to draw it. Others of the better class, the quieter and less excitable portion, engaged in basket work. They made wicker baskets, wicker chairs, wicker cradles; the slack season for trade was usefully employed in constructive work and when the fine days came they travelled all about selling their goods and often were employed in repairing some family chair that was showing evidence of hard usage.

The great bulk of this fraternity, however, were too easy-going to tackle any serious job; they found it more to their liking to wander about; their abode, a tent more or less primitive; their occupation, such odd jobs as they could obtain at farms; their wants were few and they did not ask for much. At many an out-of-the-way place they were, if not just welcome, at least received for a time for they could retail all the gossip of the districts through which they had passed and so served as a convenient source of information of a personal nature, perhaps with a little touch of malice in it which made it not unpalatable, and when newspapers with their Personal Column were not to be had the personal titbits were much enjoyed. They were never grudged a bite of food, and many a garment, particularly clothes for the children, was handed out.

Probably the greatest number of these travelling people were of the tinsmith group, for the name 'Tinker' became very general and so caused the name 'Gypsy' to disappear. To-day the name 'Tinker' is also disappearing, but for a different reason; the steadier ones who applied themselves regularly to some occupation rose in the world and they, or many of them, objected to being called Tinkers, this having a derogatory sound; while the less steady, those who did not 'stick-in' tended to become more vagrants. The disappearance of the Tinker is partly due to the character of the times; travelling is so easy now that the housewife even in a remote glen is not dependent on the itinerant trader, and what is worse for the travelling Tinker is that the great factories have taken away much of the work and many of the opportunities for the few trades he professed. Even the horse-dealer finds little he can do; with motor vehicles to be had so easily and so cheaply, horses are hardly in demand at all.

Deprived of the trades which they followed, the better disposed of the Tinkers wish to settle down, but to do so they must have some house to live in, no matter how humble, and some work to do to get food. These wants, simple as they are, are not easily gratified, houses are scarce and work not plentiful, and house-owners who have a choice of tenant naturally prefer a man with a regular occupation who can pay the rent, and employers have little difficulty in obtaining other labourers.

The less well disposed of the Tinkers, those who have wandered from place to place because they felt they could not settle and have been content to depend on the charitable public, tend more and more to lose any feeling of respect they may have had as members of a distinct community and so are becoming merely vagrants. At one time there were several recognised camping grounds where they might erect their small tents and stay for days at a time, in some places even for as long as three weeks; these camping grounds are now closed and so the Tinker is kept on the move.

For education, the standard is very low; many tinkers, men and women, can neither read nor write, and although the children attend school it is only in the winter months and as the attendances may be given at several different schools, just as the parents wander about and where they may be for a time, the educational attainment is not high.

The Royal Scottish Society for Prevention of Cruelty to Children has its own part to play in regard to these nomads and year by year it has kept in touch with them, not least in connection with the schooling of the bairns. Not much is required in this way, perhaps too little, because by Statute parents who are engaged in a trade or business which requires them to travel from place to place do all that is asked of them if they see that their children give 200 attendances at school from 1st October till 31st March — just half a school session. Even with this meagre requirement, it was at first difficult to get the gangrel parents to send the children to school at all; they, the parents, had never been at school, why then trouble about their offspring? But by keeping at the subject the parents did begin to yield, and in the course of years the Society has had the pleasure of seeing the attendances increase, and there is hope that some day the children will all give a full session's attendance . . .

It is a sad commentary upon a society which purports to be one of social progress that the challenges of depression and unemployment are really only overcome in the records of the Society through the fact that the country was once again, after twenty-one years, called to mobilise itself for war. As it had done before (as described in the previous chapter) the Society responded, as did other national social institutions to the challenge of six years of war in which, this time, the civilian and even child population were much more directly involved.

The different nature of both the attitude to this new war, the response to it and the possible effects of it are probably indicated in the Report of 1947 which could be contrasted with that of 1918 with which the last chapter closed and which contained that strong optimism regarding a new social order but which the recession and unemployment had prevented from developing.

The remarkable fact which arises from a survey of the year's work by our Inspectors is that with the advent of peace has come a disruption of home life. The effects of the war years seem to have disturbed the home and social life of large numbers of people and this unsettlement has produced many factors leading to neglect and ill-treatment of children. The policy of the Society has continued to be directed towards the prevention and alleviation of suffering by young people at the hands of their parents or guardians and towards their rescue from harrowing conditions. In this work the Inspectors, by advice, warnings, and supervision have achieved in the great majority of cases a general improvement of home conditions. Not in every instance have these methods met with success and the Society has been forced to bring several extreme cases to the Courts involving publicity which has focussed public attention on the few cases in which the good offices of the Inspectors have met with no response.

The conditions that come under our notice of overcrowding, filth, and a degradation of living which is indescribable exist in too many homes and demand unrelenting efforts. The limitations imposed by such environment on the children and on the home may have such disastrous implications that where the response of the parents has not been forthcoming it has been necessary to seek Court authority to remove the children in order that they may be brought up under conditions more likely to lead to their future well-being. The Society has been slow to use these powers and has had recourse to them only where no other way of protecting the children has been available.

A great many families have taken to squatting in former Army Camps. Unsatisfactory conditions have prevailed in many of these and still do so in some, but Local Authorities in many instances have assumed responsibility and have made them habitable and free from many of the dangers which existed. Supervision by the Society's Inspectors has had to be maintained in not a few of these camps where conditions have been far from satisfactory.

Amongst the varied complaints investigated by Inspectors many have related to children and young people outwith the control of their parents. In dealing with these the Society claims to have prevented the development of juvenile delinquency and to have helped to lay the foundations for good citizenship.

A large number of cases have arisen because parents have failed to provide towards the maintenance of their children. Many parents do not seem to realise that this constitutes a crime and carries a penalty which may include imprisonment. Cases of this kind have invariably many complications and Local Authorities do not hesitate to seek the help of the Society in securing a remedy. It is not unusual to find a deserting father living in co-habitation with another woman or claiming that his responsibilities for the maintenance of his children are met by the Family Allowances provided by National Insurance.

The ready and helpful co-operation of Local Authorities, the Police, School Teachers, and various social agencies has again proved of very great value. It was particularly gratifying to find that the suggestions submitted by the Society to the Clyde Committee on Homeless Children were very completely incorporated in the Report presented by that Committee to the Secretary of State for Scotland and forming the basis of the proposed Children's Act, 1948.

The continued lack of accommodation for the treatment of mentally defective children and the numbers who have to remain in surroundings conducive neither to their own well-being nor that of other children remains far from satisfactory. The difficulties of staffing and housing are not overlooked and it is noted that the authorities are gradually overcoming the obstacles which have prevented a more immediate treatment of a problem which has existed for a considerable time.

The misuse of clothing coupons has been the subject of reports which show only too clearly that some parents have not hesitated to sell clothing books and reduce their children to wearing ragged and inadequate garments.

This report is noticeable because it contains one of the first references to the children themselves becoming a root concern and records the consequent extension of the interest of the Society into that of prevention of juvenile delinquency.

There is also reference to the very influential evidence provided to the Clyde Committee which provided the basis report for the Children's Act of 1948 with its wide-reaching effect upon local authority work with children.

The beginning of the consequent new era for the Society in finding a *modus vivendi* for continued existence and contribution to child welfare is indicated in the Report of the following year 1948 which shows the traditional work to be continuing but in a new context of increasing involvement with the work of statutory authorities.

The criminal irresponsibility of some parents is well illustrated in the following case. The father of seven children was not only indifferent to their well-being but being short of money because of absenteeism from work took the Family Allowance from his wife to enable him to visit and entertain another woman. The Inspector found the children, whose ages were 10, 7, 5, 4, 3, 2, and 4 months, lying on damp-rotted mattresses shared with a dog and a cat, with dirty bits of blankets and old coats for coverings. The mother had lost interest in her home and the children, who were filthy. Everything was done to encourage the mother. Garments were provided from the League for the children. The father was warned of possible prosecution. In spite of everything the Inspector could do to improve matters the children continued to remain uncared for and the dirt and hopelessness became such as to render further action advisable. The father was sent to prison for 4 months; the mother for 6 weeks; and the children were committed to the Local Authority to find suitable and satisfactory foster parents. Until this should be done the Society had the children cared for in a children's home.

A case which received considerable publicity was that in which an alien was charged with the wilful ill-treatment of a young Polish girl. The Society was instrumental in removing the girl to a place of safety and with the help of the League has been able to secure for the girl a chance of following her chosen career.

The practice of allowing children to return from Approved Schools to unsatisfactory homes from which they had previously been removed was taken up with the Scottish Education Department and the use of the Society to provide prior reports has been approved.

The possible effect on the work of the Society of new social Legislation was the subject of a report by the Legislation Sub-Committee. This showed that while provision has been made for greatly increased Social Services in the field of child-care the contribution by the Society is essential and indeed is material to those services. In evidence of this it was disclosed that the parents in almost 40 per cent of cases dealt with by the Society derive their income from some form of State grant and a great deal of the Society's work in making recalcitrant parents provide for the maintenance of their children has been passed directly or indirectly to the Society from the department providing state assistance to those in need.

A deserting father asserted that his wife and working members of the family were fully able to maintain the younger children without his having to do so and successfully maintained this attitude before the Court. The serious consequences of a decision freeing the father from responsibility caused the Society to seek a fresh trial. The charge was accepted and a conviction was recorded against the man.

The Society has continued to seek to improve by all means in its power conditions conducive to child-neglect or child suffering rather than to report for immediate prosecution those instances which have resulted from maladjustments in family life and difficulties of housing and accommodation.

Emerging then during these early post-war years was the development of that statutory provision which has come to be known as the welfare state and with which the Society, like all voluntary organisations concerned with social welfare had to come to terms.

This historical profile of the Society has now reached the point where the memory of those members significantly involved can also be utilised and from this point on, the profile will rely increasingly on the experiences and recollections of those who can describe the development of the Society at first hand.

7

VIEWS OF THE SOCIETY'S WORK

This chapter is dedicated to the work of the Inspectors of the Society who occupy such a significant position in the organisation, and also to the Women Visitors who joined them in a complementary role in the most recent quarter of the Society's history. Memories recalled by some of the long-serving officers and by others who have reason to remember their work are the basis for this part of the profile record.

    On the day when the emergency meeting of the R.S.S.P.C.C. staff committee met on August 1914 to consider the outbreak of war, and the effects of the crisis, a slim tall youth of eighteen was still learning to become a butcher in his home town in Lanarkshire. Six months later,

Mr WILLIAM FINLAYSON
Appointed to the R.S.S.P.C.C. in 1917, he retired in 1965.
Today he lives in Kirkcaldy.

having joined the Territorials, he was in the Scottish Rifles and on his way to the trenches in France. As a veteran of six months in the front line, where he had celebrated his nineteenth birthday, he 'went over the top' for the third time and received severe wounds which invalided him back home to Scotland and eventually out of the army with a pension. A half incapacitated arm meant that he could not return to his trade and so, learning that the local district secretary of the R.S.S.P.C.C. had received an appeal for reliable men to be recruited as Inspectors, he applied, and found himself interviewed in the Glasgow office by Mr Paterson, General Secretary at that time.

So, in 1917, William Finlayson was appointed Probationary Inspector and retired 48 years later in 1965 as District Inspector in Kirkcaldy and in December 1983, at the age of 88, agreed to be interviewed about his work in the Society.

When he started in Glasgow Inspectors worked in pairs and he was partnered with an experienced man who supervised his work. His face still registers concern when he describes the 'terrible conditions' of the South side of Glasgow and the dock area in which he began work. Children were 'ragged, dirty and verminous' and housing conditions were 'indescribably bad'. Many of the houses were 'dens of iniquity' and many of the mothers with whom he dealt were prostitutes. As a young Inspector he soon learned that to protect children was a task requiring whole time 'round-the-clock' effort and wide understanding in order to try to change a whole way of life.

Those early years were spent in different offices because the young single Inspectors were expected to be more mobile. In 1923, shortly after moving from the West to the Leith office, he applied to become the District Inspector in Kirkcaldy. There he spent the rest of his service, married, and raised two sons, one who is now a Kirkcaldy headmaster and the other a research scientist in Australia. His wage as Inspector when he married was 27/6 a week but careful budgeting meant he could maintain his family at a modestly comfortable standard.

At this stage when Inspector Finlayson referred to the standard of living in the early 1920s it is appropriate to return to the records of the Society and to examine this point in more detail. It is not always appreciated that voluntary organisations often have to solve quite intricate staff management questions and there is interesting evidence that the Society was usually quick to face up to such questions as shown in the Staff Committee records for the 17th May 1920.

> The Meeting took into consideration the War Bonus for Women Inspectors, fresh consideration on the subject having been invited at the instance of the Edinburgh District Committee on the point whether the Bonus paid to Women Inspectors should be at a different rate from that paid to Men Inspectors. After careful consideration the Meeting decided to

recommend that, as the conditions of service and the nature of the work undertaken by Men and Women Inspectors were different, the differentiation in the rate of Bonus paid was justified and should be recognised.

The Meeting next took into consideration the question of Office Rent Allowances paid to Inspectors, a matter which had been referred to this Meeting by the Staff Committee. The principle upon which an allowance had originally been granted was that where in country districts there was no Office provided for the Society and accommodation was given by the Inspector in his own house for Office purposes, an allowance of £5 per annum was made. In course of time increases in this amount had been granted in various cases, and in consequence there was not at present any general uniformity. The Staff Committee therefore proposed that in all cases where the Society had accommodation in an Inspector's house for Office purposes a payment of £5 per annum should be made where the Inspector's Rent and Taxes did not exceed £15; £7. 10 where the amount did not exceed £20; and £10 where the amount exceeded £20. After consideration of this proposal an alternative scale was suggested by which payments should be made on the following lines: £5 where the amount of Rent and Taxes do not exceed £15 per annum; £6 where the amount does not exceed £18; £7 where the amount does not exceed £21; £8 where the amount does not exceed £24; £9 where the amount does not exceed £27; and £10 where the amount exceeds £27 per annum. It was decided to send this alternative scale to the Staff Committee and ask them to take it into consideration.

The Meeting next took into consideration the question of Inspectors' pay which had been considered informally on several occasions and recently had been brought up definitely in the Staff Committee. The Chairman drew attention to the fact that workmen's wages had again shown an upward tendency on account of increase in the cost of living, and that the desire of the Society had always been to put the Inspectors in a comfortable position and above the line of want. He proposed therefore that the Society should grant a further increase in the pay of the Inspectors. This view commended itself to the Meeting, and it was unanimously agreed to recommend an increase. After further consideration it was agreed to recommend that an additional sum of 10/- per week in their pay be granted to all Men Inspectors, and of 7/6 per week to all Women Inspectors, the increase to run from the date of the beginning of the current pay week, namely Wednesday 12th May.

The General Secretary was instructed, if the proposal was adopted by the Executive Committee, to send a letter to the Inspectors intimating this increase and at the same time pointing out the great cost entailed and the difficulty which the Society would have in meeting this.

In this connection the General Secretary intimated that he had been informed that the Inspectors desired to meet a Representation from the Executive Committee by a Deputation of their own number to explain the difficulties of their position. As it was probable that the decision now come to if ratified by the Executive Committee would obviate the necessity of any Deputation the General Secretary was instructed if he found, after the communication was sent to the Inspectors, that they still desired the Deputation to be received to arrange for this.

It was reported that the Staff Committee had purchased a piece of cloth at the cost of £18 to be kept and used from time to time for Inspectors' overcoats. This had been done to retain the cloth as it was likely to become scarce and also that the price would rise. The purchase was approved.

The minute of the Executive Committee for the 24th June 1920 describes the next stage in the development.

MEETING WITH INSPECTORS

Thereafter the Inspectors who were in attendance as a Deputation representing their colleagues, were invited to meet with the Executive in the Board Room. There were present Inspector Shedden, Ayr; Inspector McKenzie, Perth; Inspector Adams, Leith; and Inspector MacPhail, Dumbarton. On the invitation of the Chairman Inspector Shedden spoke first and stated that he had been requested to direct the attention of the Executive Committee to the difficulty which the Inspectors of the Society experienced in making ends meet in these times of high prices, and particularly those Inspectors who had families dependent on them. He recognised the difficulty which the Executive had in getting the funds which were necessary and he thanked the Executive for the increases which had been granted from time to time in the pay and particularly the recent increase of 10/- per week. As the burden of the high cost at the present time pressed hard on Inspectors with children he asked if the present War Bonus to children under 14 of 1/6 per week could be increased. Inspector Shedden stated that he had now no children dependent upon him. He also drew attention to the

Officers' Superannuation Scheme and mentioned that while at one time the retiring allowance of 10/- per week might have been a reasonable allowance this did not mean anything like the same benefit in these times, and he asked if the Executive could arrange to increase the allowance under this head. He further stated that the Inspectors would welcome the revival of a former custom of their being invited to attend the Annual Meeting of the Society and of having a conference thereafter with the Executive upon the work of the Society.

Inspector MacPhail followed and pointed out that he had a family of six children dependent upon him and he found great difficulty in obtaining all that he required on the present scale of pay even with his Army Pension. He thought that District Committees would willingly back up the Executive and provide the funds if any further payments were made to the Inspectors.

Inspector Adams spoke as one having two children and having no pension or other source of income except his salary from the Society with which he found it very difficult to live.

Inspector MacKenzie who spoke last thanked the Executive for giving the Inspectors an opportunity of stating their views as he was sure that it would satisfy the general body of their number in having an opportunity of directly representing their difficulties to the Central Committee. He suggested that in view of the increase in Rent and Taxes which would come about very soon by legislative enactment the Executive might consider if an increase could be made in the amounts presently payable for Office Rent Allowance.

Several questions were put by Members of the Executive to the Inspectors and answers received.

The Chairman expressed the pleasure which the Executive had in meeting with the Deputation and said they were fully aware from reports received from time to time of the good work which was being done throughout the country by the Society's Staff of Inspectors. He assured the Deputation and those whom they represented that the Executive were fully aware of the effect of the great increase in the cost of living which pressed upon themselves as much as upon the Inspectors. He pointed out that the Society was a voluntary institution dependent upon the public for funds and that in the shortage in the ordinary revenue, which he was afraid would be experienced this year the Society was in no different position from any other charitable organisation. He instanced in particular the Infirmaries in the large cities all of which were very far behind in their income. He promised that the matters brought up by the Deputation would be carefully considered.

The minute of the Joint Meeting of the Finance and Staff Committee on Monday 13th September 1920 provides the sequel.

> The Chairman stated that the Meeting had been called to consider the remit from last Meeting of the Executive committee in regard to the four matters brought up by the Inspectors on their recent Deputation. The four points were (1) Increase of the present War Bonus of 1/6 per week for each child under 14; (2) Increase in the amount of the Inspectors' Superannuation Scheme; (3) The revival of a former custom of having a Meeting annually between the Executive and the Inspectors; and (4) Increase in the amount of Office Rent Allowances.
>
> The Meeeting took up these points seriatim when the following decisions were arrived at.
>
> 1. War Bonus for Children. On this head attention was drawn to the recent increase of 10/- per week in the Inspectors' pay and also to the financial position of the Society and it was resolved to recommend that the War Bonus for children be not increased. With reference to a remark which fell from one of the Inspectors on the Deputation that 1/6 per week would not keep a child, the Meeting desired to point out that this sum was not meant for a child's support, but only as an addition to the income of an Inspector burdened with the maintenance of children. Further they desired that it should be recognised that any further increase in the Inspectors' pay might lead to a reduction of the number of Inspectors.
>
> 2. Inspectors' Superannuation Fund. On this subject it was recognised that something more might be done for the Inspectors as while the amount payable to an Inspector on attaining the age of 65 — namely 10/- a week up till the age of 70 when the amount is reducible to 5/- a week, when fixed at the time of the institution of the Fund in 1911 was a fair allowance, the amount would not now represent at all the same value. The Society's proportion of the premium payable to the North British and Mercantile Insurance Company at the present time amounted to £93 per annum with the Inspectors' contributing a similar amount. The Meeting agreed to recommend that if terms could be adjusted it was desirable to double the amount of the pension, and if this were approved that inquiry should be made of the Insurance Company for the terms on which such new arrangement could be carried out.
>
> 3. Annual Meeting with Inspectors. The Meeting after consideration were of the opinion that no good purpose was to be served by any such gathering, and they resolved to

recommend that the proposal be not approved. Such an
Annual Meeting would prove costly in the way of railway fares
and maintenance, and would take the Inspectors away from
their duty, in some cases for three days. It was further resolved
to point out that if the Inspectors at any time had any
representation to make upon any subject which they desired to
bring before the Executive Committee they were always at
liberty to do so and to bring the matter in writing before the
Executive with their observations when same would be fully
considered, and if it then seemed desirable to do so, a
deputation could be asked to appear before the Executive.

    4. Office Rent Allowance. This matter had been under
consideration for some time past, prior to the date of the
Inspector's Deputation, with the view of recommending an
increase in the sum payable, but difficulty had been
experienced in arriving at a sound principle upon which the
allowance should be based in order that the scheme might act
fairly between the Inspectors concerned without injustice or
inequality. . . . It was decided to recommend that when the
matters were all definitely settled the Executive's decision
should be communicated to each Inspector individually and
not to any one of their number as representing the whole.

The record must speak for itself but here in the management of staff
sixty years ago is the same humanitarian concern mixed with severe
moral principles as were applied to cases of the Society, as has been
previously described. This profile tries to indicate the extent to which a
voluntary organisation responds to and expresses the spirit of the time
and there is little doubt that those responsible for the Society, whilst
admiring and appreciating the work of the Inspectors, expected them to
maintain their position as servants of the organisation and its objectives
which were the highest priority. It demonstrates the consistency
between the internal ethos of the organisation and its external
manifestation. The Inspectors epitomised in their relation to their
clients the values and attitudes by which they were dealt within the
organisation.

Of course, staff management was not always so serious, but a
question of good husbanding of resources, because those minutes in 1920
refer to the length of cloth purchased for overcoats at a cost of £18. The
minutes of the following year refer to the fact that the cloth had already
been used up and there was a need to replenish it. Overcoats were
obviously important and a possible reason for the quick disappearance
of cloth could have been that the coats were subjected to unusual wear
and tear as instanced in the Staff Committee records of 15th January
1921 which also enable us to have some idea of the occupational hazards
of being an Inspector.

With reference to the two claims referred to in the last Report, one for the repair of the Arbroath Inspector's overcoat has been settled, the owner of the dog which did the damage having made a payment, but the other, the cost of the repair of the bicycle of the Stranraer Inspector, has not been met, the man at fault objecting to the amount charged.

The importance of uniform was also shown by the Staff Committee minutes of 21st February 1921 where reference is made to the fact that the uniform worn by the Women Inspectors was provided by the Inspectors themselves who received £5 per year as a uniform allowance. This was agreed to be insufficient and the Committee decided to increase the allowance fifty per cent. As there were five Women Inspectors employed at that time by the Society the total extra cost was £12.10 shillings.

This information from the records puts into context the description which Inspector Finlayson gave of his own domestic circumstances in these days. His boys went to the local school and then the high school. The ambition to enable your children to 'better themselves' was the goal upon which he believed child rearing should be based and which he found was invariably absent from the parents in the cases with which he worked. He is full of appreciation for the work of the voluntary youth organisations, like the Scouts and Boys' Brigade, who contributed so much to the development of his own sons, and for whom he spent a lot of his spare time working voluntarily because he was so convinced of their value.

His voluntary work could be viewed as a kind of reciprocal exchange for the great amount of help which he received from members of the local community throughout his service. These were the first people of whom he speaks when he reviews his service, people like Sir Robert Lockhart, a local linen manufacturer, who was his chairman for years, the Chief Constable who was willing to be secretary of the committee, and the nurses, teachers and policemen who served on the committees. The importance of a special relationship with the local press was emphasised when he spoke of Mr McBean, the editor of the Fife newspaper who was Treasurer of the local Society Branch committee for many years.

The committees met regularly and listened carefully to his reports of his work. They often gave advice about the difficult cases. They raised money through special events. They organised the regular collection of donations, often enrolling friends and acquaintances as the local collectors who each had a list of contributors to call upon monthly. Gradually they extended the network of support for the Society. Many church people helped as a form of service to the community.

Being the 'cruelty man' in a town where most people knew each other was not difficult. There was little criticism. It was a role well accepted and supported, even among the cases themselves. Many complaints came from wives, whose husbands were drinking their wages and failing to provide for the children. This was one of the biggest problems in the early years. He would visit the house and interview the man in the presence of the wife. He would listen to her complaint in front of the man and it was rare for the man to argue or dispute the facts in such a face-to-face situation. He accepted the view that his role was often that of a marriage counsellor.

In the days before Social Security it was essential to work closely with the parish officer who had control over the administration of poor relief. The Society Inspector often acted as investigating officer and a close co-operation developed. The recommendation of the Inspector regarding need was accepted. In special circumstances there were other local funds to which appeal for assistance could be made. Here again the trustee of the charity, usually a local solicitor, would accept the Inspector's word as justifying the need for help.

When he first worked in Kirkcaldy he needed to be a good walker. Transport within the town was often by tram and outside it by train or later by bus, but often when visiting farms or cottages in the rural areas the only access would be on foot.

His first car came in the 1950s through the generosity of a local supporter in Methil, who ran a day nursery and worked closely with the Society and, realising the need for transport, instructed him to go to a local garage and choose his car. The Jowett Javelin he still remembers with affection for the way it transformed his daily routine.

His closest co-operation and strongest support from authority came from the local police. They knew the local people and often received evidence of neglect and assault. From the Chief Constable, down, they were always willing to help. A police officer would often accompany him when investigating a complaint, particularly if the suspect had a reputation for physical assault. Sometimes the Assistant Chief Constable himself would accompany him when visiting. This example spread through the whole force, and he regularly called on the local police when visiting throughout his district.

Despite this close association with the force of law and the preponderance of assault complaints with which he early dealt he is convinced that the Society was always seen as a helping agency rather than a punishing one.

People knew that the Inspector had great authority and, no doubt, this came from the power of prosecution. They also knew, however, that this power was used only as a last resort although in the early days it was necessary to use it more frequently in order to establish the reputation and authority. In those days he would find himself in court probably three times every month.

The records of the years when Inspector Finlayson was starting his work show that this prosecution task was not undertaken lightly and was not without risk to the Inspector. The Executive Committee minutes of 25th July 1921 refer to the kind of problem which had to be prepared for when assuming authority of any kind.

> The General Secretary reported that he had received a letter from a firm of law agents in Alloa in regard to the action of Inspector Reid, Stirling, in removing two children from a mother and placing them in a Children's Home. The reason for the Inspector's acting was that the mother was unfit to have care of her children and the Inspector, before removing the children had received authority in writing from the father, a soldier at present in India. The intended procedure had been explained to the mother and had been approved by her. It was understood that a brother of the mother had now instructed the Solicitors in question to take proceedings. It was resolved that should any action be raised in court the General Secretary be authorised to take the necessary steps to defend.

The case Mr Finlayson chose to illustrate the need to prosecute was also a good example of the continuity of work of the Society and of its value as an independent organisation which could challenge the authorities. The case, he believes, is the worst in the records of the Society and one of the worst cases dealt with in the courts of Scotland. It went to the High Court in Dundee on Tuesday July 31st 1945 and lasted four days.

Foster parents, living in Dysart, were charged with severe assault of two boys in their care. The Society's case records occupy forty foolscap sides of handwriting and typescript plus accompanying letters and memoranda. The first record is on the 26th June 1943 when Inspector Finlayson investigated the allegation of neglect by the mother. It arose from the police who arrested the two boys for theft. A visit to the home showed that they were ragged and ill-fed. Inspector Finlayson visited again with the probation officer. They discovered the father was working away.

Inspector Finlayson decided to use the Society organisation and wrote to the Dundee Inspector asking him to visit the father at the place of work and inform him of the plight of his boys.

On the 28th June the two boys and the mother appeared at the Juvenile Court on the charge of theft and the boys were remanded to give time for the investigation to be completed.

On the 13th August the probation officer reported to Inspector Finlayson that one boy had been assaulted by a soldier visiting the house of the mother.

By this time the Dundee Inspector had reported the result of the visit to the father, who though concerned to help his sons, was not living in suitable conditions. So in August 1943 Inspector Finlayson, for the Society, petitioned the court that the children be taken into care. The petition succeeded and they were committed to the care of the County Council.

The next record is on December 20th 1944 when Inspector Finlayson received a report that the children had been ill-treated. Visiting the school which the boarded-out boys attended he found them in a shocking condition. He recalls vividly the horror of stripping the boys and seeing the extent of their injuries. They had been thrashed with an electric flex and the back of the younger boy had no inch of flesh which was not bruised or discoloured. Their faces and hands were swollen and they were weak with pain. He immediately removed them to the police station and had photographs taken of their condition. The photographs are still in the records of the Society and had been used at the Tulliallan Police College to demonstrate the extreme limits of physical abuse. The boys were then taken to the Children's Home in Leven for care. Whilst there they were examined again by doctors.

All of this evidence was produced in court when the case was heard. All the official witnesses, medical, police and school, agreed that the evidence of abuse was the worst seen in their experience. Newspaper accounts extended to several full columns on each of the four days of the case. The man and woman concerned were found guilty and sentenced to twelve months and nine months imprisonment respectively.

Within the records of the Society is evidence of the painstaking work behind such a case. Statements by all concerned, neighbours and local tradespeople, itemising examples of injuries noted, have been carefully collected, also the statement of the supervising official of the County Council welfare department which indicated that the authorities had had no reason for concern about the boys.

It is significant then that there is also a letter from Inspector Finlayson in March 1945 to the Head Office of the Society asking for advice and help regarding his concern about the delay in the case coming to court. He points out the strength of the evidence and questions if the delay is due to the possible sensitivity of the case in view of the national criticism of the standard of supervision of boarded-out children and retaliatory defensive statements by the authorities.

The importance of the successful prosecution was not so much in the punishment of the foster parents but in drawing further attention to the need for careful supervision of children in care.

Looking back over his service as a whole Inspector Finlayson unhesitatingly states that the greatest change was in the general conditions and health care of children. The isolated cases of severe neglect may still remain but the general standards have improved beyond measure. Improved diet and health inspection of children, by health visitors and in schools, account for the improvement, in his view. The work of the Society's Women Visitors similarly had an effect in the areas where the Society worked.

The crisis situations which still impress themselves upon his memory are the strikes of 1921 and 1926 with the brass bands playing to attract contributions for the unemployed workers and the soup kitchens which were necessary to provide relief.

Social security and the right to financial assistance changed the position of mothers of children who before then had to sink to levels of near destitution in order to qualify for help. The welfare state meant the needy could seek help with dignity.

Before that the Inspector used every device possible to gain help for families. Often the only way was to petition the courts for the care and protection of the children. Voluntary organisations which maintained children's homes and provided care, such as Quarriers' Homes and the Aberlour Orphanage, were relied upon by the Inspector for help when needed.

He would sum up the role of such organisations and that of the Society and also of staff like himself as simply being that of helping people, trying particularly to help children. Trying to provide that betterment of conditions for other children, which he had regarded as the motivation for himself as a parent, and which often the families seemed unable or unwilling to provide. That unwillingness, he agreed, was most likely the product of the conditions and experience in which the adults themselves had grown up. Only general improvement in those conditions would really remove the need for the help the Society could provide. He thought the Society would continue for as long as there was a need to express concern for the care of children. He was proud to have been involved in the work of the Society, and continued to identify himself with it in any way he could.

A further record of similar service by Chief Inspector J. Judge O.B.E. is provided in this personal report in response to questions connected with this history. His notes have been reproduced in the form provided as they illustrate the 'shorthand' used by Inspectors in their case notebooks.

> In the year 1938 when I became an R.S.S.P.C.C. Inspector, there was considerable unemployment, very bad housing conditions in large areas and allowances were low, averaging £2.12s per family with an extra 2/- (10p) for every additional child. The allowances came from the Assistance Board, Public Assistance Department and Ministry of Labour Exchange. Our main role was to deal with complaints of neglect, ill-treatment and many other wrongs. Only the Society and Police were dealing with these matters. The Education Authority had powers as Petitioners but did not require to do anything if some other party was interesting themselves. No Authority had any Treasury Grant to enable them to investigate child abuse. On receipt of any type of complaint, homes were visited and examined and children also examined.

We never accepted that a complaint was justified until we had inspected and investigated. We then maintained vigilance until the matter was cleared up and hardship alleviated.

Saturdays were always busy days; at that period our Glasgow office was kept open for callers from 9 a.m. until 10 p.m. Some Inspectors went off-duty after 1 p.m. when matters in their districts had been dealt with, others were on duty at the office continually until 10 p.m. Fathers called and paid in allowances for the children; these ranged from 4.6d (22½p) to £2. These were booked and enveloped. Mothers called within minutes or hours and collected the allowances. On a busy Saturday as many as 200 payments were dealt with. If mothers had not called by 10 p.m. the Inspectors visited as they knew there must be sickness or some good reason as the money was needed. The money was delivered. Many of these mothers had been battered. In other cases children who had previously collected from the father had been abused so we took over. Later this type of case was referred to a legal office or the National Assistance Department. Inspection, investigation, organising help; these were our main roles.

Changes really started (I think) between 1945 and 1948. Family alowances were paid and, although small, did give mothers something extra to work on. In 1948 Children's Departments were created and the Society with aid from Children's Officers was able to work much more efficiently. Free medical aid for everyone, modern drugs improved family health. Infant Life Mortality which was 170 per 1,000 in Dundee in 1906 dropped to a very low figure; other cities in Scotland were about 125 per 1.000 in 1906; they also improved. The *Children Act* 1948 took about ten years to really get going. A massive housing programme must have re-housed at least one third of our population. Diseases such as T.B. and Rickets have been wiped out. The present generation of children are bigger in stature, healthier than at any time during the past. Less overt physical neglect. Since 1970 we have had the Social Work (Scotland) Act 1969 in force and Social Workers co-operating with the Society and providing practical help for children and families when we recommended it. This has made it possible to quickly alleviate hardship and reduce the number of cases under our supervision. In April 1971 the Children's Panels came into being. The Reporter relieved the Society of a lot of Court work but we still had the investigative role to make sure Panels had all the facts. The Guardianship Act 1973 gave the mother of legitimate children equal rights in the custody and care of her children — In the past much suffering and perhaps many lives would have been saved if the father had not been the sole guardian when medical aid became critical. In my early days, some 46 years ago, we dealt mainly with poverty, neglect, ill-treatment, filth and disease and at times grossly immoral surroundings. Today we still deal, at times, with dirty conditions which endanger health, but help is readily available to alleviate the suffering. We also deal with so called battered babies and again highly skilled helpers are coming into the picture. A form of neglect that has always existed is perhaps even worse today than in the past; children left alone and unattended, often become terrified and endangered, simply because the guardians are too occupied with their own pleasures to give the children any of their time. I can describe some cases which illustrate different categories which may be of interest:

(1949) Child aged 2 years. Chest condition. Doctor called by mother. He got ambulance to move child for intensive care — father refused to allow child to leave home as he feared mother would leave him (they had quarrelled) and he used child as a lever to keep her. Doctor called at Police station and officer called Society. Father would still not agree. Removal Warrant granted to Society within minutes by local JP. Child to Hospital and made a good recovery. Petition presented at Court and then diet deserted when Solicitor took steps on mother's instruction for custody.

(1952) Child aged 8 months with young parents in house below street level. One room with little natural light. Both parents T.B.; father very advanced. Had refused hospital treatment (father bedridden). Health Visitor asked Society for help. We took immediate action. Advised parents that they must take proper treatment forthwith or we would have to remove child. Child moved to relative as foster parent and found to be quite clear. Parents to hospital. It was too late to help father who died within weeks, while mother lived for about a year. We had several similar dark, damp houses where children were not thriving and guardians refused proper treatment. By persuasion and with help of G.P. and Children's Officer guardians were moved for treatment and children to proper care.

(1952) Most cases of abandonment were dealt with by police, but at times Society were asked to help. Mid Winter about 4 a.m. Very old lady called police. Mother of two children had, some 36 hours previously left her baby with her to get messages, baby aged 6 months. Neighbours gave temporary help. Information given that the mother was going to a shipping office. Inspector arranged temporary care, 9 a.m. called at shipping office. Learned mother and child had passage to East. Contacted Passport Office (Glasgow). Mother had mentioned only one child. Ship's name supplied. Contacted N.S.P.C.C. London. They contacted Met/Police. Ship stopped while on Thames (Costs £500 per day for ship on Thames). Mother admitted deserting child as she could not take a child aged under 18 months to the country out East. Contacted Town Clerk. Arranged mother agree to all costs of rearing child in care and cost of flying child out to her when old enough and that this be entered in the ship's log by order of the Captain. This was agreed. At a later date the child with an escort from the British Red Cross Society was delivered to the mother in the tropics.

(1940) Time 8 p.m. 9 children aged from 6 months to 12 years alone in very bad home. All windows vandalised. Winter. No fire. Light cut off. No food. Five roomed Corporation house bare except one bed and chest. No other furniture. Father at 'Sea'. Mother having what was called 'a good time'. All telephones in area vandalised. I got message to police and Police Cycle Patrol brought candles. Eldest child ill. Phoned for doctor. He arrived before midnight and moved eldest child by ambulance as she was seriously ill. Local Authority promised to collect other eight children. Took no action. Neighbours brought food and coal and by 6 a.m. agreed to take over from Inspector if Police continued to visit. Inspector walked home, some miles. Wrote report. Lodged complaint with police. M.O.H. acted at once. Children removed without further examination. Mother also had to be taken to police and kept in custody as mob of neighours gathered and threatened serious injury. Society and Local Authority conferred over case and proper arrangement made in case of any future emergency.

Other cases which I remember:

1. The father of two children called and asked for some help. He was handing over his wages and got no pocket money. Home conditions bad. Gas cut off. Mother mentally sick. She simply obtained fish and chips and cooked food and handed over the wages to the shop. Woman Visitor took over. Mother taken to hospital. Gas reconnected and father assisted with family budgeting.

2. Since 1854 parents have been compelled to Register the birth of their children within 21 days. We were checking on unregistered child minding in an unsatisfactory home. Asked the mother for birth certificates relating to her own three children. She had only two. Gave a birth date for the third. Child was not on birth register. Mother then admitted that

child was born without medical aid and she feared to register.
Had managed for nearly two years without finance for child
and had no family allowance. Authorities decided that no
punitive measures be taken under the circumstances. Mother
got back dated payments of Family Allowance and called to
thank Society for clearing up the mess for her.

   3. Child aged 13 years repeatedly called on the Society to
remove her from home. She was bright at school, worked part
time and kept herself well turned out. One brother with
Borstal record, another with prison record, two sisters with
illegitimate children all made life difficult for her. School
teacher phoned to say child wanted immediate help or she
might run away. We collected child at School and took her to
Children's Officer where she made her own application to be
taken into care. Mother taken to Children's Department
where the child made it clear she would not live at home (after
a recent assault). When medically examined rather startled the
doctor when asked if there was any infectious disease at home
— her reply 'Yes — they are all daft.'

To continue with my comments on the general work of the Society
   Women Visitors were introduced by the Society in an
effort to clear up certain types of neglect and make it possible
for the children concerned in these cases to be reared within
their own homes, in reasonable conditions. Women Visitors
had small case-loads and taught childcare and homecraft, to
mothers and sometimes fathers; they gave considerable help
and supervision with demonstrations on basic cleaning,
cooking, sewing and budgeting. They did much valuable
work, kept many children happy at home and reduced the
financial burden on Local Authorities. They also gave the
Inspectors more time to deal with the numerous enquiries that
came to the offices.
   The Society is the only Scottish national agency whose
primary function is the welfare of children within their own
homes. It still deals with a wide variety of problems in order to
help children directly or indirectly. The Society has always
wished to be informed about any situation where there is
concern about the welfare of children and this concern will be
continuous and comprehensive until the problems are
alleviated. Investigations can continue regardless of a certain
lack of co-operation from parents and guardians.
   Concern for the young was the keynote on which our
Society came to life 100 years ago and this concern still
motivates our staff. I feel that they are needed as much today

as when I joined the Society in 1938. The neglect may be less
overt but the stress and the problems to be dealt with are
greater and perhaps more dangerous than at any time in
history.

I joined the Society as an Inspector some 46 years ago, in
1938. I served an apprenticeship with the Society in Glasgow
of about 5 years and then moved on to Edinburgh, Argyll and
the Isles, Wigtownshire, Stirling and Clackmannan and finally
to Dundee, as Chief Inspector in 1951. I retired in 1975. I
served under the famous Chief Inspector Heathwood. (He
joined the Society about 1900.) I also worked with Inspector
Alexander Reid who joined immediately after the Boer War.
He had the reputation of having rescued more children than
any other living Inspector of his time. I learned much from
him. There have been many changes for the better and I feel
that the Society deserves credit for assisting with the legislation
which has bettered conditions.

Those memories of Chief Inspector Judge which he wrote down in
response to written questions from the author, are vivid in the picture
they give of the work of the Society. When this history was contemplated
it was felt that the general public should be informed and have a chance
to respond similarly. A Society which has depended for so long on public
support should give that public support a chance to be demonstrated.
Therefore a letter was placed in most local newspapers in Scotland
asking for those with special examples of the Society's work to record, to
contact the author at the Society's headquarters. The response was
overwhelming and the following selection of information must be
regarded only as a token illustration of the interest aroused. Letters and
information have been utilised both to prompt study of particular parts
of the records of the Society for use elsewhere in this profile and also
directly in this section to give some indication of the way others feel
about the spread of the Society. In certain cases names are omitted but it
must be emphasised that the reputation which the Society claims that
people, even the clients themselves, are ready to identify themselves to
the Society, had been given tremendous vindication in this process.
People have not only volunteered their names and addresses but were
willing to be interviewed about painful and traumatic experiences of
their past lives. Only lack of time prevented a deeper investigation of this
wealth of information and the Society must be grateful to everyone who
responded to the invitation to participate in this record.

First, were those responses which were related to involvement in
the general routine work of the Society, the regular committed work and
the fund-raising. Typical of the way people were drawn into this work is
this letter from Mrs Cunningham of Dumfries, in her 77th year and 'still
very active in the Society'.

When I was a girl in my teens I was walking to the Office one morning, where I worked in the South Side of Glasgow. There was a great commotion at one of the entrances where a horse-drawn cart was standing and quite a few people around it. This was a family of children being removed to a place of safety and some of the crowd were quite hostile. There were a few Inspectors with the children. I had never heard of the R.S.S.P.C.C. until then and it really impressed me very much at the time. A few months after I was asked to sell tickets for the Pantomime run by Miss Bertha Waddell and her pupils in aid of the Cruelty to Children . . . I also helped at the Children's Parties which were held at the H.L.I. Halls in Glasgow as at that time most of the Inspectors were on service in the Forces. You can read from this I married one of the Inspectors. My husband was 46 years with the Society. He served in Glasgow, East End, from there to Paisley and from there to Dumfries until he retired 11 years ago. He is still on the committee but for the last year hasn't been able to attend as he would like owing to illness. We could write a book on some of our cases.

and then these extracts from a letter from Mrs Campbell of Cambuslang which describe the nature of this voluntary work:

> . . . The League of Pity began in Cambuslang about the end of the First World War, set up by Miss Catherine Todd — the aunt of one of our present members. In 1928, it was taken over by my aunt, and I have a card dated 18.1.28, as have several others.
>
> In 1943 the Cambuslang R.S.S.P.C.C. Committee was formed by Mrs Ross, with seven other Ladies, of whom three are still going!
>
> Our first event in 1943 was a Children's Party, from which we were thrilled to raise £25! (Nowadays it is in the region of £4000!)
>
> Flushed with that success we proceeded to have various other events — one of the best being a Children's Christmas Carnival, with the 'platform party' consisting entirely of children.
>
> The Carnival was opened by the then Marquis of Douglas and Clydesdale (now the Duke of Hamilton), aged 7, and I still have a newspaper photograph of him on that occasion.
>
> Another spectacular event was a Cambuslang Pageant, organised by Mrs Ross, who invited various schools, groups, etc., to act a scene from the history of our village.
>
> Every year we had a Big Event, as well as smaller offerings, and I recall another very successful one, of a

Gathering of Interesting Work — sewn, painted, tooled, etc, by local people, and also antique *objets d'art* lent by many friends. It became so large, and valuable, that we had to organise husbands to sleep in the halls for the two or three nights of showing!

All fund-raising was not of the more usual type as this extract from a very interesting letter from Mrs Steuart Corry of the Helensburgh Committee shows. After speaking of the work of Inspector Forrest who served in Dunbartonshire from 1931 to 1961 and 'who always inspired us to go on with our money-raising by his work' which illustrates the rather unique link, between the direct providers of family support and the indirect providers of funds, she describes a special activity which raised funds for the Society as follows.

In 1961 the Committee decided to write a cookery book aimed at helping young marrieds who loved cooking but who had not much time — so as we had members of our committee who were excellent cooks — we set to compile a book. It was paid for by advertisements (very hard work by members to achieve this) and we had the free help of a West of Scotland artist Angela Ker, to make us a delightful cover and suitable illustrations within. We launched our book *Clyde Cuisine* at a coffee morning in the autumn of 1962. Copies were sent all over the world — it did not take long to sell 2000 copies at 10.6d each.

Our Hon. Secretary, Mrs Hume and myself made a decision on the number of copies fearing they would not sell! 5 years later there was a request for yet another edition so out of this was born *Cordon Clyde 1966–67*. . . . This time we were brave and had 4000 printed — they all sold at 12.6d.

Once more in 1972 we were asked to do yet another book . . . *Encore Clyde* at £1 . . . launched at the opening of our Sale in George Street, Edinburgh. When Lord Wheatley RSSPCC Chairman presented me earlier that year to Princess Margaret, the President of the RSSPCC, I had no idea how I could ask her for a recipe but all came very easily, and after assuring me she was not a cook I asked her if there was any special recipe she enjoyed . . . Her Royal Highness seemed delighted and very kindly arranged for a recipe for avocado soup to be sent to us — so I will give you the recipe:

COLD AVOCADO SOUP FOR 6

3 or 4 avocado pears (depending on size)
1 pint consommé
$\frac{1}{2}$ teaspoon full each of pepper, salt and sugar

pinch of Garlic salt
Teaspoon of Worcestershire sauce
Dessert spoon full of horseradish
A little dry sherry

Method: Put all ingredients into a blender or sieve together. Chill for an hour or more, serve with spoon full of cream on top.

To be served with Cavitello Bianco — Val D'adigo — (Mr Maurice Kidd (Treasurer of the Scottish Children's League) kindly put suitable wines for all our recipes in this edition.)

Some of the letters were from people who simply wished to give information which might explain parts of the Society's history, as for instance, Mrs Mitchell of Dumfries, who referred to the contribution of her father James Farquarson J.P., who was Secretary of the Aberdeen Association of Social Service from 1921 to 1945. He served also as the secretary for the Aberdeen City and County Society for the Prevention of Cruelty to Children. He was associated with using the symbol of heather in Heather Days and was one of those within the Society who felt strongly that the autonomy of the Branch was to be preserved at all costs against the attempt to develop the strength of the national organisation. When the R.S.S.P.C.C. was formed in 1922 (on the granting of the Charter) he 'took umbrage at the money collected in Aberdeen being sent to Edinburgh'. Apparently on one occasion he 'travelled to Edinburgh to ask that money collected in Aberdeen remain there, only to find when he arrived there that everyone was out playing golf!' There is still some family suspicion about 'haid yins up in Edinburgh'. Evidently Mr Farquarson with Inspector Cockburn and later Inspector John Mennie collected heather in the Society's Austin A7 van and then arranged for sprays to be given to donors on Heather Days.

Whether or not this was the actual origin of the practice it indicates both the strength of feeling and the degree of commitment behind the volunteer work of the Society.

There were many contributions from people who simply wished to record the contribution of other people to the development of the Society as for instance Sheila Gordon of Angus who wrote:

During the 40's and 50's the Misses Forsyth-Grant who resided at Burnside House, Angus every year produced a Nativity Play at Christmas and an Easter Play at Easter with the girls of the village taking part. The proceeds always were sent to the Society and each girl always received a letter of thanks from the Society.

The need to maintain limitations upon voluntary involvement and the fact that things are not always easy are expressed in a comment from a correspondent in Helensburgh who wrote:

> My connection with the R.S.S.P.C.C. began in 1930, when I was persuaded to become Branch Secretary in Clydebank and Dalmuir. Conditions in the area were quite appalling, and there was no welfare state or National Health Service to cushion the effects of mass unemployment and impossible housing conditions. I was asked to accompany the Inspector on some of his visits, and, as an eighteen year old, born and brought up in a Yorkshire country village, found myself quite overwhelmed by the sights and smells I encountered. In retrospect, I am certain that my presence, or lack of understanding did much more harm than good. From time to time there have been suggestions that committee members should accompany the Inspector or Health Visitors on their rounds, and this I have resolutely opposed, because I am convinced that it is no task for amateurs.
>
> Since the help that the Society tried to bring produced, at that time, more resentment than gratitude, a mass meeting was arranged, to be addressed by Mr Cumming Forsyth, the then General Secretary, to try to explain that the Society existed not to *expose* cruelty and neglect, but to try to alleviate the impossible conditions and that the *Prevention* of Cruelty to children meant exactly what it said. To my despair or dismay, not one single member of the Community turned up in the Clydebank Town Hall that afternoon.

Others, apart from the officials of the Society themselves, recall with appreciation the work of the Inspectors. It was obviously not unusual to have long service because Miss St. G. Bell recalls the service of her own father Mr J. Bell who served as Inspector from 1907 until 1942. She also referred to the work of Inspector Reid of Stirling who was a pioneer of Boys' Clubs and gave considerable time to taking young boys to camp. She also remembered the work of Inspector MacKenzie of Perth with the tinker fraternity to which reference is made elsewhere in this book.

Then a letter which indicates the trust the general public had in the Society:

> I was a bus Conductress in Traction House, Motherwell for 12 years. While travelling on my last journey from Uddingston to Motherwell, I very often saw a wee girl walking on the pavement just before midnight. I stopped the bus and asked her what she was doing and she told me she was looking for cigarette ends for her father, whom I found out was the

man her mother lived with in a caravan site . . . I also noted
she had bruises on her face and arms. I asked her what had
happened, had she fallen downstairs etc.? The wee girl told me
her step father hit her, so right away I contacted the Police. I
gave my name and address. The Police contacted the welfare
and R.S.S.P.C.C. I was told by a policeman that the
organisation would do everything they could . . . The one thing
I abhor is people who are cruel to kids or anyone else for that
matter and I wouldn't hesitate to report cruelty.

The same lack of hesitation in volunteering information in this
history was true of those who had been cases themselves, as, for instance,
in this account which shows the willingness of an Inspector to bend the
rules in order to help towards a long term goal.

My husband was an alcoholic and we had four children, my
youngest being 26 years old now. When they were young we
had a terrible life with my husband and I had to contact
R.S.S.P.C.C. on many occasions. As my home was clean, and
by hook and by crook I made sure they never exactly starved,
there wasn't very much they could do but try to advise my
husband, but to no avail.

Anyway one Inspector in particular gave me a bit of
advice on the side. He told me not to pay the rent but keep
putting the money away. Pay no attention to letters or eviction
notices so long as I had the money to pay arrears. I did that
and on the day we were to be evicted, acting on the advice I
got, I told my husband I had the money to pay as long as he
signed the house over to me. It was the happiest day of my life
when I saw my name on the rent book. After a year I threw
him out and never looked back.

I got a job, brought them up with no fear of a drunken,
abusive father coming in and although it was a struggle, they
have all done well. I often think of that Inspector, I don't
know his name, but he was so full of sympathy and
understanding at that time. His advice made my life and the
life of my children a lot happier.

And then this revealing letter into the effect of family separation
which could be used as a case study for all students of social welfare and
also a salutary reminder to professionals of the effects of their actions.

I shall put details brief. I myself was in care, about the time
1962–64 my family split up. I was in a home with my brother
and sister. Then fostered out at different times. The strange
thing as I have got older, which I am 29 years, I looked back
and it caused a lot of my emotions to get very mixed up and
caused me to run into sexual emotion at an early age hoping I

could find the love which I realise now. I have been married twice. I also put my own daughter into care. All our family were only split for one year and we were brought back as a family when my mother returned. I believe any child coming through any break up has a lot to do with the way they grow up. If something is taken away from you at a small age you sometimes rebel yourself.

I am sorry my letter has not being phrased right but this is another thing that happens. As being split your mind is not at school but trying to understand why you have something one minute and the next you are in a home. Yet I have done the same with my daughter. She is now 11 years. I would even let you have a word with her on how she felt.

The research for this profile did not provide the opportunity to give the support which would have been necessary to investigate the feelings of the daughter concerned. But nevertheless it is important to recognise that the mother herself realises that the daughter would have a contribution to make and that her feelings and interests need to be considered regarding her future.

The pressure upon families in situations like those investigated by the Society is made apparent in another letter which also indicates that the intervention of the Society was not always welcome and appreciated.

You had an article in our paper regarding to any one who had any contact with the R.S.S.P.C.C. in the sixties. Well I admit I was one of the many, and I am not proud to admit this, as I found the experience very embarrassing and really did bring me down to nothing. I have three sons . . . When they were small I suffered a lot of depression being on my own. I got to the stage I had to get out. And that is exactly what I did. I had young kids who were only too glad to let me get out. However, one night I arrived home to meet the police and R.S.S.P.C.C. in my home. Naturally my first impression was that they were there to remove my kids into care. I actually went out of my head and hit out at the R.S.S.P.C.C. and was on the threat of being lifted by the Police. However, things cooled down and I was able to find out that someone had phoned in to tell them my babysitter was under age. A few days later I had the welfare officer up and there it all began, being pestered and watched. I could not get any peace so I made up that I could not cope with the kids and they were taken into care. Naturally my kids were away a couple of weeks when up I marched to the home they were in and took them home. Soon after I arrived home bang goes the door. Welfare. Cruelty. I was demented by this but this time I was determined to hold on to my kids and I won. But needless to say, they were still

watching me. I have no nice things to say regarding your
R.S.S.P.C.C. men at Christmas. We did not get much help
when others were able to tell me how much help they got from
them.

   I came in 1979 and at Christmas time was told by my
social worker to go down as there were a few things there for
me. To my disgust I recognised one of the men from there. He
was one of the men who raided my cupboard. I felt really
terrible and wanted to just run but I had my kids with me.
Funny when we left there my oldest son asked me what was
wrong. I could not bring myself round to telling him. I was
shaking like a leaf. A couple of months ago I was in my sitting
room with my kids and the door went. And one came rushing
in to tell me there was a man at my door. Before I could get up
from my chair the man was in the room. He then told me who
he was and that he was from the cruelty. I just about died as I
was unwell that morning. He told me he had a phone call
saying I was drunk and my kids had nothing to eat. He was
certainly surprised to see I was alright and promised I would
hear no more about it. And so far I have heard no more.

Some of the information suggested that even the close supervision
which Inspectors thought they were giving to cases was not always as
effective as it appeared to be.

   I am replying to your request in the August edition of the
Falkirk Advertiser for information on the contribution of the
R.S.S.P.C.C. to society.

   As a Social Historian I am sure you will be aware of the
pitfalls of 'biased history'. My main reason for writing is an
attempt to overcome this and perhaps act as a voice for
society's 'failures', too inarticulate or too scarred to respond.

   My family was in the 'care' of the Society between the
years of 1958–71. Despite this I experienced a childhood of
violence, extreme hunger and sickness, due mainly to the
classic unemployed drunken father who regularly spent all the
dole money on drink. Whenever an Officer from the Society
called, my father feigned blackouts and, as it appeared to us,
succeeded in deceiving the Officer. A visit to Head Office in
Edinburgh as late as 1969 did nothing to relieve conditions.

   I am quite willing to be interviewed so long as you are
prepared to write a balanced view of the Society 'warts and
all'.

   That letter suggests that possibly social work is too concerned to
protect itself from those who are affected by family difficulties and that
research into the after effects would not be resented by those who have

undergone painful experience. From this we could probably learn a great deal that would be beneficial for practice. Certainly it is evidence to encourage the developments which now make it possible for young people in care to organise themselves to express their own needs and difficulties to those in authority.

From the response it is also obvious that there are people who genuinely regard the Society and its Officers as having a very significant and positive effect upon their whole upbringing.

> My attention has been drawn to your appeal for information regarding the R.S.S.P.C.C. and wonder if you would be interested in my experience of help given as early as 1924.
>
> After many years of abuse from my foster parents I was removed from their home in Campbeltown at the age of almost fourteen by Mr George Riddell of the Greenock branch of the Society.
>
> The only place that could be found for me because of my age was at a Home in Ann Street, Greenock run by the Discharged Prisoners Aid Society.
>
> Mr Riddell visited me often and this benefited everyone as he somehow persuaded the ruling committee to allow the church choir to give concerts and parties on festive occasions. (An innovation in those days.) I had been doing reasonably well at school in my last two years in Campbeltown and he again used his charm (influence — call it what you will) to get permission for myself and some others to attend Holmscroft Evening classes.
>
> I left Greenock on 6th June 1927 to work as a laundress at Bellsdyke Hospital, Larbert and during this time we corresponded regularly. Two years later, I began work at Cartlock Hospital, Glasgow and I have a very grubby tattered reference which he so kindly sent to me then dated 22nd April, 1929.
>
> When he visited Glasgow he arranged to see me and always gave me five shillings which I am sure he could ill afford. When I was to be married he invited my late husband and I to his home and approved of my choice.
>
> He kept extolling my character and was totally unaware that he had formed it. I would have laid down my life for him and still know that without his help and encouragement the paths my feet have trodden would not have been so tolerable.
>
> On a visit to Greenock many years ago, I was grieved to learn of his death, but I am sure there are many persons like me who treasure his memory and are proud to have known such a dedicated man who served his life in caring for those ill-used by mankind.

The information received included much about individual Inspectors and the next item probably shows in a rather different way the kind of men they were. It is yet another example of their long service and it also gives some indication that in their lighter moments many of the Staff had abilities which were creative and not necessarily directly related to the work. It was sent by Mr Bell and relates to his grandfather who served for thirty years from 1900 to 1930. There is a newspaper clipping which states:

R.S.S.P.C.C. PRESENTATION

After service, which began in 1900 Inspector James Burns has retired from the Royal Scottish Society for Prevention of Cruelty to Children. His first 18 years with the Society were spent in Dumbarton, where he had charge of that area; and then he was transferred to Kilmarnock, where he worked for a further 10 years before being called to Glasgow Office three years ago.

Colleagues last night presented him with a smoking cabinet, while Mrs Burns received an umbrella.

And it is accompanied by a typescript poem as follows:

Auld freen, Noo that we ken your leavin,
An' feelin sure your auld heart's grevin,
To think nae mare you'll join the scribble,
Montrose Street daily clash, and quibble.

We felt we coudna let you leave
Without stapping something in your neive,
That when you turn o'er in bed,
Will mind you o' the Cruelty Shed.

Expect Na, Jeems in this oration,
A first class bletherin dedication,
To roose you up, and ca you good,
Its just a rhyme, that's understood.

To trace your history with the corps,
We hie back thirty-two years and more,
When in the prime of life you came,
But faith, you still are soond an game.

The auld yins a hae featsome stories,
O doughty deeds and ancient fories,
An if we got you in the mood,
Your stock would just be quite as good.

Dumberton saw you at your best,
For cases then you had the zest,
Five in one day your record bold,
Stands a challenge though its old.

Kilmarnock next the land o' Burns,
Where Rabbie had his playfu turns,
I'm thinking Jeems, had Rab been leevin,
Your Office Record he'd been thevin.

But when you came to Glasgow toon,
Your record had gaen somewhat doon,
But faith you took nae lang to settle,
And very soon you showed your mettle.

At first you were a wee bit grumphy,
Nae doot ye felt a trifle humphy,
The young yins primed with notions new,
Jest tried to pit you in a stew.

Wi' mony a game and prank contrived,
They let you know you'd just arrived,
But aye you gave as good's you got,
And after a that means a lot.

But then ye ken the work's the thing,
In that we a your praises sing,
We'll min your jovial sonsy face,
An growl when dealing with a case.

You made a rotter feel fu sma,
When reading him the cruelty law,
An just as mild could be your sermon,
When some pair soul was real deservin.

There's yin will miss you, pair auld Alf,
In siding we his Pension gaff,
An Alecks cheek nae mair you'll hear,
Big Willie will hae't a to bear.

The Ladies too, will miss your chaff,
Your pawky yarns and hearty laugh,
I'm sure they thocht you quite a treasure,
Although they hadna got your measure.

Noo Jeems you'll hardly ken yersel,
Wi a this gush aboot farewell,
But let me say we fairly feel it,
An trust you'll hae nae weary meenit.

An min you though your no beside us,
We'll always hae your form to guide us,
Montrose Street Chronicles are fu,
O doughty warriors like you.

An then you've never been so blate,
You've taen the Hill both soon and late,
Just tak your stick and aince mair dander,
When'ere you feel you've time to squander.

It was not only the Inspectors and staff of the Society who were long serving but this applied to the records too. As indicated by a letter from Mrs Budge in Forres, Morayshire.

> Regarding your letter requesting information about the history of the Society, I have a minute book which goes back to 1901. I am still using it, as there are quite a lot of pages to be filled. The Inspector had been called up in 1916, but in 1918 the meetings have been resumed. In 1902 the money sent to headquarters was £24.16.6d. In 1982 we sent £2148.4.3d. There were 9 cases in 1901 and 5 in 1981, in the Forres area.

She also describes cases reported in the book, for instance this one on 7th October 1901.

> Inspector reported that a boy aged $14\frac{1}{2}$ years, whose parents were dead, had been found sleeping in an unoccupied house in Kerr's Close, Forres. He was destitute and covered with vermin. He had been sleeping in stables and outhouses for months. The boy was sent by the Society to the Industrial Boys' Brigade, Edinburgh.

There was also evidence of the fact that the Society and its officers were held in esteem by those local authority officers with whom they had to co-operate. Typical was this letter from Mr F. H. J. Earnshaw of Perth.

> As County Children's Officer for the Joint County Council of Perth and Kinross from 1948 to 1969 I was closely associated with the local Inspectors of the Society, particularly the late Mr James Stocks and the late Mr Tom Farquhar. Also, Mrs Zena MacDonald the first 'Woman Visitor' appointed for this Area. I would have liked to comment on the contribution made by the aforementioned persons as staff of the Society as well the general interest they took in all matters relating to the poor and needy families in our Community . . .

This link with the public service was also exemplified in a different way by ex-Inspector Robbie of Hamilton who served from 1950 to 1960 as Inspector in the Society and then transferred to the public service to be Mental Health Officer for the Burgh of Hamilton. He wrote to say that he regarded his period with the Society 'as one of the greatest experiences of my life'.

One of the most significant developments in the history of the Society was recorded in the Annual Report for 1955 which stated:

> During the year the Society introduced by way of experiment a scheme for following up in certain cases the preventive work done by the Inspectors by the appointment of Women Visitors. Preliminary reports have shown the value of work of this kind.

Reference to this development was made by an Ex-Inspector Mr Sutherland of Glasgow who in a very interesting description of his work with the Society said:

> ... I can enumerate changes that have taken place during that period.
>
> The first was the introduction of 'Women Visitors' to the work of the Society. This was not hailed by some members of the inspectorate (which consisted of men only), probably on the grounds that it was an invasion by women on the domain of Man. It however, showed a success, having afforded an opportunity for more involvement in work of a social nature in certain cases and where a Woman Visitor was more suited to deal with Mothers who were largely responsible for neglect and inadequacy in the handling of money ...

Others like Mr Robertson of Glasgow wished to emphasise the contribution of women to the work of the Society as shown by the service of his aunt Miss Christina MacKinnon who served as a Matron of the Glasgow Shelter and later the Crookston Home and later still at Challenger Lodge in Edinburgh. The person most fitted however, to describe the work of women in the Society was Mrs E. L. McIntosh from Glasgow who served as a Woman Visitor from their inception until she retired as the Chief Woman Visitor in 1973 when she was honoured by the Queen as her record (provided in answer to written questions from the author) describes.

> *Question.* What special contributions did Women Visitors make to the work?
>
> *Answer.* The introduction of the Women Visitor's Service I feel gradually changed the emphasis from the punitive to the preventive, with a strong accent on rehabilitation of multi-problem families in their own homes.
>
> *Question.* What was the most important aspect of the work of the Society from your point of view?
>
> *Answer.* The work of the Society went on unhindered in many ways as the staff could go where 'angels feared to tread' in as much as they were not restricted by the legislation which colleagues in the statutory local authority posts were.
>
> Another of the aspects unique to the Society's work was the continued support given to the family, i.e. when a parent such as a father had been found guilty of neglect and even, dare I say it, imprisoned, the family were supported and often the father visited in prison. We tried to have a goal in mind as a united family, emphasis always being in working to keep the family as a unit. This often

involved re-housing, the children perhaps going into care
for a period and co-operating with the statutory agencies
to achieve our goal.

Question. Could you list one or two cases where you felt there
was particular interest?

Answer. I found it difficult to single out particular cases from
the many, but obviously such case situations as the single
parent father with a wide and varied selection of problems
remains uppermost. Such a case was Mr H. with seven
children, one of whom suffered from leukaemia. He was a
bitter man who felt life had dealt him a raw blow. His wife
had left him when his seventh child was three years old
and he had struggled to maintain the family unit with
great difficulty. He did have one positive aim in mind and
that was to keep his children, with the help of a Woman
Visitor. It was a long battle and he had over the years
several Women Visitors. One had always to be consistent
in our approach to Mr H and my own contact stood with
him over the years. His children grew up — one of the
boys had to be taken into care and, sadly, the child with
leukaemia died — but in the end Mr H made it. He
regained his pride and eventually felt a sense of
achievement in keeping his family together. Latterly, the
one practical service that we could give to this father was
to babysit for him and give him a night out.

Another single parent father who springs to mind was a
Mr McC. whose wife left him on Christmas Eve, leaving
him with three young boys approximately 7, 5 and 3 and
a little girl. Mr McC's opening statement was that he
intended to commit suicide. However, with the help of the
parish priest and some encouragement from granny who
agreed to look after the little girl, we gained Mr McC's
trust and with some persuasion the three boys were taken
to Dundonald Home. The promise to Mr McC. was that
as soon as the youngest was school age, they would come
home. This father maintained contact over the years and
never missed a Saturday visit to Dundonald to see his
children. When the youngest one was five, the children
came home. Despite the great rejoicing, there were many
ups and downs with these children at home as they were
lively youngsters and quite a handful, but the proverb 'All
for one and one for all' applied with these children and
they survived to grow into independent teenagers and the
case closed.

I would like to add a happy ending to the case but,
sadly, the father died — a cruel blow to these youngsters

PAST AND PRESENT

(a) Staff leaving 142 High Street, Edinburgh.

who by this time were reaching the stage of leaving school and needing the support of their father. Granny was visited and arrangements made with the local authority for a related fostering arrangement and she in fact took the three boys.

(I still hear from Granny and the next generation is doing very well!)

There are many situations when a child suffers a non-accidental injury. I am convinced that given the right support to a family at this stage when the stress level has reached breaking point, further injury to the child can be avoided. It does however need a special kind of person with a commitment to the work, a caring for the people and a limited caseload. These families tend to be isolated and have no friends to advise them and can be completely lonely. They need all the help and support they can get

(b) Inspector taking statement from child.

but, by and large, they need a parenting type of help as rarely have these families faced any discipline and even a basic routine is totally alien to them.

Question. Are there other significant memories you have of any aspect of the work?

Answer. I felt that it was important even from the very earliest of days to introduce some form of basic training for the Women Visitors. This was always of great interest to me

(c) Two Inspectors.

and I tried whenever possible to have my staff visit other agencies and places of interest that they were likely to come across during their day to day work. Initially the training was fairly modest but over the years it grew and I am enclosing the final programme of training which I

(d) Ian MacGregor, Group Officer, Inverness (1984).

drew up and completed twice a year and in the latter stages, some interest was shown in this course of lectures by the Scottish Home Office.

Another thought that comes to mind is that often we learned from our families. We tried to encourage the mothers to have some self-esteem. They tended to see

(e) Matt Stewart, Group Officer, Glasgow (1984).

(f) Sheila Milne, Inspector and George Quested, Group Officer, Edinburgh (1984).

themselves as an appendage to their families. To encourage the mothers who, in the Woman Visitor's opinion, had really tried hard to improve their surroundings and had co-operated well over a period, we suggested a night out. This grew in popularity and for a

time we ran a club for which the mothers chose the topic
for the night. It was interesting that just as popular as
having someone to advise on hairdressing, cookery or
making paper flowers, these mothers enjoyed a cup of tea
and a blether. One thing they also enjoyed was the fact
that father was duly installed as babysitter for that night!

Question. Do you have any view about the relationship between
voluntary organisations and the statutory authorities?

Answer. There is little doubt in my mind that voluntary
organisations and the statutory local authorities should be
able to work alongside each other.

During my twenty years of working with the Society,
we had a service to offer the local authorities — that of
rehabilitating a family and attempting to keep the family
unit together. I can only speak for this time and say that
we received maximum co-operation from the statutory
authorities and my staff were never refused either
financial or material help that we asked for. In return we
kept the social worker involved notified of the progress or
otherwise of the family.

Perhaps it is necessary for leadership in the field of co-
operation as if the small problems are not ironed out from
the top then they tend to mushroom to a fungus.

In conclusion, I do not think I can do any better than
to quote from an article in one of the daily papers from
1965 in which I stated:

'Sometimes I wish I had never got mixed up with the
Society.'

'You can be content not doing anything for anyone so
long as you remain in ignorance of how much needs to be
done.'

'It's all very fine to be kind and do good for people in
far-off lands but for people on your own doorstep that's a
different matter.'

'I wonder how many people know anything about the
disease of poverty, that terrible sickness that makes people
slip back?'

'We've got into our heads the quite erroneous fact that
in this welfare state there is no one in real need of help or
kindness.'

'There's as great a gulf between the "haves" and the
"have-nots" as there is between black and white.'

'I wish sometimes that the 'haves' could go out with one
of my Woman Visitors and experience for themselves the
dreadful smell of poverty.'

Although this article appeared in 1965 I would state

quite categorically that the service is as necessary today for returning self-respect to these families.

Recognition for the work done by the Women Visitors' service was achieved by the award being made of M.B.E. to myself in 1973. This honour, although granted to me, was I feel given for the work of the Women Visitors carried out in all parts of Scotland.

8

A FORMER GENERAL SECRETARY'S VIEW

It is part of the institutional rituals of most voluntary organisations that the chief officer is often designated Secretary because the traditional ethics of such organisations is that the official is the Secretary to the Executive Committee which is the managing group of volunteer members. The task of helping such a voluntary group to be effective as the managing and policy making body of an organisation is one of the most difficult professional tasks within modern society. The post requires someone who embodies the highest professional expertise in the sphere of activity within which the voluntary organisation is operating but also someone who is adept and skilled at making such expertise available for use by interested and involved voluntary members who can only spend limited time on the task of managing and supervision. The expertise must be presented in such a way that the voluntary group can make knowledgeable and responsible decisions in the field of activity. The Secretary then has to be equally capable of translating these policy decisions into the work of the organisation in a responsible and efficient way in order to achieve its objectives. The post requires also the ability to portray the organisation publicly so that the work attains credibility and public support. This work has to be extended into the community so that existing members continue to maintain their involvement, so that new members join and develop the organisation and so that society at large expresses its support in terms of goodwill, and material and financial resources.

Organisations are as effective as the quality of the personnel directing the affairs but however eminent and able, dedicated and energetic the members of the organisation and however efficient their elected executive may be it is the quality and performance of the Secretary which translates so much voluntary effort into demonstrable results.

Add to all this the fact that most voluntary organisations operate upon minimal resources, usually less than are required to be effective judged by standards of normal provision elsewhere and that the Secretary is concerned to husband those resources, stretch them over a

173

variety of activities and yet maintain a high standard of service and it is difficult to imagine how voluntary organisations succeed in finding the personal paragon to embody all the necessary qualities.

Yet they do and the R.S.S.P.C.C. has been particularly effective in this respect. There have not needed to be too many in the history of the Society because most of the distinguished men who have followed the founder James Grahame, who occupied the position as Managing Director in the earliest years, have given considerable length of service in the position.

One of the longest serving was Claude Cumming Forsyth who began service with the Society in 1931 and retired in 1968 but, who is still able to recall his memories of that long period. Claude Forsyth was a lawyer, well established in the legal work of the railway organisation, with his feet well placed on the ladder of bureaucratic achievement. All he needed to do was to stay and perform his duties and his status was assured. Like many young lawyers of the time he responded to calls to help with voluntary legal advice at the Edinburgh Legal Dispensary. Here his duties led him into contact with the R.S.S.P.C.C. through giving advice to needy cases and the work of the Society impressed him. The Society was looking for a Secretary. So he took the massive step from the security of the bureaucratic structure, to the flimsy insecurity of a single-handed post with a voluntary body. Why did he do it? He admits, with a twinkle in his eye, that he was probably 'a round peg in a square hole' in the railway bureaucracy, although somewhat ruefully he conjectures about the position he might have had if he had stayed and the financial security it would have provided. The consequences of this step into the voluntary world meant to forsake the security of well protected salary structures and public service pension schemes and the possibility of alternative attractive posts which could have claimed his interest. The willingness to do so went with the individualism which the post at that time required and with the readiness to receive satisfaction and reward from working with the volunteer members to develop a service to the community.

In his less guarded moments Claude Forsyth can wax eloquent upon the vagaries of some of the distinguished people who have given service to the Society. The distinction and commitment which enabled them to help the Society often went with personal idiosyncrasy and with attitudes which required the skill of the diplomat to cope with and to translate into effective relationship with the rest of the Society and with the public at large. There is no doubt that he possesses this diplomacy and, if pressed, he will agree that it is the essential requirement of the servant of a voluntary committee coupled with the ability to take the occasional patronising attitude, the occasional failure to recognise the value of expertise and service, and the occasional slight which can be components of the relationship between the respected and powerful volunteers and the paid servant of the voluntary organisation.

C. A. CUMMING FORSYTH, O.B.E., B.L.
General Secretary R.S.S.P.C.C., 1934–68.

A few moments of discussion with him will also convince anyone
that this willingness to absorb a degree of condescension does not mean
that Claude Forsyth, or the ideal General Secretary, is by any means a
"yes" man. Far from it he has always prided himself on having his point
of view and expressing it, even when it was not palatable and not easy to
accept.

In particular he has always been an uncompromising critic of
pretentious and inefficient beaucratic professionalism. He has never
been convinced that so-called professionalism has universally improved
the standard of care. He has always been critical of the impersonal
elements which the development of statutory provision has introduced
to the lives of the families which he considers were the main concern of
the Society.

In the early days the milieu of the volunteers, the committee
members, the convenors of the lady collectors, the collectors themselves,
became his world. Each year as Heather Day, the Scottish Children's
League annual flag week came round, then Cumming Forsyth as the
single headquarters official was the hub of frantic voluntary activity.

Building patiently throughout the year, developing District Committees who would extend and supervise the work of the Society in each area of Scotland, identifying possible supporters, encouraging and advising them, he spent many miles of travelling to sustain them with his presence at their meetings. He is full of admiration for the work of these voluntary committees but obviously his capacity to extend his work into the social life of the areas he visited was an asset to these developments. There were no hours of work, no conception of on- or off-duty. Even the need occasionally to take his aged father who lived with him on some of his lengthy travels in his cherished car was symptomatic of the extent to which he was prepared to live his work.

Claude Forsyth was in his own view, however, outmatched in his dedication and his involvement by the Inspectors of the Society. His reminiscences of these men, everyone in his view a sterling character and a unique personality, could constitute a book in itself. He smiles as he speaks of, for example, Inspector Mackenzie of Perthshire who patrolled his area on a push-bike and prided himself in visiting regularly every school in his entire area.

Each Inspector was an individual who expressed his own personality in the social commitment to the work of the Society. They embodied strong moral convictions and an uncompromising view of the social standards they felt they had to uphold. Claude Forsyth is convinced of the importance of the personal qualities of these officers and is somewhat sceptical of the so-called professionalism of the modern trained social worker. These officers, he says, understood people and had the capacity to relate to a variety of backgrounds because of their own life experience. He respects the personal discipline which so many of the officers embodied. Probably, he feels, it was not accidental that many of the officers were ex-policemen or ex-servicemen. Their experience and their trained objectivity contributed to the strong image of firmness but fairness which 'the cruelty man' developed amongst all Scottish communities.

Reminiscing about the different Chief Inspectors, in Glasgow, Edinburgh and Dundee it was again their ability to control and exact high standards of reliability and efficiency which Claude Forsyth emphasises.

As General Secretary he was both the main selector of Inspectors and often their trainer and also the final authority for disciplining officers. He only remembers the need to use the ultimate sanction of dismissal in two cases.

Even then, he makes the careful and sympathetic point that they were 'not dismissed' but 'firmly asked to find another job'. One suspects that, receiving the quarterly reports presented regularly on each Inspector, he knew each man intimately enough to render the reports largely superfluous.

The Inspector of the Society was an important person and,

particularly in country districts, could wield immense power in his area. There was a safeguard over this power and that was the relationship with the parish clerk who invariably knew the families well and also knew the Inspector. This close relationship between the parish clerk and the local Inspector was cemented in a number of ways and Forsyth speaks amusingly of the common interest in fishing which in his view made one such partnership in Elgin a particularly effective and productive one.

The General Secretary spent much time travelling to visit committee members. Usually the meetings were in the evenings so there was not much spare time. The committee members were hospitable and the General Secretary, as he said, did not need money but he needed the capacity to cope with the varieties and vagaries of that hospitality. One suspects that Claude Forsyth was well able to contribute as, for instance, to the ceilidh which he remembers took place regularly at the Grant Arms Hotel, Grantown-on-Spey on each of his annual visits to that township.

The importance of the school teacher in Scottish society is verified by Forsyth who emphasises that there was rarely a committee in Scotland that did not have a teacher in its midst. The Inspector of the Society always endeavoured to mention a close relationship with each school in his area and the report of the Inspector was a valued instrument in assessing the background and needs of children.

Just as important as the school was the good relationship Inspectors had with the police. The Inspector had to be able to construct a good report and to substantiate it with factual evidence. Their ability to do so was respected by the courts and by the police who would, therefore invariably provide assistance and support.

It is here that Claude Forsyth is most critical of modern social work. He respects the professional expertise and the developed standards of social work provision but he considers that the capacity to collect evidence and marshall it into an authoritative report to the court has been lost. As an aside he mentions that 'the cruelty man' was also always known to be available on a 24 hour basis. The police never hesitated to call upon the services of 'the cruelty man' whatever the hour of the day or night. The Inspectors prided themselves on this ready availability and upon the extent to which public officials availed themselves of their services. Forsyth mentions, in particular, the respect there was between the old public assistance officials and the Inspectors.

The question had to be put and now was the opportune time. Some people thought that the Inspector was punitive. Did Claude Forsyth think that the Inspector was or should be punitive? 'Never' was the answer. The Inspector had to be firm but he was essentially concerned with the protection of children. In interviewing within the family situation this was the prevailing principle which guided the action. Obviously such situations were fraught with emotion and tension and the role of Inspector was always open to criticism. But Claude Forsyth is firm in his opinion. Most cases come to 'the cruelty' from the clients themselves. People refer themselves to 'the cruelty man' for help. Families call in 'the cruelty man' to intervene in their difficult relationships. This is not the response you would expect if the image was one of punishment. Forsyth is certain that his experience suggests that the firmness of 'the cruelty man' is respected. The use of the 'warning' by 'the cruelty man' might suggest a punitive approach but it was accepted by the clients as part of the process of continual concern expressed by the Society. The mere availability of 'the cruelty man' was an important deterrent to deviance in many communities in Scotland.

Some of the Inspectors themselves had experience of what it was to be neglected. Forsyth remembers at least one who was deserted by his parents and brought up in residential care.

The work of the Society with the tinker families of Scotland is a particular matter of pride with Claude Forsyth. The 'traveller' families were very difficult to work with and one or two of the Inspectors of the Society, particularly in Argyll and Perthshire, were probably the people in Scotland with most experience of their way of life and of their needs and difficulties.

Other special problems which this former General Secretary notes over the whole period of his service as contributing to the tasks of the Society were those associated with alcoholism, which he views as a major contributing factor to the neglect of children. So often intervention or a crisis call for the Inspector arose from drinking bouts and drinking quarrels. The experience and reputation of the 'cruelty man' was crucial in this type of intervention and cannot be easily usurped by the more diffuse availability of the professional services. The role of the Inspector was as a guardian and protector of the rights of the child and yet often he could act as mediator, adviser, and counsellor in the dynamics of family problems.

Although Forsyth was the General Secretary throughout the thirties he was never aware of a special effect of unemployment upon the task of the Society. He, therefore, had no view on the likely effect of increased unemployment upon the work of the Society at the present time. He saw the development of Children's Departments and welcomed them. In his time he contributed to some of the changes because he gave evidence to and served upon a number of the working parties and investigating groups which suggested changes in the legislation and services regarding children's welfare.

Probably it is not generally known but Claude Cumming Forsyth had determined to write a minority report following his membership of the McBoyle committee in 1962. He wanted to emphasise the importance of the child protection service to be based upon and integral to the education service. Only strong pressure from official sources designed to make the report unanimous made him decide to suppress his

SEPTEMBER 1968

Retiral of R.S.S.P.C.C. General Secretary — Claude Inspector Judge, O.B.E. of Dundee (standing right centre Cumming Forsyth, 1934–68. Also in the picture are Mrs E. under umbrella). With Mr Cumming Forsyth is his wife, McIntosh, M.B.E., the former Chief Woman Visitor (sitting Isabel. opposite Mr Cumming Forsyth) and the former Chief

convictions. But they were still there and interestingly were expressed
almost in the same form by the Kilbrandon Report which prompted the
legislative reforms expressed in the *Social Work (Scotland) Act* 1968.

Some of Forsyth's more scathing criticism of the shortcomings of
social work and professional child care obviously have their origins in
this view of child protection and child welfare. There is no hesitation in
his assessment that social work is often too diffuse and aimless in its
approach to these questions. The greater expertise and understanding of
a service concerned to concentrate upon the all-round development of
the child would have been preferable. In his view social work often has
neither the approach nor the understanding to get near to the needs of
families which have always been the concern of the Society. He regrets
the fact that the theory of statutory services working with voluntary
organisations to provide a complementary and co-ordinated service has
never been achieved. He cannot understand why the professional
services have often been so jealous of voluntary organisations and effort,
so rejecting of the work of organisations like the Society.

He recognises that the challenge of working alongside the
professional services has made the Society examine its own work and
focus it more clearly in the areas of work for which it is especially suited.
He is glad that the Society has developed and improved the training of
officers but equally glad that the Society has continued to emphasise
that the Inspector has a special and unique contribution to make to
social welfare.

In Claude Forsyth's view the voluntary organisation enables the
community to demonstrate that it has a conscience and a concern about
welfare. Even the painful task of raising money, which was the constant
preoccupation of his years of service, he considers to be beneficial. He is
full of admiration for the efforts of the voluntary committee members he
worked with over the years. He mentions how each profession
contributed its expertise to the Society, pointing out that although he
always found it difficult to find doctors with sufficient spare time to serve
on committees he could invariably rely on their wives to take on active
role in the local fund-raising.

Finally he emphasised that the full time official is dependent often
upon his committee for support and advice. He considers he was always
well served in this respect. Particularly important, he emphasises, is the
role of the Chairman of the Executive Committee who really makes the
work of the General Secretary possible and effective. In his view it is the
supportive partnership between an understanding and able Chairman
and the permanent official which determines whether the organisation
can really utilise the full potential of its membership and financial
resources.

9

A FORMER CHAIRMAN'S VIEW

Appendix A, in tracing the development of voluntarism and the necessary components of the voluntary organisation, gives emphasis to the need for public figures to signify by their support the credibility and importance of the organisation and also to the significant role of the chairman of the executive group who is usually the effective head of the policy-making of the organisation and has to contribute the professional and expert authority to that task. The Rt. Hon. the Lord Wheatley P.C., LL.D., Lord Justice Clerk, who held the post of Chairman from 1956 to 1979 epitomises and embodies both of these requirements. Distinguished lawyer and jurist, and renowned also for a convinced political, humanitarian and religious view of society, he brought to the affairs of the Society the weight of that public authority and concern, as so many of his fellow Scottish leading professionals do to the cause of voluntarism as it widely expressed itself.

His answer to the inevitable first question to him, regarding the association of a judge with the possible punitive image of the Society, was a convinced, firm and knowledgeable rejection of the suggestion. He pointed out that the Society only used prosecution as a preventive measure and that one of the objectives in the use of a judge's powers of disposal was the individual and a general deterrent to prevent a recurrence of the offence. In his view there was no conflict between his position as a judge and his being associated with the prevention of cruelty. On the contrary, in associating himself with the Society which has the care of children as a major objective, he was being consistent with his professional task which was concerned with promoting the protection and well-being of society by a firm maintenance of its agreed values and standards.

He pointed out that throughout its history by far the greatest proportion of the work of the Society had always been with the identification and treatment of the neglect of children. The deliberate and extreme acts of cruelty to children had always been a small minority of cases, but these had presented the most perplexing and sensitive problem to the Society. During his period of office, the complexity and

THE RT. HON. THE LORD WHEATLEY, P.C., LL.D.
Vice President, R.S.S.P.C.C.
(Chairman, R.S.S.P.C.C. Executive Committee, 1954–79.)

deep-seated causes of such behaviour had been recognised by the involvement of the Society in the wide-ranging research activity to try to discover more knowledge which would be helpful in prevention and treatment. An outstanding example of this was the establishment of the Special Unit in Glasgow concerned with the treatment and prevention of non-accidental injury to children.

Returning to the theme of neglect he recognised that the work of the Society was largely with the poorer or disadvantaged members of the community. He was aware that such members of the community were at greater risk of being seen to be or accused of being neglectful, and were more exposed to scrutiny and to investigation than the rest of society. He was in no doubt, however, that neglect, perhaps in different form but with no less detrimental effect, can be found in the more affluent and more economically fortunate sections of the community, but this was less likely to be discovered or brought to the attention of authority. Recognition of this increased the need to emphasise the humanitarian and preventive aspects of the work. In this respect he welcomed the evidence he had that the 'cruelty man' was still the first 'port of call' for help in many instances. It emphasised the continuing role of the Society, not in competition with the local authority and professional services, but as a different access point for help and assistance. The value of 'the cruelty man's' personal experience and his knowledgeable and continuing relations with the community were invaluable assets in this field of social work.

As Chairman of the Society over the years he had been very conscious of the effect which the increasing professionalism of the local authority services had upon the Inspectors employed by the Society. He was also aware of the effect which this had on the Society in its need to emphasise its role as a complementary system to local authority provision. He was proud of the fact that the Committee had been able to find a positive solution to this problem in developing the training function of the Society. This emphasised the specialised role of the Inspector, as a special investigating officer of the Society, who utilised the particular methods and approaches of the Society in aiding the clients.

In this connection he acknowledged with appreciation the help of the School of Community Studies at Moray House College of Education, Edinburgh, which, as an agency concerned with the development of professional social work training, had directed these professional training resources to the assistance of the Society in developing the professional role of the Inspector, rather than in insisting that the generic principles of social work should necessarily be embraced completely by the Society.

This willingness of the Society to continue to emphasise its own approach had preserved its role in the field of child care. At the same time the Society had always been very conscious of changing social conditions and the need to review constantly its role within the community. The policy-making group kept thinking ahead, and this was being demonstrated by the increasing emphasis within the present work of the Society upon specialist activities and projects which were being designed to meet special needs.

As Chairman of the policy-making group he realised the importance of preserving, protecting and promoting the public image of the Society. The image of the Society had to be successful in attracting the support of both the concerned financial contributor and the professionals in this field. There had been an ever increasing dependency on legacies which, for any particular year, were imponderable. While from one point of view legacies can be a reflection of public opinion and support they represent an attitude at the time they are made rather than the time at which they are paid. Nevertheless, the steady and increasing flow of legacies over the years was testimony, in his view, to the high regard in which the Society always has been held. In an interesting side discussion on this issue there arose fascinating subjects for research as well as the direct suggestion that the proportionate support of Society effort by legacy income should probably be investigated.

    Subsequently the financial department of the Society provided the following figures which not only reflect the changing pattern of income and expenditure over the years but also the tremendous growth in the contribution made to the welfare system by this voluntary society.

ROYAL SCOTTISH SOCIETY FOR PREVENTION OF CRUELTY TO CHILDREN

1900

Source of Income	Percentage of Income	Source	Percentage of costs
Subscriptions etc.	88%	Salaries	70%
Legacies	5%	Shelter maintenance	21%
Grants*	3%		
TOTAL £5,600		TOTAL £5,129	

* = income received from parents whose children were sheltered.

1925

Subs. etc.	77%	Salaries	60%
Legacies	10%	Travel	9%
Board contributions	2%	Printing/Stationery	5%
		Waterproofs & cycles	2%
		Shelter costs	10%
TOTAL £23,500		TOTAL £22,000	

1950

Fundraising income	48%	Salaries	53%
		Motor Bicycles/Cars	1%
Board maintenance for children in Homes	11%	Travel	7%
Legacies	37%	Printing/Stationery	3%
		Home costs	15%
TOTAL £66,000		TOTAL £50,000	

1982

Fundraising income	56%	Salaries	61%
Grants from Local		Transport	16%
Authorities and Central Government	9%	Printing/Stationery etc.	5%
Legacies	28%		
TOTAL £743,000		TOTAL £800,000	

This brought attention back to the necessity of a voluntary organisation to be responsive to changed conditions. The development of the Woman Visitor scheme was, in Lord Wheatley's view, a good example. Increasing evidence in cases of the lack of ability to cope with home-making and budgeting drew attention to the need for educational and supportive activity to supplement the investigative activity of the Inspectors. The Women Visitors developed good relationships with families. Local authorities were quick to appreciate their worth and recognised this by providing grant-aid to extend the scheme. As their work became better known and more appreciated then the picture became part of the standard service provided by local authorities.

In Lord Wheatley's view the importance of being a voluntary organisation is this ability to experiment, or to attend to particular problems, and to use the support of members in specially significant ways. All of this freedom could be limited if there were too much dependence on statutory funds. On the other hand very few voluntary organisations can provide a satisfactory supplementary service to statutory effort without help from public sources. In his experience government departments have aways been favourably disposed towards voluntary effort if responsibly exercised and he had much admiration for the ingenuity of officials in devising ways to help deserving voluntary effort. On the other hand he recognised that there were many demands upon a limited national public purse and that it was increasingly difficult for officials to determine priorities for funding.

He was convinced that the most important function of the Society was the direct preventive work it performed in the community. That this work was crucial and effective was shown by the way in which so many cases were self-referred or referred by friends and relatives of the clients. There was obviously a confidence in the community that cases would be treated sympathetically and that resort to the Society was seen as an effective way of preventing neglect and ill-treatment of children.

One factor in achieving this was by making the organisation of the Society as effective as possible at communicating between and involving every component of the Society. It was especially important that a voluntary organisation should not appear to be bureaucratic but that it should be personal and made easy for everyone associated with it to contribute to the work. Accordingly he had always emphasised the need for a flow of information generally, but particularly between the Inspectors and the Executive Committee who should not be seen to be remote and inaccessible. It was also important that district committees should feel closely linked to the centre and that there should be a good flow of information to and from the headquarters to the districts and the members.

Lord Wheatley could not say enough in praise of the local and district committees and their members. They were the important contacts between the Society and local communities and the general public. They did much of the routine work of the Society, a lot of it, such as collecting money and fund-raising, not very exciting but vital to the Society. The ingenuity and industry shown by many of them in their fund-raising efforts were as heart-warming to him as they were productive to the Society. It would be easy for the local networks to become moribund or just a mechanism but he was pleased to say that they always appeared to him to be vital and lively. They participated in the discussion at Council and were quick to communicate about issues of concern in their area. They took a jealous and protective view of the work of the Inspectors in their areas and these relationships were co-operative and productive.

The Executive Committee was a special example of this kind of service, and he wished to pay a tribute to all who had served with him in its work. It could be an onerous responsibility, particularly when finances were low and commitments were large. The Society had always been fortunate in having people who gave of their time and energy simply because they had a genuine interest in the work.

Lord Wheatley looked back on his first association with the Society when Claude Forsyth was the General Secretary. It was a different organisation then. Typical of so many voluntary organisations it revolved around the one lynch-pin — the General Secretary — 'Claude was the Society then'. As Chairman he realised that the organisation was becoming more complex and had to diversify responsibility. It had developed considerably since then as needs had emerged and new challenges had to be met. In bringing in Arthur Wood in 1961 as assistant, understudy and eventual successor to Claude — they had laid the foundations for the development into the modern complex organisation. He doubted, however, if they had fully realised the extent to which the Society would grow in the next years, but that decision in 1961 had since 'proved to be a winner'.

'Would it continue to grow?' — was a question which had to be asked. It was difficult to conceive pragmatically a society so completely free from social problems that there would not be a continuing need for voluntary organisations. Lord Wheatley feels that voluntary or-ganisations make a positive contribution to social well-being. He believes in people having the opportunity to demonstrate their concern for others and to show a willingness to assume responsibility for others. Yet he is also a great believer in public provision. He wants to see a just and humane society making provision for all to have an equal opportunity for fulfilling a meaningful life. But, in his view, there will always be gaps where voluntary effort and the voluntary organisation can make their contribution. In any event he is sufficiently old-fashioned to believe that welfare is not something which can be provided by simply turning on a tap of money or resources. There is moral value in feeling responsible not only for oneself but for one's fellow beings. There is also the importance of the Christian responsibility to work towards a better society and to the highest possible standards of co-operative and corporate life.

What would he see of the way the Society might go in the future? Prevention through the removal of causes for neglect was the obvious path. He feels that whenever possible the family unit is the appropriate context in which children should be given the opportunity to develop happily and to the limit of their potentiality. As the Society moved into its second century of activity he hoped that it would continue to make its significant contribution to creating better opportunities for all children to enable them to have a secure upbringing free from cruelty in any shape or form.

10

INTO THE MODERN SOCIAL WORK ERA

PART I — *The views of the present General Secretary*

If it is true to say, as the knowledgeable undoubtedly would, that during the period of Claude Cumming Forsyth's occupancy of the position of General Secretary, the R.S.S.P.C.C. consolidated its national and district committee structure, became a sound national organisation and established a reputation as a significant contributor to policy thinking in child welfare, then it is also certainly true, that the period since Arthur Wood took over as General Secretary has seen the Society develop as a complex welfare organisation, extending and developing its special expertise and unique knowledge. The year of takeover was significant in that it was the year of the *Social Work Scotland Act* 1968 which ushered in a new era in local authority social work provision and organisation. Claude Cumming Forsyth had contributed to the deliberations which led up to the Act, by his distinctive membership of the McBoyle Committee and by the suggestions he stimulated from the R.S.S.P.C.C. in response to the proposals of the Kilbrandon Committee and the White Paper which preceded the 1968 Act.

Cumming Forsyth handed over the General Secretaryship to Arthur Wood at the time when the Act had to be implemented and when voluntary organisations had to find new answers to their situation within the organisation of social welfare. Arthur Wood who was Assistant Secretary from 1961 to 1968 is very appreciative of his grooming under his predecessor, over years of gradually assuming increased responsibility, sometimes as he now recognises, being thrust in 'at the deep end' or left 'holding the fort' thanks to the faith of his predecessor and his willingness to delegate. Wood, after law studies and a law apprenticeship, had six months with an insurance firm before being brought in to bolster up the 'one man band' of Claude Forsyth and to ensure continuity for the organisation.

During these years of supporting Claude Forsyth and learning from him, Arthur Wood assimilated much of the tradition and spirit of the organisation which had been integral to the experience of his senior colleague. Even now he has in the corner of his office one of the famous

188

On the cheque:

Clydesdale Bank PLC 17th October 1983

R.S.S.P.C.C.

£6,000-00

Six thousand pounds

or order

R.K. SLOAN.

Ronnie Sloan

ARTHUR WOOD, O.B.E.
The R.S.S.P.C.C. General Secretary since 1968 receives a cheque for £6,000 from Ronnie Sloan, Edinburgh Actuary, who raised that amount for the R.S.S.P.C.C. by running as Superman in the Edinburgh Marathon.

Inspector overcoats which he can remember were still made in his early days with the R.S.S.P.C.C. from measured yards of a bale of special cloth (mentioned in Chapter 7) kept in the head office, and provided to an Inspector when he joined the organisation. How the overcoat was rescued and kept remains a mystery, although the tradition was that if an Inspector left the Society he should have returned his overcoat. During his period of service the treasured overcoat was first replaced by a clothing allowance and then this was assimilated within the salary scale, by a process of negotiation with the staff. As Wood describes this development then it epitomises the change in the organisation which marks his period of office — from the paternalism of the provided overcoat to the conferring of status in a process of negotiation between equals respecting each other's position.

During the immediate post-1968 period Arthur Wood recalled a number of issues which required the attention of the R.S.S.P.C.C. Internally these included staff training, and the necessity to increase the Society's professional social work complement for the purposes of management and consultancy and the development of the Society's committee structure with the growth of smaller sub-committees to deal with special aspects of the Society's activities. Externally there were the particular trends relating to problems such as the battered child problem — later to become known as non-accidental injury to children — the marked trend from the late 70s of self-referrals to the R.S.S.P.C.C. and the continuing review of the Society's tasks taking into account the ever changing needs and the services available to meet these needs. Overall there was the continuing problem of funding on which everything depended and the need to seek additional sources of funds and to pursue different as well as tried methods.

As it happened training had been of particular interest to Wood during his period as Assistant Secretary (when for a time he had been a member of the Training Committee of the Scottish Advisory Council on Child Care). In the early 1960s training was organisational, carried out in each area by the Chief Inspector and other senior staff. Inspectors came to Head Office at the end of their probationary period of twelve months to sit a written test devised by the General Secretary and to be interviewed by the Staff Committee. As Arthur Wood freely admits the test was mainly on organisation, legislation and procedures as was to be expected since it was designed by two lawyers! Gradually however, the stimulus provided by the McBoyle and Kilbrandon enquiries was providing an awareness of the need for more conscious preparation in the field of probation and child care and this was reflected in the R.S.S.P.C.C. whose interest was given much practical support by Mr M. Corner, then the Chief Officer of the Child Care and Probation Inspectorate within the Home and Health Department. Corner encouraged the R.S.S.P.C.C. in training activities probably sensing an affinity between the role of the probation officer and the 'cruelty man' and perhaps anticipating that the experience of the Society and its officers would be invaluable in the expansion of welfare provision which was to come. Certainly many officers who gained their experience in the R.S.S.P.C.C. were later to serve with distinction in child care, probation and allied services, like Mr T. Hinshelwood who became the Principal Probation Officer in Glasgow. Accepting the risk of a drain upon its staff resources into the better paid and wider career network of the statutory service, the Society, nevertheless, recognised the benefit of these co-operative training activities with other authorities. Wood himself went on a Home Office in-service course during this period and then helped to establish a pattern of in-service courses within his own organisation. A course — prompted and organised by the Child Care Inspectorate, at the Palace Hotel, Edinburgh, in 1966 was the first of these and, within the Society, has the status of folklore. The success of the Society's participation in this course and the response to it by the officers concerned led in time to the achievement of a grant from Central Government funds to institute the regular in-service annual pattern. The Society also forged a relationship with Moray House College of

Education, which by then was establishing full-time professional social work courses of training, and the expertise of tutors involved in this professional training was used to develop the in-service training of the Society Inspectorate.

Another task assumed by Arthur Wood at this time was to develop the interest of the Society in research. The Executive Committee had become aware of the N.S.P.C.C. research developments and the Chairman at the time Lord Wheatley, thought that the Scottish Society should investigate its own activity more closely. A chance conversation between him and the Principal of Moray House College led to an association between the two organisations in research activity. The college provided the expertise of sociologists who acted as consultants to the Society in examining some of the questions and issues which were arising from its organisation and practice. A study of the role of the Inspectorate yielded factual evidence of the amount of time spent in routines such as travelling and record writing and gave the staff committee of the R.S.S.P.C.C. the *raison d'être* for instituting wider transport provision, recording machines and better access to typing of records. This benefit to the Inspectors in their daily routine probably facilitated their ready and active co-operation in the research activity next undertaken which was a detailed investigation of the cases handled by the Society. In addition to the interesting information published in *Neglected Children — a Study* by B. J. Ashley and H. Cohen, which provided the Society with useful evidence of its continuing significance in the field of child welfare immediately after the implementation of the *Social Work (Scotland) Act*, the survey drew attention to the need for standardised recording of case material and the research questionnaire provided the basis for the comprehensive revision of the records developed by Ray Starrs the R.S.S.P.C.C. Social Work Executive Officer, which now gives the Society a strong data base for its policy decisions.

By this time, in the early 1970s Arthur Wood was firmly in the position of General Secretary and beginning to help the organisation to move into a position as an acccepted voluntary movement within the increasingly professionalised field of social welfare. The choice of path was not easy because there were questions to which there were no obvious answers. The dilemma was apparent within the training exercises of the years around the institution of *Social Work (Scotland) Act* as already discussed. The development of a professional element within the training of the Inspectors was welcomed by them because they felt the need and could see the benefit but at the same time it threatened them and raised their defensiveness regarding their apparent non-professionalism and their fears of rejection by the newly developing professions. The research activity already referred to had given evidence to indicate that the Society and the Inspectors probably made a unique contribution to the welfare of children and that their approach was particularly effective and welcomed within certain communities and by certain families. The answer, therefore, within the training policy was to focus on the areas where the Society had a unique and effective contribution to make and to build and improve upon it.

The developing emphasis on training and staff support was given a further impetus in 1971 with the appointment on a part-time basis of Daphne McCuaig as Social Work Consultant. This psychiatric social worker did much to help fieldwork staff through the traumatic period of establishing a confident relationship with professional social work colleagues and her influence coincided with the development of the policy of seconding Inspectors to full-time courses leading to professional social work qualification. This development in turn led to the need for the creation of a professionally trained middle management capable of providing social work support for the staff who were returning from training and for ensuring that the Society would utilise their experience to the full.

If the seeds for this development were sown by the influence of Daphne McCuaig it was her successor Ray Starrs who was responsible for implementing the policy in practice, first of all as Social Work Adviser and latterly as Social Work Executive Officer in an established management role. In time another similar post was created in Strathclyde Region where half of the Society's work is concentrated. More recent appointments had been that of a Development Officer with the responsibility for maintaining and analysing trends, community needs and social work policy in order to assess where the R.S.S.P.C.C. might undertake new initiatives, and in 1983 an Information Officer whose task was to ensure the Society had the essential data to help it with decision-making regarding such initiatives and who would also provide a flow of information to those outside the Society such as other social workers, children's panel members, students, school students and the public. Also in 1983 the Society was enabled with grants from Central Government to appoint a full-time Training Officer, another example of government support which had its beginnings back in the 1960s. With the revision of case work recording and procedures by Ray Starrs (as already referred to) and the creation of middle management posts from within the fieldwork establishment of the Society there was created within a remarkably short time an organisation which was equipped for the 1980s both in terms of the service which it could provide and in relation to developments taking place outwith the R.S.S.P.C.C.

Looking back to external factors affecting the work of the Society, Wood considers the internal changes to have been of vital importance. In the late 1960s for instance there was growing attention to the problem of the battered child and with the help of the N.S.P.C.C. the Scottish Society were able to attract Professor Henry Kempe of Denver to a conference at Moray House College. Kempe had been the paediatrician responsible for connoting the phrase 'battered child' and as this was one of the first Scottish conferences on the theme, the auditorium was packed with over three hundred representatives from social work, health services, police, education and voluntary organisations. This initiative was to be matched by the Society nine years later with the setting up of the first Special Unit in Scotland for non-accidental injury to children in Glasgow at the Overnewton Centre (this was also to provide a unique experiment in partnership between the R.S.S.P.C.C., Strathclyde Region, the Greater Glasgow Health Board and Central Government who shared in the funding). In the intervening years however, increasing concern and a number of tragic cases on both sides of the border had led to the introduction of procedures and co-ordinating arrangements involving all the relevant services. All this led to increasing demands and expectations on the R.S.S.P.C.C. and had further implications for training and support for staff and for collaboration.

Nevertheless while extreme cases of physical abuse were of great public concern (and thereby could also command potential financial support for activity to prevent it) Wood stressed that the Society had always been careful to indicate that these only constituted around ten per cent of its overall work. Increasingly in recent years much of the Society's work was protective and supportive with families who brought themselves to the Society because they wanted help and support. The development of statutory care had not removed the demand for this supportive function — in fact the reverse — because of the vulnerability of children to a wide range of circumstances and because certain people in any community would always seek the help of a voluntary organisation like the R.S.S.P.C.C.

The increasing trend of self-referrals had led and was still resulting in a change, not in the Society's role, but in the variety of tasks which were carried out. Wood referred to the interesting developments of the experimental work at the R.S.S.P.C.C. Melville House Family Centre where project and group workers were developing a co-operative response to the needs of families and integrating this with the establishment of an information and training unit which would be consultative and educational both to other parts of the R.S.S.P.C.C. and to outside organisations. Wood saw this as an example of the way the work of the Society could develop. Other Branches of the R.S.S.P.C.C. might not produce exact copies of such work because the strength of a voluntary organisation was that it could both experiment and diversify. The Society did not need to standardise its provision but should always be in a position to recognise local and regional differences and have the flexibility to respond accordingly.

Looking at the value of diversity and experiment and linking it with the possibility of considerable independence, Arthur Wood recognised the danger that a voluntary organisation could be tempted to become too varied and pursue too many different goals. It was sometimes

MELVILLE HOUSE FAMILY CENTRE (1984)
Melville House at 41 Polwarth Terrace, Edinburgh. Formerly the Children Shelter, it now comprises a Family Centre and (in the extension) the Head Office of the R.S.S.P.C.C.

difficult for staff who were heavily involved and in direct contact with extreme need to avoid following the variety of possibilities which could emerge for a response from the R.S.S.P.C.C.

Traditionally in a voluntary organisation this was the function assumed by the voluntary policy makers to ensure that the organisation remained 'pure' and committed to its objectives. The Society had recognised in the last few years that it was becoming increasingly difficult for one Executive Committee to assume the whole task of supervising a complex differentiated organisation.

Therefore it had begun to use two variants of organisational structure both of them designed to allow supporters with specialist interest or professional expertise to contribute from that basis rather than simply from the more general or diffuse commitments of support in membership of the organisation as a whole. One variant was by the involvement of these different interests in specialist sub-committees providing advice and recommending on policy as in the case of fund raising, staff, training, legal issues etc. The other variant was by increasing the involvement of the Council — arranging for it to meet more frequently and providing in advance the necessary packaged

MELVILLE HOUSE FAMILY CENTRE
Group activities are a basic element of the Melville House approach.

information so that realistic debates could cover policy or professional issues. This movement towards a greater involvement of the Society supporters on issues of a national or organisational nature, was in recognition of the need to keep as broad a base of support as possible. District Committees had tended to become largely fund-raising in their focus and therefore might not be sufficiently rewarding to individuals who had particular interests in policy and practice. The proposed new system which strengthened the Council would provide a genuine opportunity for participation for those whose interest was to seek that and would allow the Society as a national organisation to benefit from the opinion and involvement of as widely representative a group as possible.

As General Secretary therefore, it has been necessary for Arthur Wood to address the implications of the ever changing scene in child care and social work and the need to ensure and service an effective system of committees for the Society's management. In addition it had been necessary to review with increasing emphasis in recent years the whole question of funding.

As already referred to it was necessary for the R.S.S.P.C.C. within the general field of social welfare to professionalise itself in terms of becoming more consciously analytical of its situation, more specific about its objectives and less pragmatic about its policies. To do this effectively it requires financial resources on a regular and continuous basis otherwise even well-planned and long-term strategy could be adversely affected by *ad hoc* decisions enforced through financial crisis.

Historically, the R.S.S.P.C.C. had usually had success in the fund-raising field, but as Lord Wheatley emphasised more than once in the Society's Annual Reports, a heavy reliance on legacy income was very difficult to manage in terms of prediction for future policy decisions. When Arthur Wood joined the Society the Headquarters staff incorporated the crucial position of Financial Secretary, occupied at that time by Lyall Horsburgh, a long-serving official of the R.S.S.P.C.C. who retired in 1979 after more than thirty years' service. Lyall Horsburgh was expected to maintain a tight financial management and give a detailed account of even minor expenditure to the Finance Committee on a monthly basis. On the fund-raising side there was usually a Headquarters organiser who combined support to District fund-raising activities with the role of Assistant Secretary. In addition, there were three area organisers in Scotland based at Aberdeen, Glasgow and Edinburgh.

Wood considers that one of the major changes in his period of office has been the professionalisation of the process of fund-raising. By this he is quick to stress that he does not mean the use of outside professional fund-raisers, nor does he imply a reflection on the many voluntary members throughout Scotland who, through committees and other groups sustained support for the Society over so many years. Wood is, in fact, referring to the Society's willingness to adopt a more analytical approach to the strategy required to achieve genuine long-term funding and an income which will eventually match expenditure. The General Secretary believes that the R.S.S.P.C.C. is close to solving this problem in terms of organisational method if not yet in terms of results. He points to 1979 as a critical year when, faced with a record deficit of nearly £100,000, it was necessary for the Society to actively consider its future direction and to make in effect a choice between cutting expenditure by reducing service for children or finding ways to obtain additional funds. In the event they chose the latter course, accepting that this would be likely to mean an initial increase in expenditure to achieve the returns sought for. The strategy was firstly to review and increase the support which could be given to the network of District Committees and Friends Groups throughout the country and to ensure that their most successful activities were used to the maximum effect throughout the Society. Secondly, to try and close the gap between expenditure and income, there would be a drive to seek new sources of funds from areas which had not been previously tapped by the R.S.S.P.C.C. Thirdly to create the most positive climate for such a strategy to succeed more initiatives would be taken to use the opportunities provided by the press and media and to promote the R.S.S.P.C.C. as widely as possible.

Like his predecessor and in common with all office bearers of the Society Arthur Wood has always had a great respect, admiration and

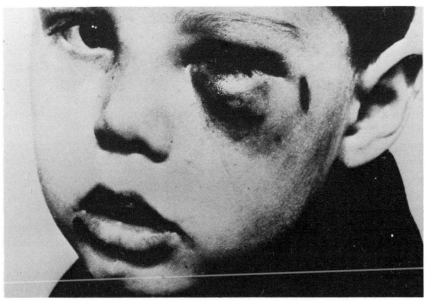

NON-ACCIDENTAL INJURY TO CHILDREN
This and other forms of violence in the family represent
ten per cent of the Society's work.

affection for the members of the one hundred or so District Committees and Friends Groups and for the members of the Scottish Children's League, the junior branch of the R.S.S.P.C.C. Together they formed the voluntary network of the Society's main support. They are, as Wood puts it, the 'life blood' of the R.S.S.P.C.C. and without their commitment the Society could not continue. In the years gone by the relationship between the General Secretary and District Committees and between the Committees and the local Branch Inspector provided a sufficient framework of support in most cases. In recent years however the complexities of life both within and outwith the organisation had changed that relationship to some extent; hence the need to ensure a strong and effective local support for all such groups. This objective is at present being addressed through the role of area organisers (whose number has been increased) and they will have a crucial responsibility for providing a link between the Head Office of the Society and every District for fund-raising purposes, not only through sustaining their regular efforts but also by ensuring that they are given effective back-up through the provision of suitable promotional and public relations material of the Society, as well as regular information.

With regard to seeking new sources of income two recent developments were cited by Wood. Firstly the membership scheme which invites supporters of the R.S.S.P.C.C. to commit themselves to an annual subscription of £5 minimum with a particular encouragement to consider the use of covenants. To some extent this is a return to the original principles of the Society as a voluntary organisation whereby supporters who are emotionally attracted to the objectives can identify with it and belong to the organisation. The importance was also stressed of giving members a return for their commitment through the provision of regular information about the work of the Society.

The other development cited was the use of sponsorship from commerce and industry, in particular by costing the expenditure on an average R.S.S.P.C.C. Inspector and encouraging firms either individually or together (i.e. in a club) to sponsor an Inspector for a certain period of time. The sponsors involved collectively could be encouraged to meet occasionally to share in the experience of the Inspector and again the responsibility of the Society for providing regular feedback and information was crucial.

So far as public relations were concerned, fund-raising as Wood appreciated was dependent upon the image of the R.S.S.P.C.C. and the work it was doing. Obviously most people were sympathetic towards work with children and therefore the Society had the advantage of working in a generally supportive context. However, it was essential to ensure that the image was keeping pace with activities and there was an important responsibility therefore to keep the public informed. Many people for instance associated 'cruelty' with only the extreme cases of physical abuse — understandably because of the publicity which this tragic problem received. However in terms of R.S.S.P.C.C. experience, physical abuse only represented about ten per cent of the caseload and recently the Society had been concentrating on publicity about its work

ALMA THE ELEPHANT

The nine-foot-high pink elephant, constructed by the R.S.S.P.C.C. for Centenary Year and adopted by Round Tables in Scotland for fund raising purposes in aid of the Society. On the left is Douglas Turner, R.S.S.P.C.C. Promotions Organiser with Raymond Binnie, past Chairman, Area 39, Round Table.

in the preventive field. In public relations terms the R.S.S.P.C.C. had been greatly assisted by the voluntary support of Polecon Co. Ltd. whose professional advice and practical involvement had been of significant value especially in relation to press liaison. Their contacts had also enabled the Society to engage the support on a voluntary basis of individuals from the business and industrial sector who contributed their expertise and their experience on many different aspects of the management of the Society.

Looking back over all the developments since 1968 an inevitable question to Arthur Wood was to ask what all this had meant to the role of the General Secretary. He felt that the most important change was that from the necessity of being a 'Jack of all trades' he was now supported by a team at Head Office with appropriate professional expertise. The main task of the General Secretary to be the translator or interpreter or communicator between the staff of the organisation and the managing committees remained. In his view this meant that as the manager of the professional staff team it was probably helpful that he was a generalist with no professional axe to grind. Thus he could act as a reasonable test of the likely response of committee members who of necessity were in most cases at a greater distance from day-to-day operations. If the specialist staff could explain a proposal to him as General Secretary and convince him of the case for a new development for instance, it was also likely that the support of the committee could be obtained. Another benefit of the expertise available within the Headquarters team was that instead of having to be himself a sponsor of new ideas he could rely on others to pick up indicators and feed them into the management team where they would be tested, processed and developed to the point where they could be suggested as policy to the committee. However Wood also stressed that not all developments came through that channel and there were other occasions when ideas and initiatives came from committee members. Then the reverse process applied in that the staff had the responsibility of refining the idea, assessing it and, if it proved effective, building it into practice.

Wood also felt that a major part of the General Secretary's role was to explain, promote and where necessary defend the Society's work to the outside world. He recognised that the diffusion of responsibility allied to delegated management could increase the difficulties in his fundamental responsibility to answer for the organisation. So far in its history the R.S.S.P.C.C. had managed to remain involved in many contentious areas of activity, to support some developments, to oppose others and sometimes to have a minority position but it had also avoided becoming 'tagged' with a particular political or ideological label, holding always to its focus on the Prevention of Cruelty to Children.

In a sense the General Secretary saw the voluntary network of support as representing the 'check' and himself in certain circumstances as representing the interests of the voluntary members in a complex area of work when the increasing demands on the Society's professionals could lead in the heat of the battle to forgetfulness and the fact that at the end of the day the organisation belonged to the voluntary members. It was for this reason in particular that Wood was especially interested in the new proposals for increasing the significant role of the Council in discussions of policy in the future.

In summary, after 23 years with the R.S.S.P.C.C. Wood could not realistically contemplate the likelihood of there being a time when there was no need for the organisation. He accepted the aim of the Society had to be to remove the need for its existence but felt that the dependence and vulnerability of children made this unlikely. The tasks of the R.S.S.P.C.C. would undoubtedly keep changing as they had in the past but as this profile demonstrates the Society had been remarkably prescient when defining the original objectives which still remain.

As a solicitor Wood has obviously had a particular interest in legal aspects of child protection and as a member of the former Scottish Child Law Group had been considering the need and the possibility of a legal information network which might be available to the community generally, including children, with special reference to child protection and children's rights. With the demise of the Scottish Child Law Group, Arthur Wood sees an opportunity for the R.S.S.P.C.C. to fill a possible gap by further developing its information resource at Melville House. This development has been given further impetus by the setting up of an R.S.S.P.C.C. legal committee comprising representatives from the Universities, the Bar, Procurator Fiscal service, private practice and the Children's Panel service.

Looking to the future it was the General Secretary's view that the most important trend at present was the increasing number of self-referrals to the R.S.S.P.C.C. with the opportunities that provided for co-operative and preventive work with the whole family. The Society was still being placed under pressure by demands which required crisis intervention and it was likely that the R.S.S.P.C.C. must continue to provide an avenue of immediate help to those who either would not use the recognised statutory sources or who for whatever reason were not satisfied with the response. Ways had to be found to make further progress in the field of prevention and seek methods which at the end of the day would reduce the circumstances whereby children were exposed to unnecessary suffering and which would create the kind of positive relationships within families which might avoid the need for any outside body, whether statutory or voluntary, to intervene.

Arthur Wood had been particularly impressed by the comment of a mother when interviewed on television about the way in which she had been helped by the R.S.S.P.C.C. Her response was 'the most important thing the Society did was to make us independent'.

To the present General Secretary that seemed a satisfying objective to reach for as the R.S.S.P.C.C. entered its second century.

PART II — *The View of a professional Social Worker*

As indicated in the previous section the Society began to plan during the early 70s a conscious process of in-service training and staff development. Ray Starrs entered the service of the Society in 1973 with the task, as a professional social worker, of building upon the *ad hoc* development work begun by part-time consultancy. He is quite clear that he entered an organisation in which the staff were already beginning to examine their role and function, stimulated by the research activity referred to earlier in this profile. This was taking place in a wider context within which social work in the statutory field was still establishing itself and determining its own attitudes and roles, in which professionalism within social work practice was extending its influence and its training and qualifications; and also in which reorganisation into larger local authority units and new health administrative units was causing re-examination and re-formulation of policies.

The precise demands for new thinking by the R.S.S.P.C.C. within this total process of change were stimulated by the renewed attention given to child abuse by the repercussions of the Maria Colwell and Richard Clark cases. The intensification of local authority awareness of statutory responsibility was such that there were possible suggestions that there could be no role for voluntary organisations like the R.S.S.P.C.C.

The R.S.S.P.C.C. had to show itself capable of responding to the changing situation of which it was a part and also of making a significant and relevant contribution to the developments which were taking place. The questions which were emerging regarding the appropriateness of residential care for children in need was leading to greater awareness of the importance of providing support for families and the Society had to show itself capable of that task.

Continual change tends to produce anxiety and this was true for both social work and the Society. Workers were desperately needing to define their role.

Ray Starrs utilised the documentation which the Society had collected as a result of its research activity. He wanted the Society to answer three questions. What is the Society doing? How is it doing it? What should it be doing? The material collected by the research provided the basis for the answers to these questions. It also enabled decisions to be made regarding allocation of resources and staff development. The Society, therefore, could quickly establish a field work structure within which officers had a clearly defined role based upon a clear conception of the way in which the Society could make its best contribution to welfare and the tasks they were required to fulfil.

Having established the basic structure it was necessary to build a middle management structure to support and facilitate the work. He used the annual training exercise, developed in co-operation with

Moray House College as a consultant training agency, for this purpose. This was linked with a process of secondment of selected staff for professional training as social workers so that they could return to fill key posts in the overall staffing structure.

It was considered important that all staff should receive developmental training appropriate to their function and this was gradually established within the Society. The Society recognised it had a variety of roles and functions and, therefore, it was not only social work training which was required but a varied package including group work and community education skills. What was more important than the precise specialisation was the quality of performance that was produced by training.

At the same time communication within the staff of the Society had been improved by group and team meetings, middle management and supervision meetings and by allocation and assessment meetings. These had a training and development function and were aimed at producing a consistent approach to the tasks of the organisation.

This progress enabled the appointment of specialist officers to intensify the work of the Society in different areas of work. The first of these was W. Brown, appointed as Development Officer, who enabled the Society to see the strong link between experimental and pioneering projects and the improvement of the general work of the Society. This pioneering work led to the appointment of a Training Officer and further professional advisory staff.

The opportunity presented by the closure of Melville House as a residential children's unit was seized upon by the Development Officer to establish a national resource unit for the Society. The concept was that of an 'engine-room' for the whole organisation. With a resource unit the Society could experiment, collect information, review practice and develop specialised research. The Melville House unit has to be seen as responding to and providing for the needs and questions of the whole organisation.

It was essential that it did not become an elitist establishment separate from the rest of the work. It must remain firmly rooted in the on-going work of the Society and must be realistic and relevant to the objectives of the Society.

These objectives were being continually clarified in relation to changes within social welfare but it had never been necessary to change them. The role of the voluntary organisation within the field of welfare was clearly confirmed by the Wolfenden Report in the mid-70s.

In the last ten years the increased attention given to non-accidental injury and child abuse procedures had made the Society clarify the principles upon which its own support was offered to the community. The Society was showing itself very ready to co-operate with the increasing trend towards recognising the capacity of the community to accept responsibility for care. A voluntary organisation was very well

AN INSPECTOR CALLS

(a)   (b)

equipped to help the community to develop its capacity for caring. In particular the voluntary organisation had to come to terms with the competition for scarce resources and had to show how best to use these resources and to share and co-operate with others in developing them.

The Society was recognising that it had great responsibility in working in the field of individual's rights and in protecting the rights of children and families. It was no longer appropriate to make these decisions for people but instead to provide support for people to take responsibility for their own decisions. This recognised that the role of the Society extended into areas of health and social care as well as law enforcement. It also meant (and this was important) that the Society had an educational function. Within these wider remits, however, the Society continually had to remind itself that its express purpose was to protect children from abuse and neglect. Its special expertise and

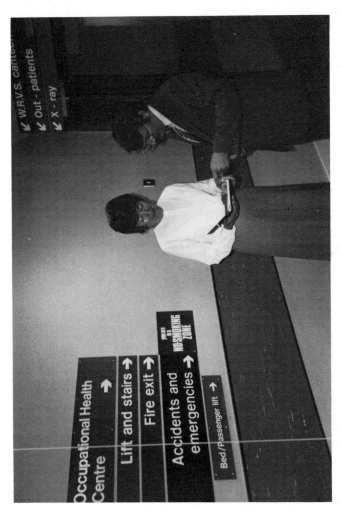

(c) Checking with the hospital department.

interest, therefore, was to inform these other areas of community care and act as a stimulant to action, as a watchdog over action, and as a promotional body.

The emerging question for the Society, therefore, was one of balancing its educational and developmental role with its watchdog, protective, or investigative role. The Society had a great opportunity to use its learning from its work with children in its work with the community. The same principles which emerge from a study of children's needs can be utilised in the development of caring policy within the community. Independence and responsibility are learned within a caring and secure environment within which relationships based on honesty and openness can lead to sharing and co-operative endeavour.

The Society is learning this lesson from its own work and may be able to help others in their turn to discover the truth of these principles. Ray Starrs is hopeful that it can.

I I

THE NEXT STEP . . .

It is doubtful whether it is appropriate at the conclusion of this profile to try to look too far into the future for the R.S.S.P.C.C. and the issues with which it is concerned. It is certainly the responsibility of an analysis like this to try to indicate in summary the discernible trends which have been recorded.

Despite a natural degree of reluctance on the part of those influential in the Society to suggest as individuals the future path of national policy, there is nevertheless an indication of an organisation which will proceed steadily in the process of refining itself and organising itself to focus upon the crucial issues of child protection which are presented to it.

The process of adaptation to need and to the social context and to the developing social attitudes which this profile has tried to emphasise has resulted in an organisation which began as directive and controlling, gradually changing through an emphasis on paternalistic care to a use of professional guidance and finally to the acceptance of supportive self-help and the possibility of client contribution in the care of others. Thus the change has been gradually from that of assuming responsibility on behalf of the community towards that of involving the community in caring for itself.

The past decade has seen a dramatic increase in welfare provision by the state in accordance with its statutory responsibility to 'promote social welfare'. There has corrrespondingly therefore been a con-siderable review of the Society's work and tasks and while the primary activities of the Society (involving intervention in crisis situations and giving short-term support) continue there has been an increasing concern and awareness of the need for different approaches to 'prevention' of cruelty to children and experimentation has taken place with various projects to equip parents and children for family life.

It is likely that the forseeable future will witness further developments in these activities, aided by the resource which has been set up at Melville House Family Centre. In addition the Society's interests in legal aspects and the collation and provision of information will enable it, as in the past, to comment on and influence trends in child protection. At the time of writing the Overnewton Centre in Glasgow — the Special Unit initiated by the R.S.S.P.C.C. in 1978 in response to the problem of non-accidental injury to children — is secured financially until 1987 and, whether or not it continues as a separate entity thereafter, its experience may well provide opportunities for further exploration into aspects of child abuse. Meantime governing all these developments the Society's revised committee system should give greater opportunity for a wider involvement of expertise and interest from the community.

If the future follows similar trends to the past different operational activities may well lead the Society to focus on particular issues related to the protection of children and the prevention of neglect or abuse.

In considering what may be the major issues, the Society could follow its historical origins and consider developments in areas beyond the United Kingdom in the field of child protection and it would therefore be legitimate to make some reference to developments which are taking place in other countries which might also provide an indication of some of the possible future steps of the R.S.S.P.C.C.

In the United States of America for instance there has been the development of mandatory reporting and the independent representation of the child in the legal process. The R.S.S.P.C.C. floated the idea of mandatory reporting as long ago as 1973 but the concept has received little active consideration in the United Kingdom. The machinery for independent representation of children is of course built into the Children Act 1975 but at present (March 1984) has still to be implemented.

Moving to countries where general social conditions and welfare provisions have been similar to our own, it is interesting to note that in Sweden for instance there have been considerable developments. There is, for example, this description of a different approach to the needs of children which has similarities to the record in this profile but may also have some suggestions for the future. The description is taken from *Current Sweden* published by the Swedish Institute in 1979.

> Violence breeds violence. If a parent beats his child, there is a risk that the child will use violence in his future life to achieve his aims. Corporal punishment shapes the child to an authoritative pattern and seems unfitting in a Society which aims to develop the child into a peace-loving, independent individual.
> With these thoughts in mind, an overwhelming majority of the Riksdag (the Parliament) — 259 to 6 — recently outlawed corporal punishment in Sweden by adding a new clause to the Parenthood and Guardianship Code:
> 'The Parent or guardian should exercise the necessary

supervision in accordance with the child's age and other circumstances. The child should not be subjected to corporal punishment or other humiliating treatment.'

The Commission on children's rights proposed this clause to clarify that society can no longer accept the use of violence as a method of upbringing.

In 1920, when *husaga*, the master's right to flog his servant, was abolished in Sweden, the law still stipulated that parents had the right to punish their children. In 1949 the word 'punish' was replaced by 'reprimand'. Not until 1966 was the right of the parent to resort to violence deleted from the *Code of Parenthood*, and the punishment of children of more than 'insignificant corporal correction' considered maltreatment, to be judged by the same rules which apply when 'adults commit acts of physical violence towards adults'.

The new law (in force since July 1st 1979) does not imply that any parent who gives his offspring a box on the ear or smacks his bottom will be immediately drawn into court. The educators, psychologists, sociologists, doctors, social workers and lawyers who supported the legislation, intended to establish a norm for parents and guardians and to initiate a wider discussion of the dangers of violence in all its different forms to which children are constantly exposed in everyday life.

'Even in our well-advanced welfare system, despite our high standard of living, our far-reaching school reforms, the low infant mortality rate and the considerate care of immigrants', Rigmor von Euler explains, 'the conditions of the child are far from ideal'. Rigmor von Euler is Sweden's (and probably the world's) first Ombudsman for Children and is employed by the Swedish Save the Children Federation. 'People must be informed again and again about the dangerous consequences of the physical and mental punishment of children. A recurrent general programme to educate parents and guardians about their rights and their responsibilities seems essential and should be initiated as soon as possible. . . . Surveys have clearly shown that the "battered child syndrome" also exists in many modern Swedish suburbs, where youngsters are predestined to become hard, unfeeling adults, putting their own interests first, often neglecting those of their own children.'

Some Members of Parliament opposed the new law arguing that it was 'unnecessary and even dangerous', because by removing the Biblical right of the father to chastise his child, 'many well-meaning parents would never learn how to behave.' Sixten Pettersson (Cons) put them right. 'In a free

democracy like our own we use words as arguments not blows',
he said during the debate. 'We talk to people not beat them. If
we cannot convince our children with words, we shall never
convince them with a beating.'

Another concept which has been developed in Sweden is that of the
Children's Ombudsman (mentioned above). 'Society assumes in the
first place that parents care for their children and know how to satisfy
their needs, and takes action in the child's best interests only when the
parents fail to do so', says Rigmor von Euler, who is retiring from her job
as Children's Ombudsman after seven years of trail-blazing work.
'There is still a lot of cruel repression and maltreatment. Legislation has
to create a climate where the family can flourish. But we cannot rely
upon legislation to afford adequate protection to the child either. The
child needs his own spokesman to safeguard his rights.'

'Ombudsman' is a Swedish word for representative or
delegate. In English and other languages it is identified with
'an official empowered to investigate complaints of
bureaucratic injustice'. The role of the Ombudsman of the
Swedish Save the Children Federation, however, is merely that
of a spokesman or advocate without legal or political power,
charged with protecting children's rights through
investigation, recommendation and information.

'One of my tasks is to help the individual child in
immediate need of assistance,' declares Bo Carlsson, 33, a
former teacher, sociologist and local politician, who succeeded
Rigmor von Euler as the Swedish Children's Ombudsman on
May 1st 1983. 'My over-all aim is to make the public aware of
children's precarious situation and to be a thorn in the flesh of
reluctant bureaucrats and authorities.'

He intends to exert pressure on local authorities to
improve the children's environment, he wants the expression
'what is best for the child' to be more clearly defined and he
insists that the child's own wishes should always be considered
before a final decision about custody or public care is taken.

Continuing the efforts of his predecessor to create a more
effective organisation to assist children in need of moral and
legal aid, he would like to introduce the institution of the
Children's Ombudsman on a municipal level throughout the
country. 'There should be someone paid by the local
government, with sufficient authority to intervene, and to act
as the child's spokesman in court, on social committees, in the
town planning office, everywhere where the fate of children is
at stake or when parents dispute the custody of their children
or when the child is sent to a public institution or a foster-
home, or to assure adequate play and leisure facilities in new

residential areas. Children should always know that there is someone outside the family on call to help them if need arises.'

Another of the Scandinavian countries, Norway, with a similar approach to welfare provision as in this country, issued in 1981 the following memorandum explaining its reasons for instituting the provision of a Children's Ombudsman which was implemented in September 1981.

ON THE BILL RELATING TO A CHILDREN'S OMBUDSMAN
INTRODUCTION

In February 1981 the Norwegian Storting adopted an Act on a Children's Ombudsman.

In the Bill containing the proposal for the new Act, the Government outlined the following background and reason for the Bill.

Children are an important as well as a weak and vulnerable social group. Good intentions, plans and regulations are not enough to safeguard the interests and needs of children. What we have learned from the UN Children's Year is not least an affirmation of that. The wishes and requirements of children have a fairly low degree of penetration. When confronted with groups with strong organisations and spokesmen children often lose out when important decisions are taken. This is particularly apparent when children's and adults' interests clash.

The Ministry's Bill for the establishment of the post of a Children's Ombudsman is in the main based on the views expressed in the Report of the Committee dealing with legislation relating to children (Nov 1977: 35, The Act Relating to Children and Parents).

THE OMBUDSMAN'S TASKS

The Ombudsman will not have the final authority, but will initially act as an independent body looking after the interests of children.

The Ombudsman's duty is to further children's interests in relation to the authorities and private individuals and institutions, and to follow the development of the quality of childhood.

The Ombudsman is to ensure that the rules and regulations in force for the benefit of children are obeyed in practice. The Ombudsman may also suggest new regulations.

As a permanent hearings instance, and on his own initiative, the Ombudsman may assess the effects of various reports and plans on the quality of childhood.

The Ombudsman shall also make sure that the authorities provide satisfactory information on the rights and needs of children. Everyone shall be entitled to turn to the Ombudsman — children, individual adults, organisations, public bodies etc.

The Ombudsman will not relieve the public administration of its responsibility to safeguard the rights and interests of children. The Ombudsman may bring pressure to bear in order to get that responsibility attended to more efficiently.

In promoting the idea of a Children's Ombudsman in Norway the Ministry there pointed out the following reasons for suggesting that such an office was required.

Children lack the opportunity to safeguard their *own* interests by taking part in political activities, professional bodies, and so on. Children will, moreover, not have the same means of assessing plans and decisions as do adults, and of forming an opinion on how things will affect them.

The professional and industrial bodies play an important part when decisions are made in our society. They are frequently consulted in advance, and quite often proposals are amended so as to become acceptable to those who have been consulted. Children, as a rule, lack such means of influencing events.

Fairly often we see that the regard for children's requirements is contrary to other social considerations. In urban planning matters, for instance, children's requirement for playgrounds may clash with the need for a site for building purposes. When the authorities make their decision in such matters, the well-organised demands of the developers will reach those who make the decision, while attention is seldom given to children's need to play.

Children are also in a much weaker position than those who are of age and adults with regard to securing their legal rights. Children, for instance, do not have the opportunity to make a formal protest against plans made, as do any adults involved.

Children's lack of capability to attain their goals by political means, implies that there is no way for them to bring about a change in their factual and legal position if that position does not protect their interests adequately. Children do not have the vote and consequently they cannot react by helping to replace a party or an individual candidate.

Many parents have made a major effort to improve the quality of childhood. They have campaigned to preserve

children's playgrounds, to make roads used by children on
their way to school safer, to provide more kindergartens and
better schools. They have also done a number of other things in
the local environment. But parents also lack unifying and
effective organisations whose main task it would be to
formulate demands for a more children and family orientated
policy on the part of the authorities.

The public bodies looking after children's interests are
generally weak. Moreover, they largely do not have the legal
authority to intervene against plans or decisions conflicting
with the interests of children. Some of the work in progress in
the public administration, to strengthen the position of
children has already been mentioned. The Ministry considered
it important to intensify the efforts of the Administration on
children's affairs.

The Ministry found there is a definite need for a strong,
independent body whose duty it will be to safeguard children's
social interests in the wider sense, both in relation to the
authorities and private individuals and institutions.

The Ministry came to the conclusion that a Children's
Ombudsman would be the most effective solution. An
Ombudsman will have greater authority and penetration than
a council or a committee. The Ombudsman will also have far
greater opportunity to continually follow plans and reports
prepared by the authorities and private and public
institutions. An Ombudsman will be able to react far more
quickly than a council or a committee, which, after all, will
only have a limited number of meetings during the year.

The Ministry, furthermore, considered it imperative that
the Children's Ombudsman will be a *visible* institution for
children and others requiring the Ombudsman's help in
certain matters.

In the United Kingdom probably the greatest stimulus to developments in relation to the rights and interests of children in recent
years was the work which took place before and during the International Year of the Child 1979. In Scotland as in most other countries a
conscious attempt was made to emphasise the theme of *listening to
children*. All over the world policy makers, administrators, professional
child care workers and adults, especially parents, were encouraged to
consider the potentiality which children had to understand and to
contribute to decisions about their future. Adults were faced with the
challenge to find new ways of communicating with and consulting
children and to accept the responsibility for informing them and
educating them in such a way that they would be responsible for their
own actions. The Scottish Committee adopted the slogan 'count me in',

given to them by a class of primary school children, reminding all and sundry that children were not simply the passive recipients of decisions and action by others on their behalf.

Stimulated by this approach but responding to wider movements of self-assertion by children and young people, there has emerged around the same time in the United Kingdom both a significant development in forming organisations of school pupils and also a coming together of groups of children and young people in residential care to express their points of view to the respective authorities who have the responsibility for them. Within these movements there have been assertions of view that often the professionals who intervene to interpret the needs of children and young people were considered by the young people themselves to have a distorted view of their situation and needs and therefore to represent them inadequately.

Despite the experience and the evidence of the International Year of the Child however, there are still many situations where the opportunity for children and young people to articulate their needs and views about their future is not fully provided.

A hundred years after the foundation of the R.S.S.P.C.C. therefore there are still many relevant issues to debate regarding the best ways of promoting and protecting children's interests and even recent history provides its controversy. The creation of Children's Hearings in Scotland for instance is seen by many as a most progressive development; yet there are questions as to whether in searching for less formality to encourage participation some element of protection of rights provided by the more formal process of law may not have been lost. Others would question as to whether the really disadvantaged, for instance those who so often formed the clients of the R.S.S.P.C.C., are able to function within this less formal structure so that their real interests and needs remain unrevealed. The unimplemented machinery for independent representation for children has already been referred to while other issues such as assumption of parental rights by local authorities and the question of access to children in care are currently the focus of attention from the point of view of the protection of children's interests.

As an independent agency operating under the authority of Royal Charter, the Society, looking to the future, seems soundly placed to follow the legitimate role for a voluntary organisation as suggested by the recent Barclay report: providing a specialist service for vulnerable children; fulfilling a watchdog role on their behalf; focussing on prevention of unnecessary suffering; and carrying on innovative and pioneering work in terms of approach and method.

The setting up of the Society in the last century was triggered off from the ripples caused by the plight of a child called Mary Ellen. It is appropriate to finish this profile then with another story, told by Astrid Lindgren the celebrated children's author during her address while being awarded the Peace Prize of the German Book Trade (Deutschen Buchhandels).

> A young mother, firmly believing in the Biblical wisdom of 'he who loves his son, punishes him', and who considered that her little boy had deserved a good spanking, sent him into the garden to collect a rod. He came back after a long while, crying: 'I could not find a stick, but here is a stone, you can hit me with that.' The mother looked at her boy and started crying herself. Suddenly she saw it all with the eyes of the child, who must have thought, 'My mother wants to hurt me, so she may as well use a stone'. For a long time they hugged each other, then she put the stone on the mantelpiece and vowed: 'No violence!' Perhaps we should all put a stone on our mantelpiece to remind ourselves and our children: 'No violence!' It might be a tiny contribution towards peace in the world.

The Royal Scottish Society for Prevention of Cruelty to Children will surely continue to make its own distinctive and unique contribution to child protection, as it moves forward into new areas of work and need.

POSTSCRIPT

by Rev. H. M. Ricketts, M.A., B.D.

Chairman, R.S.S.P.C.C. Executive Committee

I have gladly accepted the invitation to try to write a short Postscript to this book, principally because it affords me an opportunity of offering to the author the warmest thanks of the Society. Had Mr Brian Ashley not been one of our very good friends from the days when he was Director of the School of Community Studies at Moray House College of Education, Edinburgh which he has demonstrated by his interest and by his writings over many years, it might have been difficult for us to approach him to undertake this work and even more difficult for him to accede to our request. Mature students who are presenting a thesis say, for a Ph.D. degree are usually given a fairly free hand as to their choice of subject, while scholars of the experience and calibre of Mr Ashley can please themselves as to what subject matter they wish to turn their mind. But in the case of this present Centenary history of the R.S.S.P.C.C. he was not entirely allowed free rein. There were certain aspects in its policies and in their implementation which the Society wished particularly to have underlined. Mr Ashley has thus, willy-nilly, had to steer his barque between the Scylla of writing in a way that would be acceptable to sociologists and social historians, and the Charybdis of what, for lack of a better expression, might be termed the day-to-day work of the Society's officers, which would appeal to the rank and file of its members. That Mr Ashley has succeeded so ably in this act of navigation is fully evidenced by the foregoing chapters, and for that, as well as for accommodating himself to our wishes, we offer him our congratulations and sincere thanks for a task so generously undertaken at no cost to the Society.

Institutions which are established with a view to their being long-lasting are rarely the product of the spur of the moment. This has been clearly illustrated in the case of children and the efforts made in seeking to prevent cruelty towards them. This abuse of children goes back a very long way, and it is wrong to assume, as some suppose, that betterment in the treatment of them only came in with the dawn of the Christian era — although the Prophet Zechariah did have a vision of the re-built Jerusalem with 'boys and girls playing in the streets thereof' (Chap. 8, v.

6). Ancient Greece led the world of its day in culture of every form but its attitude to children was appalling. Nowhere was this more so than in the city of Sparta, which boasted of being able to field the strongest army in the country. Baby girls counted for absolutely nothing; for military purposes they were useless. Boys were in quite another category. If, at birth, they were of apparently acceptable physique, good and well. But if they appeared weak and sickly, the heads of the city were called in and if they decided to give an ailing male child a second chance, he was put into an earthenware pot, carried above the snow-line on Mount Taygetus and left there over-night. If on the morrow he were still alive, he was taken downhill to the city and restored to his mother with whom he remained until the age of seven. Thereafter he was drafted into a special wing of the armed forces which trained what we would call Boy Soldiers. Admittedly that is a severe and isolated case, but the fact remains that, until comparatively recently, children and their rights were consistently ignored. As the author of this book has shown, they were regarded as mere chattels, the property of their parents who could do and deal with them as they pleased.

Brian Ashley has been at great pains to set out how this attitude to children, especially from the eighteenth century onwards, gradually underwent a welcome change, which owed much to that century's philosophers and social experimenters. We all know that the U.S.A. is a very young country compared with ours and that most of their culture and institutions were taken over initially from Western Europe. But it has to be conceded that the U.S.A. through the celebrated case of Mary Ellen, stole a march on us by establishing before we did a Society for Prevention of Cruelty to Children; incidentally, Mr Ashley quotes a longer and better version of the Mary Ellen affair than most of us had ever known. But the fact remains that a wind of change was blowing in many countries and it was only a matter of time before New York's example would be followed elsewhere.

The story of the founding one hundred years ago of what eventually became the R.S.S.P.C.C. makes fascinating reading. The references to specific cases investigated by the Society's Inspectors revive many memories. But perhaps most important of all is the attention drawn in this book to what extent the Society has developed throughout the century. It would seem that, for the greater part of that long span, the Society continued more or less as in its formative years. Changes there were, of course, many of them induced by two World Wars. But one can confidently say that the most and the greatest changes of all have occurred in the last twenty to thirty years generated to some extent by Government legislation, which increasingly recognised the rights of children and enforced their acknowledgement. The greatest mile-stone of all was the coming into effect to the Social Work (Scotland) Act of 1968, which *inter alia*, laid firmly upon the statutory authorities the care and welfare of children. Contrary, perhaps, to some expectations this

REV. H. M. RICKETTS, B.D.
Chairman R.S.S.P.C.C. since 1979.

piece of legislation was not mistrusted by the R.S.S.P.C.C. but welcomed. There may have been some who thought that the passing of this Act spelt the end of voluntary agencies which relied so heavily upon public generosity to keep them afloat, while the statutory bodies would continue to have access to a seemingly bottomless purse. But things have not evolved as one expected fifteen years ago. True, the difficulty of trying to balance the books is still with us, so far as the R.S.S.P.C.C. is concerned, but the present national recession has also placed financial restraints on the various regional authorities in Scotland, so that they

THE COUNTESS OF MAR AND KELLIE, O.B.E., J.P.
Chairman R.S.S.P.C.C. Centenary Committee, 1984.

too are unable to do all that is laid upon them to do, and what they would like to do so far as the care of children is concerned.

All of which brings us back to the question which many have been posing: 'Has the R.S.S.P.C.C. any right to use the word "celebrate" in connection with the present Centenary?' What is there to celebrate? Have we made any real advance in the last hundred years? In 1968 the Social Work (Scotland) Act gave us cause to hope that with many more Social Workers in the field the instances of cruelty to children could be more closely monitored and the numbers substantially reduced. For several years past the number of children involved in cases referred to the Society's officers have averaged around 10,000 per annum and there seems to be little prospect of a significant reduction in that number. Indeed if it were financially possible to increase our field staff, those numbers would undoubtedly rise. In a word statutory authorities and voluntary agencies even working together are hardly making a sizeable impression on the situation. There are various reasons given for this state of affairs. Among them may be named unemployment, men more about the house than at work, with all the problems that can bring — frustrated, readier than usual to cuff their children — and their wives — alcoholism, gambling, a general lowering of standards, and much else besides. So, are we not bemusing ourselves by regarding the events of this Centenary year as a 'celebration'? I do not think so, and that for two reasons. Firstly, taking 10,000 as the average annual number of children to come into contact with Inspectors (in the 20s there are instances of the number exceeding 20,000), by a simple computation one arrives at the conservative figure of one million children who have been protected by the Society from being the victims of further cruelty. That is something in itself to be proud of and grateful for. That alone would justify the Society's existence for a hundred years. Secondly, and more importantly, the Society has not been standing still, resting on its past achievements and content to conserve the aims and use the methods of former generations. This had become increasingly evident in the past ten years. Prevention of Cruelty to Children remains, and always will remain, the primary object of the Society. But whereas in the past this aim was achieved by the Inspector calling on homes where cruelty to children had allegedly taken place, warning parents and sometimes bringing them before the courts, the vision of the Society is now being widened unbelievably as to new and better ways of combatting cruelty to children. The accent is still on prevention, but the means of making it effective are being concentrated on the parents as well as on the children. Due to the shift in policy on the part of local authorities with regard to placing children deprived or otherwise at risk, into accredited places of shelter, the two children's homes which for years had been part of the Society's establishment became redundant. There were no second thoughts what to do with Dundonald in Ayrshire. But what of Melville House in Edinburgh, a splendid building but standing empty with no foreseeable future? Gradually a new use for it evolved. What Eddleston in Peeblesshire could do in the country, Melville House could surely accomplish in the city. 'Tall oaks from little acorns grow.' Beginning with a minumum staff the centre has developed into a hive of activity. Social education, parentcraft, home management, and many of the domestic problems which the former Women Visitors sought to solve are now regular features in the Melville House syllabus. Perhaps the most heartening break-through is that fathers and mothers who may have been at logger-heads with each other are encouraged to come to the

(a) Young volunteers enjoy the sunshine.

NEW SETTLEMENT CAMP, EDDLESTON

(b) The Kitchen/Dining Hut, Bunkhouse and Games Hut.

centre *together*; often they are accompanied by their children, leaving behind them an atmosphere of strife and sharing for an hour or two the peace and friendliness of an entirely different situation. A follow-up of this style of therapy has already shown that this new approach is effective and that after such a 'night out' parents and children return home with a clearer conception in their minds of what family life can be. Is that not, then, another reason why the Society should embark upon its second century with a new hope in its heart, this example of new approaches in its sights — to be repeated in different ways in other areas of Scotland and with confidence in its future?

Britain is the country par excellence in Western Europe for charitable institutions. Some other countries do boast some but these have mainly been motivated by and are carried on under the aegis of the Churches. Charitable organisations are essentially a British institution. The R.S.S.P.C.C. is proud to be one of them. Brian Ashley has put himself to a great deal of trouble in researching a century's collection of minutes and other records, and in interviewing those still with us who have been active in the work of the Society at all levels. May I once again thank him for the magnificent contribution he has made to the story of the R.S.S.P.C.C. and express the hope that the people of Scotland will continue to support one of its own best-known charities which has done so much for the good of Scotland's children in the past and means to go on doing so in the future.

APPENDIX A

THE SHAPING OF VOLUNTARY ORGANISATIONS

The social and economic conditions within the nineteenth century, which are described in the early part of this History together with the philosophical and religious ideas which were developing at the same time, meant that this century also witnessed the peak of charity, benevolence or philanthropy. This was the context within which the voluntary organisation, as it is now seen in British society and which our study is concerned to understand, became the accepted vehicle for the expression of much of that philanthropy. During this period the form, structure and ritual devices of the British voluntary organisation emerged and were shaped by the trend of that philanthropy and the reactions to it and the tensions surrounding it. The same social and economic currents which produced the needs to which philanthropy and voluntarism were a response also strongly influenced and conditioned the responses themselves.

Brian Harrison in his essay 'Philanthropy and the Victorians' (*The Peacable Kingdom* O.U.P. 1982, pp. 217-259) quotes 'that of 640 London charities alive in 1860 no less than 279 were founded between 1800 and 1850, and 144 between 1850 and 1860; by the 1860's they were raising annually about as much as the total annual expenditure of the poor law system in the whole of England and Wales.'

The massive development of philanthropy was, of course, due to the increasing effects of the economic and social developments during the century upon the masses and the awakening social consciousness within society. This awakening consciousness of need allied to the philosophical, religious and political ideas which were developing led to an increased recognition of a degree of social responsibility which either had to be expressed through independent individual action which was so integral to the spirit of the period or through some form of collective action which was emerging as an alternative stream of response and which became stronger as the century progressed. In the extreme forms these two alternative responses were in conflict with each other and antipathetic to each other. The tension between them strongly influenced the way philanthropy and voluntarism developed and has continued within the voluntary movement ever since.

As Harrison points out the three great social reform movements of the nineteenth century (the attacks on Sabbath breaking; intemperance and animal cruelty) were part of a general awareness at the beginning of the nineteenth century in that they all featured in the Vice Society's *Address to the Public* in 1803. All, however, became the subject of distinct and separate

223

movements which developed throughout the century. In this they demonstrated the first principles of voluntary movements in that they develop and
gain strength by attracting their own adherents who, because of their own
interests, support and join particular organisations. Philanthropy, voluntarism
or altruism is not so likely to manifest itself as a generalised capacity so much as
a specialised focus based on interest.

In his essay 'Animals and the State' (ibid. pp. 82–122) Harrison analyses
one of these movements in describing the development of the R.S.P.C.A. which
was founded in 1824 and which conducted, in his view, a classic campaign
during the nineteenth century. It is a significant analysis for our study, in that in
its organisation and the methods it adopted as, for instance, in the use of
Inspectors, the careful prosecution of selected cases in the courts, the close
relationship and understanding with the police, and the willingness to work
towards legislation and state action, it probably provided, consciously or
unconsciously, a basic model for the development of a voluntary organisation
concerned with an attack on cruelty to children. Probably even more
significant however for a study of the prevention of cruelty to children is that the
movement to attack cruelty to animals developed over fifty years earlier. This
may appear to say something strange about the vagaries of the Victorian social
consciousness and social conscience but it is probably more clearly evidence of
the ambivalence about responsibility and how to organise it, to which reference
has already been made. The sensitivity of philanthropy and voluntarism
towards intervention into the stronger and more sacrosanct of institutions of
Victorian society, particularly the strong social institution of the family, which
was seen to be the bastion of Victorian individualism and Victorian values,
probably explains this slower awakening of responsibility for the welfare of
children who were seen to be clearly the responsibility of the family. This
sensitivity and ambivalence about the rights of children persists through the
history of child welfare until the present day. As will be seen later the sensitivity
about intervention which was the necessary concomitant of the strong
Victorian emphasis upon individualism was the source of much general
suspicion regarding philanthropy and voluntarism.

As we study the emergence, development and persistence of a voluntary
organisation which was founded towards the end of the nineteenth century and
has had a continued existence of one hundred years, it is helpful to us to
understand the tensions, criticisms and emotions which shaped and tempered
the voluntary movement during the nineteenth century. Harrison's excellent
analysis of Victorian philanthropy in the essay already referred to can provide
us with a basis for understanding such a voluntary organisation.

Harrison firstly makes the point that it is almost impossible to estimate the
extent of philanthropy because the exact nature of contributions, the way they
are made and re-distributed and the exact way to define them is difficult to
identify. The non-monetary contributions within philanthropic and the
voluntary movements in the form of voluntary labour, contribution of ideas and
expertise, and the gift of time and effort are immeasurable.

This fact is still true of the voluntary movement and is even more
significant in a society which increasingly measures all effort in economic terms
and defines the economic contribution to society in terms of participation in the
so-called productive sector. The immeasureability of voluntary effort in terms
of these criteria, in arguments about society's resources, appears to be used as an

excuse for omitting all such effort from the calculation of the nation's balance-sheets. An alternative view is emerging and researchers at Linkoping University in Sweden, using the criteria of the productive sector and the respectable methods of collecting 'hard data', have developed respectable and accepted figures which challenge the tendency to ignore this massive contribution to society. Their figures show that if the real burden assumed by voluntary effort within child care, within the family, within the relative and kin network, within the neighbourhood and within the voluntary movement is genuinely costed then it can challenge in magnitude the so-called productive sector. If this view were to be taken then the right of the productive economy to dominate considerations of national importance would also be challenged. It is possible, however, that this concealment of effort and this unwillingness to place voluntarism genuinely alongside other efforts within society had its origins in the strong independence and individualistic separatism of Victorian phil-anthropy. Harrison also differentiates between the philanthropist who contributed his own money to alleviate social misery and his own efforts to benefit others and the social reformer who campaigned to redistribute the resources of others towards the general good. In recognising these two aspects of welfare movements which often merged in voluntary organisations, particular-ly when philanthropists realised that their individual efforts were insufficient to meet the magnitute of the need, Harrison helps us to identify different aspects of the voluntary organisation which persist even now; namely the capacity to attract private philanthropy to redirect resources to the benefit of others together with campaigning for educational objectives directed towards changing the circumstances which produce the need.

Motivation for philanthropy or altruism is always an intriguing basis for discussion and analysis. Religion could be seen to be the predominant motivating force for Victorian philanthropy. In particular religion ensured that the developing affluence of Victorian prosperity was directed into philanthropy and voluntarism as a means of salving conscience, earning salvation, or demonstrating gratitude. Religion awakened conscience and directed responsibility and surplus wealth into philanthropy and voluntarism. Legacies, commemorative gifts and memorials were established as ways of showing concern or support and recognising personal and family tragedy whilst personal involvement in voluntary effort developed as a means of coping with difficulties, tragedies, or showing deep-seated concern about social and community issues.

In his analysis of Victorian philanthropy, Harrison shows that it provided opportunity for three important groups in society, until that time excluded from political and policy-making influence, to develop their significance and potential. These three groups, the professional middle classes, the new non-conforming religious groups and the educated women, in making their important contribution, established traditions for the voluntary organisation which have continued since. Harrison says that whereas the aristocratic class featured in Victorian philanthropic movements in order to demonstrate the respectability and the significance and national importance of the movements, much of the organisation and financial management was carried out by the middle class. The new professional classes could show their public mindedness and responsibility by contributing their expertise to the voluntary movement. Similarly the non-conforming religions could develop local and community efforts to improve social conditions. Educated women found in voluntary organisations the opportunity to use their potential and to demonstrate their ability in ways which were denied to them elsewhere in nineteenth-century society.

Already, therefore, in the nineteenth century, these characteristics of the voluntary organisation which emerged due to the social circumstances were emphasised and established and have continued as a basic assumption of such organisations even when the original reasons have disappeared. So the need to involve the aristocracy to demonstrate interest and support and to emphasise significance is still apparent, although this is now less of a token involvement but has become a particular expression of public service. The immense contribution of the professions has, if anything, increased in terms of ideas and expertise and the tremendous dependence of voluntary effort upon women has continued even when there are many more opportunities for women to demonstrate potentiality and ability and to earn status and recognition. The present day voluntary movement is, however, showing signs of a new attitude to service and caring which does not necessarily depend upon the association of these responsibilities with the role of women. However, young people of both genders are now demonstrating their willingness to assume responsibility for care.

As has been indicated already, philanthropy and voluntarism received their main stimulus from Victorian independence and individualism and this was transmitted into the fierce independence and defensiveness of much of the voluntary movement. Developing at the same time, however was often a gradual recognition of the need for the assumption of public responsibility and state intervention. Eventually, therefore, many voluntary organisations developed an express objective of demonstrating need and meeting need in order to provoke or be replaced by public initiative. This has continued into the recent experience of the voluntary movement. Often a result of this transfer of objectives within the voluntary movement is the way those drawn into and involved in a movement begin to learn more about the nature of the need and in educating themselves as to the most appropriate way to meet the need, discover that it may, in fact, require a very different response from the original orientation.

Harrison refers to a special aspect of this developmental change within the voluntary movement in describing the gradual change from pure altruism towards an increasing recognition of similar issues such as the elimination of poverty, the improvement of sanitation and the development of all forms of education.

This movement towards remedial, educational, preventive and more interventionist programmes was partly prompted by the deep feelings underlying Victorian attitudes to relief in that it was seen, not so much as degrading for the recipients, but as more likely to encourage indolence, pauperism and to discourage effort. Therefore there was a strong improving moralistic and even punitive element allied to the compassion of philanthropy. As, therefore, philanthropy became more aware of the size and intransigence of the problem it often found it difficult to be critical or reproving of those in difficulty and had to take account of the situation which surrounded and produced the need. Attention was directed to the study of the problems and causes which produced them. Instead of the immediate *ad hoc* response of benevolence to the presenting symptom it became necessary to take a longer view and a more secularised and scientific response. But as philanthropism and voluntarism began to recognise the need for a more secular and interventionist programme then it became subject to more detailed criticism as to whether it was the appropriate response or the appropriate vehicle for the response. Simple *ad hoc* benevolence was difficult to attack except in so far as it might be criticised for unintended consequences, but recognition of the need for intervention and the assumption of the right to intervene could be attacked more directly.

Harrison itemises a number of criticisms which began to crystallise and first of these was that of inefficiency, arising from competition and duplication among many organisations, from the need to develop participative structures which would maximise the involvement of many volunteers, and from the over enthusiasm of a crusading zeal. This criticism of inefficiency, particularly significant in Victorian society which prided itself on the application of rational principles within economic and commercial affairs and which was also accepting of the directive authoritarianism of the powerful and knowledgeable individual, has remained with the voluntary movement ever since even though participative structures have become more generally desirable. The need for co-ordination and co-operation within the voluntary movement is still in constant tension with the separatism, specialism and focussed interest which attracts adherence and support. The fierce independence and separatism which led to the vast excesses of competition were more typical of the Victorian philanthropy than the modern voluntary organisation, which, as seen in this History, is financed from changed sources and, therefore, has to yield more easily to the demands for rationalisation.

Victorian voluntarism was also attacked because it was seen often to be based on ignorance of the real issues. Haste and urgency in pursuing the immediate problem rather than acquiring real understanding and specialist skill and knowledge was seen to be typical of the benevolent response. Voluntarism often emphasised the immediate and practical help rather than a critical and objective study of the problem.

Allied to this was the need to impress the subscribers whilst at the same time meet the needs of the beneficiaries. When the source for philanthropy was the individual who needed to be convinced of the worth, status and significance of the support given then often organisations were tempted to demonstrate these qualities through the organisation itself. When the methods for collecting and attracting philanthropy were often through lavish social gatherings and similar means of bringing the affluent subscriber into contact with the movement then there was often opportunity for criticism of wasteful extravagance.

Those social reformers who wanted to see more public responsibility and more state intervention advanced the cause of public welfare against that of voluntarism and philanthropy because it was seen to be more expert and less wasteful. The attacks on voluntarism were supported by the evidence which was often available, that the enthusiasm and individualism of the voluntary movement often could be counter-productive in that the desire to be seen to always do well was often used as an excuse to conceal failure or inadequacy. Fear of competition or over emphasis upon a particular commitment led to dismissal of alternative ideas and attacks upon rivals' claims for resources. The developing emphasis upon scientific evaluation and collection of facts and use of controlled experiments also led to criticism of the individual entrepreneurship and charismatic quality of much voluntarism together with a suggestion that it depended too much upon sentimentality and conviction.

Harrison also points out the importance in this context of an increasingly confident socialist movement which wanted to see a socialist welfare state which would eliminate the need for the philanthropist and replace him with trained professionals. This was the increasing trend within the twentieth century and the voluntary movement as it continued within the new century had to be capable of coping with this view of its role in society.

Reviewing this brief analysis then we note that the strong individualism which characterised the beginning of the century and developed into the strong emphasis upon enterprise and initiative prompted and shaped the massive development of philanthropism and the voluntary movement and provided a tremendous stream of endeavour which towards the end of the century had to cope with increasing scientific awareness, increasing rationalisation and increasing public and collective responsibility. Already, however, by the end of the century the platform for voluntarism was firmly built and the main structures which formed the shape of the voluntary movement were already erected upon that platform. Most voluntary organisations which developed after this point utilised the platform and the structures and changed and amended them in ways which suited their objectives.

Finally, then, in this Appendix it is possible to list some of those characteristics of voluntary organisations which tend to be repeated throughout the movement and to suggest the reasons for their continued usage.

Firstly there is the 'trigger' which transforms a vague awareness or consciousness into the initiative which then becomes an organisation or movement. This 'trigger' can be an individual, or a group of similarly minded individuals, or a particular event. Usually, however, an individual is associated with the initial trigger. The success of the 'trigger' in focussing consciousness is in exposing that consciousness in such a way as to stimulate interest, motivation and adherence in others. Observing the characteristics it would appear that the successful formula is the gradual development of a small group of like-minded individuals, who by interaction develop and sustain their interest over the formation period. The formation phase depends on the trigger and the initial group of adherents successfully translating their own interest into a publicly respectable and publicly attractive organisation. It is at this stage that the noticeable commitment of public figures becomes important and explains why the voluntary organisation relies upon the use of a number of positions which are assumed by members of society who recognisably demonstrate public significance. Members of the aristocracy and others who occupy recognised positions which do not require explanation, therefore, give the movement at this stage, this quality which places it beyond question.

Recognising the need for efficiency, for dependability, and authority in terms of attracting subscribers and adherents the movement must now attract a managing group with expertise. Indeed it invariably proves that these two requirements, the need for public figures to develop public support and public significance and the need for dependable and authoritative management are reciprocally related during the formation stage. Public figures are unwilling to commit themselves to support an organisation of which they do not have knowledge and confidence; and people with expertise and authority only commit themselves to a movement which begins to prove its utility.

So the committed group who develop the trigger initiative usually steer the movement through the formation stage until there is the necessary commitment of the other two groups to enable a formal demonstration of involvement. By this time also there has been an opportunity for adherents to develop as a membership of the movement.

We can, therefore, identify the main organisational forms and rituals of the British voluntary organisation. The membership of the organisation constitutes the adherents or supporters who are attracted by a particular focus for their general motivation towards social consciousness, responsibility or activity. These members may be subscribers in terms of money, resources, or effort and they may express their support in terms of passive interest or active involvement. So the organisation has to provide structures for the expression of these different forms of support. It does this usually in the form of opportunities to enrol or register as supporters. In return the supporters will usually receive some form of recognition and also communications regarding the aims, objectives and activities of the organisation. A particular form in which this is done is by the annual general meeting which is an opportunity for all concerned in the movement to gather together to demonstrate their support; to renew each other's commitment by collective activity and to receive information about the organisation. This annual general meeting is usually the ritualising of the original public formation meeting which is brought together at the end of the formation phase to announce the public support of the new movement.

This original formation meeting gathers together with public figures who have agreed to support the initiative, the committed group who have manipulated the initiative, the authoritative experts who will demonstrate its continuing viability, and its early adherents. This formation meeting receives and approves the constitution which usually states the aims and objectives as the formalisation of the original initiative, and which establishes the structure of the organisation. This structure recognises the needs of the organisation for the support of significant public figures and, therefore, there are positions within the organisation which are designed to be occupied by these public figures who cannot be expected to devote a great deal of their time and effort to the organisation but are prepared to allow their name and their position to be used by the organisation. Next comes the important managing group which has to be seen to give the organisation authority and expertise. Equally, however, it must be seen to be a group with the support of the membership and to be under their influence. Therefore this management group is seen to be representative of the membership and elected by them to undertake responsibility and conduct the affairs of the organisation on their behalf. Some organisations have an intermediate device between the annual general meeting and the management group. This intermediate structure recognises the need for maximum participation by the membership and the necessary formality of the annual general meeting. Therefore this intermediate group which has a degree of representativeness but some selectivity from the total membership meets probably quarterly and receives more regular reports than the annual Report presented to the annual general meeting. From this selected membership group, often called the council, the management group usually called the executive committee is elected.

The three most crucial positions in most voluntary organisations are firstly the Honorary President, who is the public focus of the organisation and should epitomise the public significance of the organisation. The other honorary officers of public significance are supportive to the impression created by the President. The President usually demonstrates public support and significance by presiding over the meetings of the whole organisation, often only the annual general meeting. Presidents can, of course, and often do, involve themselves in much more of the activities of the organisation. Secondly there is the Chairman of the Management group, usually the Executive Committee who is usually the leader of the organisation, through the chairmanship of the policy-making structural groups within the organisation. It is a publicly responsible position because it is essentially the position which determines the accountability of the organisation to the membership, and to the wider public and the community. Thirdly there is the Secretary who is the executive officer of the managing group and responsible for translating the policy into executive action. As the organisation grows and develops this officer is the one who is most quickly taken into a full-time position and is seen to be in the controlling position responsible for the supervision of executive and other positions which develop to carry out the functions of the organisation.

Meetings of the organisation and of groups within the organisation are usually recorded through the writing of minutes which are formally acknowledged and approved as the records of the proceedings. These minutes are often confidential to the groups of which they constitute a record but they provide a valuable source of information as to the aims and methods and responses of the organisation.

The ritual of the annual general meeting is important because through it the organisation makes a public declaration of its objectives, its philosophy and the support it has within the community. The ritualised procedure of the annual general meeting, through utilising the honorary officers, declares the status, respectability and public significance which have been achieved by the organisation. The managing or executive group who have assumed responsibility for the development of the policy and activity of the organisation on behalf of the membership between meetings of the membership uses the annual meeting as an opportunity to present a Report of that activity to the membership. This Report provides an opportunity to explain to the membership and through them to the general public how the affairs of the organisation are being conducted. The receiving of the Report and the response to it, though often formal and ritualised, provide the membership with some opportunity to participate and to influence the direction of the organisation.

By analysing these records of the organisation, the minutes of meetings, memoranda and the annual reports it is possible to build up a profile of the development of the organisation. The selection of extracts from the records can be allowed to describe the ethos and activity of the Society.

What has emerged in this History is a picture which is the idiosyncratic view of an individual researcher but which hopefully does some justice to an organisation which is an interesting representative of that continued movement of voluntarism which received its significant impetus in the nineteenth century.

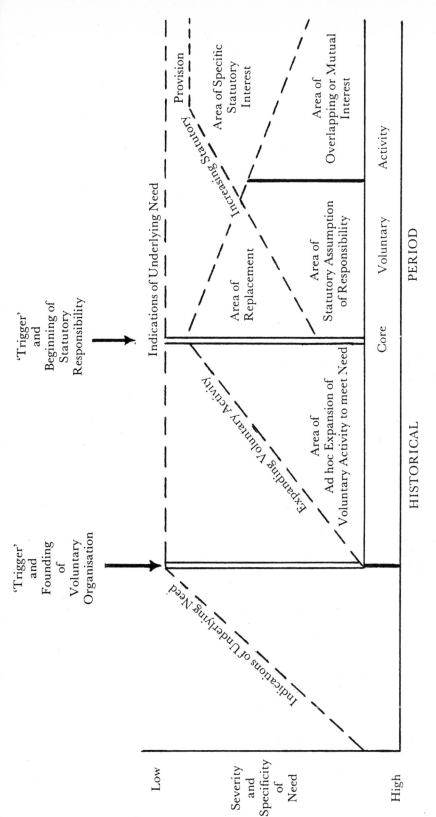

Diagram showing relative development of voluntary activity and statutory responsibility.

APPENDIX B

This obituary notice appeared in the *Glasgow Herald* on 27 January 1917.

Notable Glasgow Citizen

DEATH OF MR JAMES GRAHAME

We regret to announce the death, which took place on Thursday at Fort Augustus, of Mr James Grahame, formerly of Auldhouse, Pollokshaws. Mr Grahame, who was 84 years of age, was for many years one of the most prominent citizens of Glasgow. He was the fourth son of the late Mr Thomas Grahame, W.S., Joint Keeper of the Particular Register of Sasines for the Shire of Renfrew and the Regalities of Glasgow and Paisley. He was educated at Dumfries Academy and the High School and University of Glasgow.

Mr Grahame, who was formerly a member of the firm of Messrs Grahame, Crum and Connal, stockbrokers, was identified with many philanthropic movements, notably the West of Scotland Society for the Prevention of Cruelty to Animals, of which he was honorary secretary for more than 30 years. In 1876 he assisted in forming the Glasgow Association for the Higher Education of Women, and was one of the first honorary secretaries along with the late Miss Galloway, LL.D. He assisted the late Professor Sir Thomas M'Call Anderson and the late Dr A. B. Buchanan to start in 1861 the Glasgow Hospital for Skin Diseases in which he held successively the offices of honorary secretary, director, chairman, vice-president, and president. He was for a time one of the directors of the Royal Asylum for the Blind, Glasgow, and was a past president of the Perthshire Charitable Society and of the Glasgow and Stirlingshire and Sons of the Rock Society. In 1884 he founded the first society in Scotland for the Prevention of Cruelty to Children in Glasgow. The society then formed has extended its operations all over the country, and is now known as the Scottish National Society for the Prevention of Cruelty to Children.

In politics Mr Grahame took an active interest. He founded the Renfrewshire Liberal Association in 1873, the West of Scotland Liberal Association in 1876, and assisted in forming the East and North of Scotland Liberal Association in 1877, and was till 1880 the honorary secretary of the consultative committee of these two bodies. In 1886 he started and was first hon. secretary of the West of Scotland Liberal Unionist Association, and was a member of the Liberal Unionist Council in London. In the same year he (as a

Liberal), together with the late Mr John Cunninghame (as a Conservative) formed the West of Scotland Imperial Union Club. He filled the position of assessor to the Earl of Lytton in Glasgow University Court, 1887–1890, when Lord Lytton was Rector. He was for a long period a member of the Royal Company of Archers, the King's Bodyguard for Scotland, and received from Queen Victoria the Diamond Jubilee Medal in 1887. Mr Grahame retired from business a good many years ago, and resided at the Abbey Lodge, Fort Augustus. Mr Grahame's surviving son is Major J. C. Grahame, D.S.O., Highland Light Infantry.

APPENDIX C

NATIONAL CHAIRMEN AND GENERAL SECRETARIES 1884–1984

N.B. From 1884 to 1890 the work of Prevention of Cruelty to Children in Scotland was carried out mainly by a Society in Glasgow and a Society in Edinburgh which joined in 1889 to become the Scottish National Society for Prevention of Cruelty to Children (originally split into the Western and Eastern Districts). In 1895 the movement became part of the London based N.S.P.C.C. as the Scottish Branch.

CHAIRMEN

1884–1894 James Grahame, C.A. (of Glasgow Society & Western District)

1884–1894 James Colston, J.P., D.L. (of Edinburgh Society, also amalgamated with Edinburgh & Leith Children's Aid & Refuge)

1895–1905 Sir Henry D. Littlejohn, N.S.P.C.C. (Edinburgh & Scottish Branch)

1899–1905 James Kirkwood, N.S.P.C.C. (Glasgow & Scottish Branch)

(Here the Scottish Branch became separate from the N.S.P.C.C. in England and became the Scottish National Society for Prevention of Cruelty to Children (S.N.S.P.C.C.))

1906–1920 James Kirkwood, S.N.S.P.C.C.

(In 1921 the Society was granted a Royal Charter & became the R.S.S.P.C.C.)

1921–1934 F. J. Usher of Dunglass

1935–1938 A. P. Melville, W.S.

1939   James Johnstone (Acting)

1940–1946 Lord Stevenson, O.B.E.

1947–1953 Earl of Mansfield

1954–1979 Lord Wheatley, P.C., LL.D.

1979–   Rev. H. M. Ricketts, M.A., B.D.

GENERAL SECRETARIES

1884–1886	Major Lyson, Glasgow Society
1886–1888	H. A. Roxburgh, Glasgow Society
1884–1888	John MacDonald, Banker, Edinburgh Society
1889–1894	John MacDonald H. A. Roxburgh } Joint Secretaries, S.N.S.P.C.C.
1895	James Grahame, C.A., Managing Director for Scotland
1896–1904	John MacDonald (For period described as Managing Director)
1905	John Hamilton, C.A.
1906–1910	Ninian Hill
1911–1913	C. T. Gordon, Advocate
1914–1933	R. T. Paterson, LL.B.
1934–1968	C. A. Cumming Forsyth, O.B.E., B.L.
1969–	Arthur M. M. Wood, O.B.E., M.A., LL.B.

APPENDIX D

R.S.S.P.C.C. STAFF STRUCTURE AND TASKS

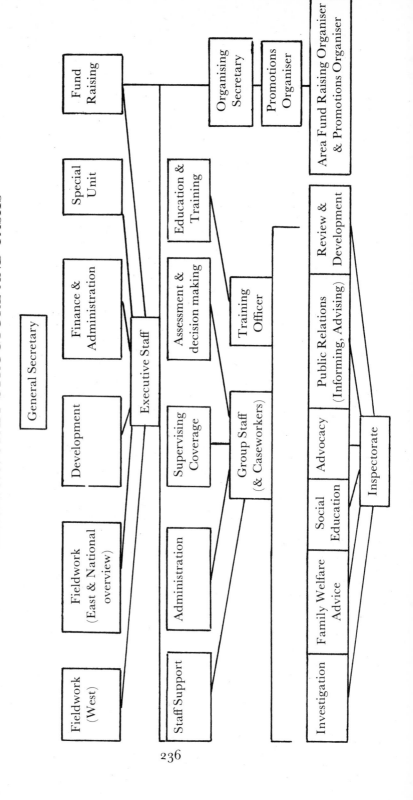

APPENDIX E

ANNUAL RETURN
1st December 1982 to 30th November 1983

Number of family crises brought to the attention of R.S.S.P.C.C.   4,734

Who contacted the R.S.S.P.C.C.?
The family 2,584 (55%)
The general public 1,311 (28%)
The public services 839 (17%)

Why was concern being expressed?
Neglect 1,859 (40%)
Family violence 439 (9%)
Assistance................ 2,436 (51%)

What types of family were involved?
Two-parent families
     (four categories).........2,240 (53%)
Single-parent families
          (four categories)2,014 (47%)

How many children were involved?
10,368
Male 5,364
Female 5,004

Age groups
Up to 5 years.................... 3,455
Between 5/12 years 4,481
Between 12/16 years 2,432

What was the nature of R.S.S.P.C.C. intervention?
Crisis Support.................... 3,909
Long-term Support................. 825

How much direct contact was made with the families?
Home visits 19,711

How much material help was given?
Cash Grants...................... 1,045
Grants in kind................... 1,768

How much communication was there with public services?
Informal contacts with all services 27,061

Formal meetings in accordance with agreed formal procedures as Case Conferences, Children's Hearings and Courts etc. 1,827

Reports to public agencies......... 1,732

How many families were referred to public services by R.S.S.P.C.C.?
848

237

APPENDIX F

ROYAL CHARTER: ARTICLE 3

OBJECTS, PURPOSES, AND POWERS OF THE CORPORATION

The Object of the Corporation is the Prevention of Cruelty to Children, and particularly:

1. To prevent the public and private wrongs of children and young persons, and the corruption of their morals.

2. To take action for the enforcement of the laws for their protection, and for any necessary amendment thereof.

3. To seek out, investigate, and report upon all cases in which children and young persons unable to protect themselves are being neglected, ill-treated, or dealt with in any manner causing or likely to cause them unnecessary suffering, as also all cases of wilful assault, ill-treatment, abandonment, or exposure, and to take steps to bring to an end all such cases of wrong-doing.

4. To repress and aid in the repression of any case of children or young persons being employed for the purpose of begging or receiving alms, or of singing, playing, performing, or offering anything for sale for the purposes of inducing the giving of alms.

5. To take steps to prevent any child or young person residing in or frequenting or visiting any place of immoral surroundings, and for removing such child or young person therefrom.

6. To institute, maintain, and carry on schemes of self-help, or schemes of an ameliorative or remedial nature, relative to the work of the Corporation, for the purpose of improving the physical, moral, or mental welfare of children and young persons, and for bettering the conditions of the parents and guardians of children and young persons.

7. To do all such lawful things as are considered expedient for or consistent with the attainment of the Objects of the Corporation.

N.B. This was the wording as it appeared at the time of the granting of the Royal Charter (1921). An updating has been proposed by the R.S.S.P.C.C. Council for approval of the Privy Council in 1985.